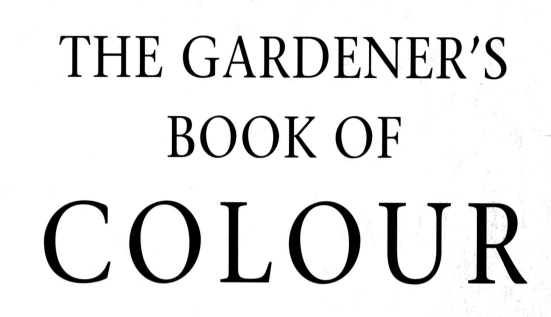

THE GARDENER'S
BOOK OF
COLOUR

ANDREW LAWSON

FRANCES LINCOLN

NOTES ON PLANT DIRECTORIES

The plant directories that appear within the chapter on *Single Colours* comprise brief descriptions of the most prominent plants illustrated in the book, together with a selection of plants that are highly recommended for gardening with colour. Plants have been placed within broad colour categories, but it should be emphasized that related colours merge together imperceptibly, and the delineation between them cannot be precise. Also plant colour can be variable. The distinction between blues and violets is especially difficult and depends on factors such as the maturity of the flowers and on light conditions. Colour photography brings different hazards. The human eye is sensitive to certain wavelengths of light, and colour film has slightly different sensitivity. Film, for instance, will pick up bands of infra-red light which the eye cannot see. Some 'blue' flowers reflect infra-red, and so they appear pinker in photographs than they do in reality.

The heights and spreads of plants, indicated as H and S in each plant entry, represent the average dimensions of a mature plant. The spread is a measure of the diameter of a single plant, which is the recommended minimum planting distance between two plants. Soil, climate and plant husbandry will have a bearing on these dimensions and they may diverge from those indicated.

The hardiness zone, quoted as Z in each plant entry, is a rough guide to the appropriate minimum temperature a plant will tolerate. The chart on page 192 shows the average annual minimum temperature of each zone.

Frances Lincoln Limited
4 Torriano Mews, Torriano Avenue
London NW5 2RZ
www.franceslincoln.com

The Gardener's Book of Colour
Copyright © Frances Lincoln Limited 1996
Text copyright © Andrew Lawson 1996
Photographs copyright © Andrew Lawson 1996
Artwork copyright © Frances Lincoln Limited 1996

British Library Cataloguing-in-Publication data
A catalogue record for this book is available from the British Library.

First Frances Lincoln edition: 1996
First paperback edition: 2002

ISBN 0 7112 2054 9

Printed and bound in Hong Kong by Kwong Fat Offset Printing Co. Ltd

9 8 7 6 5 4 3 2 1

PAGE ONE Colour demarcation. This garden is divided into areas devoted to different colour combinations. Here the 'cool' colours of violet-blue *Clematis* 'Perle d'Azur' and pale pink *Rosa* 'New Dawn' give way to 'hot'-coloured daylilies and monarda beyond.

PREVIOUS PAGES Colour echoes. Bicoloured pink and white *Lupinus* 'The Chatelaine' has been cleverly partnered with *Rosa* 'Wife of Bath' in which the bud and the fully-open flower echo the same two colours.

OPPOSITE Primary contrast. Red *Tulipa praestans* with blue *Muscari armeniacum* and blue *Chionodoxa lucilae* make a bright combination for spring.

Contents

THE POWER OF COLOUR

Colour is the most potent weapon in a gardener's armoury. Nothing in a garden makes more impact. It can stop you in your tracks or it can beckon you onwards. It can suggest coolness and warmth, and it can evoke different moods. You can even use colour to manipulate the sense of space. Understanding the power of colour will help you not only to put a personal mark on your garden but also to orchestrate the profound ways that colour can act upon the emotions, so that some parts of your garden will become areas of repose while others will be exhilarating or – if you wish – even shocking.

Yet despite the infinite variety of colours, the sensory cells in our eyes can only distinguish between them on the basis of five choices. How red? How yellow? How blue? How dark? How light? The brain organizes these relatively crude signals and creates from them the images of extraordinary subtlety and beauty that we experience. Although physicists can explain different colours in terms of wavelength of light and physiologists can describe the cells in the eye that respond to colour, we are still very much in the dark when it comes to explaining how the brain responds to the messages it receives from the eye. Memory and symbolic associations, without a doubt, play a very strong part in our experience of colour. Certain

LEFT Red and yellow flowers seem to give out heat and draw the eye, like flames in a garden room. Hot colours are bold, aggressive and showy. In mixed company, they can overpower their neighbours, which is why it is a good idea to grow them all together, in isolation from cooler colours, in one glorious, fiery display. Here, in early summer, red and yellow columbines (*Aquilegia* hybrids) fill the foreground, with yellow tree lupins (*Lupinus arboreus*) and red roses (*Rosa* 'Dusky Maiden') behind them, while another rose (*Rosa* 'Parkdirektor Riggers') is just visible on the wall beyond. Used in an enclosed space like this within a much larger garden, a planting of hot colours creates an area of excitement that is a stimulating part of a garden stroll. If this were a complete garden in itself though, you might find the effect of the hot colours disquieting and you might not be inclined to sit out among them for too long.

colours can give meanings and create atmosphere in a garden. The idea that we 'see red' when we are angry, 'feel blue' when we are sad, and 'are green' when we care for the environment, are blunt metaphors but they derive from fundamental distinctions between these colours. You may find that red has an agitating effect wherever it appears in the garden, and that blue is calming and dreamy. Green, perhaps because it makes us think of the countryside, tends to make us feel comfortable. Yellow can cheer us up because it reminds us of the sun. The chapter on *Single Colours* looks at the qualities that are associated with particular colours, and the dramatic effect that these colours can make in the garden

We also often associate colours with familiar things. For instance, reds, oranges and yellows remind us subconsciously of fire and heat. For this reason we think of them as 'hot' colours. The warmth of these colours can even affect us in a physical way. Indoors, we can paint our rooms red or deep yellow to make them seem warmer. In our gardens, a planting of hot-coloured flowers can have a similar result. On the other hand, we associate blues and violet-blues with the colours of the sky, the sea and distant hills. They remind us of water and space and we think of them as 'cold' colours. In our gardens, cold colours tend to have a calming effect.

The 'temperature' of colour is important to gardeners because the hottest colours tend to jump forward in space and to dominate their cooler neighbours. Hot colours may even give the illusion that they are in front of their neighbours, when in fact they are side-by-side. The opposite is true of cool colours. Cool-coloured flowers can seem to contract in size and withdraw in space. There are times when you can exploit the spatial distinctions between

RIGHT When a colour scheme is dominated by blues, the eye and brain are subliminally reminded of images of cool water and distant hills. Compared with the hot colours seen in the garden opposite, this planting appears calm, subdued and peaceful. This is a garden of repose. True blues appear in the delphinium and in the *Geranium pratense* 'Mrs Kendall Clark' beside it. Tufts of violet-blue catmint (*Nepeta* 'Six Hills Giant') visually bind together the pink roses ('Magenta' with 'Reine Victoria' in the foreground, 'Commandant Beaurepaire' on the right, and 'William Lobb' growing up the obelisks at the back). Pink *Geranium endressii* and old-fashioned Cheddar pinks (*Dianthus gratianopolitanus*) clothe the terrace walls. All the pink flowers have been selected for the blue bias of their colour. The greens of the foliage, too, look bluish in the cool, shaded light of a summer afternoon. The colours meld together and the effect is subtle and comforting.

hot and cold colours. For example, you can deceive the eye and make a garden appear longer than it really is by planting hot-coloured flowers at the near end, and blues and violets at the far end.

It is not so much individual colours that are important in the overall garden picture, but how they are put together. Each colour has an influence on how you perceive its neighbouring colours, and so it is the relationship between them that catches your attention. The most successful schemes involving more than one colour fall broadly into two categories. If the colours of the plants are similar in some way, they make a harmony, and if the colours are quite different, they make a contrast. These two approaches create widely differing effects – harmonies tend to be soothing, while contrasts are usually stimulating. The basis of these colour combinations is explained in the chapters on *Harmonies* and *Contrasts*.

The way that you use colour in your garden is as personal to you as the decoration of your house. We all interpret colour differently, according to our background and circumstances. We all have different tastes, and there are no rules about right and wrong. What seems subtle to one person may seem dull to another. You might consider a colour scheme bright and cheerful, whereas your neighbour regards it as garish. What matters is to use colour in your own way, absorbing any help and examples that you find useful.

You are bound to be influenced most of all by what you have seen. You can pick up useful ideas about colour from garden visits and from garden pictures in books and magazines, but be receptive also to ideas from outside the sphere of gardening. Paintings, textiles, and fashion design can point to new ways of using colour in the garden. Within garden design itself there are changing trends in approaches to colour. The Victorians liked the combination of rich colour and strong pattern. A more restrained approach originated with Gertrude Jekyll in the early years of this century and reached its apogee with Vita Sackville-West's white garden at Sissinghurst Castle in the 1930s. Today the 'state of the art' may be in the use of bold, rich colour, and wild plantings with grasses whose colour effects are judged successful to the extent to which they reflect nature. With all these conflicting influences you will be most successful with colour by being true to your own preferences.

Whether you make your colour associations by instinct or by following examples that you have seen, it helps to have an understanding of how colour works, so that you can refine your colour sensibilities and find new directions by experimentation. While there are no strict rules and regulations governing the use of colour, there are underlying principles that you might like to draw upon for guidance. However, if you reject them altogether you will be in

RIGHT It is surprising how far you can extend an illusion of space with colour alone. The scarlet oriental poppies (*Papaver orientale*) in the foreground catch the eye like warning flags and their colour makes their position plain at the very front of the border. Beyond, clumps of delphiniums with catmint behind them make a shimmering haze of blue, suggesting a distance far greater than that which separates them from the poppies. By exploiting the illusion that hot colours seem to come forward in space, and cool ones to recede, you can make your garden appear longer than it really is. And if you want a long, narrow garden to appear wider, try planting blue flowers along the sides, while avoiding alignments that emphasize perspective.

good company, because some highly original gardeners have found that to be adventurous with colour involves flouting all preconceived notions. The chapter on *Mixed Colours* looks at some daring plantings and analyses why they work despite going beyond the usual colour conventions.

Before you make your final decisions about colour schemes, it is vital to match your colour combinations to both the opportunities and the limitations of your particular garden. Your success with colour will depend upon good plant husbandry. Before you choose any plant, make sure you can satisfy any special needs that it may have for full sun or shade, or for soil that is acid or alkaline, well-drained or boggy. The temperature extremes in your district will have the most influence upon your choice of plants. Discover whether the trees, shrubs and perennials that you want to grow are likely to survive over winter by checking the hardiness zone. Above all, be sensitive to your climate and quality of light. You might find that strong, bright colours are needed in tropical climates where the light is very clear and the prevailing vegetation colourful. Muted colours can look insipid in these harsh conditions but reveal their subtlety in the softer light of temperate regions.

It is also important to be flexible and to adjust the colour choices for your garden to take account of your immediate surroundings. Begin by taking a look at the materials of which your house is built, and at the hard landscaping of your garden – the walls, fences, and paths. These permanent structures impose their own demands upon the plant colours that you introduce. If your house is built of red brick, for instance, a scheme of vermilion or terracotta reds with greens could be appropriate. It is worth remembering that many of your garden fixtures – from pergolas and fences, gazebos and garden sheds, down to the least garden chair – can be tied in to your colour schemes with a coat of stain or paint. White is an obvious colour candidate, but it is stark and bright and can eclipse surrounding colours. Blue-green, green or grey are proven choices for garden furniture, but you might be more daring and try a colour that makes a complete contrast, such as bright blue or even rusty red.

The colours of surrounding buildings, especially in the city, and even the trees in neighbouring gardens will influence your colour selection. In the country too, bring the colours of the borrowed landscape into your schemes, to ease the transition from the garden into the surrounding countryside. Gardens look best in partnership with their environment and not in conflict.

The most challenging goal for gardeners is to keep the colour interest alive in every season of the year. You can choose, broadly, between two planting approaches, and your choice will depend partly on the size of your garden. If you have plenty of space you

ABOVE These two plantings have been carefully designed to complement the colours of the architecture against which they are seen. A good solution for a white building, *top*, is an all-white planting that uses flowers such as Himalayan balsam (*Impatiens glandulifera*), tobacco plants (*Nicotiana x sanderae*), and white hydrangeas (*Hydrangea paniculata* 'Tardiva'), as well as a tree with white-variegated foliage (*Aralia elata* 'Variegata'). A perfect choice of plants to surround a brick-built pavilion, *above,* is a copse of azaleas (*Rhododendron kaempferi*) with flowers of a dark salmon pink that makes a near-match with the color of the brick. The underplanting of ferns (*Matteuccia struthiopteris*) is clever, too, because their fresh green matches the color of the emerging foliage of the azaleas.

can devote separate areas of the garden to distinct seasonal effects. By grouping together plants that peak at the same time, you can be sure of an intense incident of colour when that time comes. Each one might be quite short-lived but if you have space for enough incidents and you spread them through the year, there should always be at least one colourful corner in the garden for every season. This way you would have separate 'gardens' for winter and spring, and beds or borders that come to a peak at different moments through the summer and autumn.

If you have a small garden, the second approach for achieving successional colour is the one for you. In a small space you cannot afford to leave parts of the garden inactive for very long; you need to keep the whole garden working for you through the seasons. The way to do this is to select plants that will grow up through each other and perform in sequence on the same piece of ground, as seen in the three photographs shown here. Use shrubs, bulbs, herbaceous perennials and annuals together in mixed borders, with the widest seasonal spread among them. In any one border the year might begin with early bulbs – aconites, snowdrops and crocuses under winter-bare shrubs, with narcissi and tulips following on. By the time the spring bulbs have gone over, herbaceous plants have pushed through to take their place. As the summer progresses, fill any gaps with annuals, or place a container to hide an empty space. To keep control over your colours, decide on a particular scheme for each section of the garden – it might be an all-white scheme, for instance, or a more complex mix of colours – and use only plants within this colour range in each season. This is labour-intensive gardening, because you need constantly to cut back plants as they go over, to make room for the newcomers in the cycle. Overall, though, it is a regime that ensures that you will be able to enjoy your chosen colours on the same patch of ground for the longest possible time.

You do not have to rely on flowers alone for all-year colour. Foliage provides colour over a longer period and changes interestingly with the seasons. For winter colour, evergreen foliage has a part to play and so do coloured bark and stems, fruits and berries, seedheads and even the mosses and algae that grow on garden surfaces.

Gardening is a partnership with nature, and even when you are very experienced, nature can sometimes have the last laugh. A combination of plants that flower together in one region may have staggered flowerings in another. Even in the same garden the succession of flowering can be inconsistent from one season to the next. The lesson is that however clever your planting, you should leave room for the happy accident and welcome the unplanned effect that may turn out better than the one that you had intended.

ABOVE In the author's garden, successional colour is orchestrated in a small space with foliage contributing to the effect in every season. This border is loosely restricted to blues, violets and mauves contrasted with yellows and lime-greens. In spring, deep purple 'Queen of Night' tulips, lilac *Allium rosenbachianum* and a froth of forget-me-nots are set against the foliage of *Spiraea japonica* 'Goldflame' and *Philadelphus coronarius* 'Aureus'.

ABOVE A few weeks later, perennial geraniums (*G.* x *magnificum* and *G.* 'Johnson's Blue'), anchusa and *Iris sibirica* reinforce the violet and blue thread which has also been taken up by the slightly later-flowering *Allium aflatunense* 'Purple Sensation'. More yellow foliage comes into play now too, with Bowles' golden grass (*Milium effusum* 'Aureum') in flower, and the small tree (*Robinia pseudoacacia* 'Frisia') putting on leaf.

ABOVE By late summer, the scheme is dominated by the tall pink and mauve-flowered annual *Cosmos* 'Imperial Pink'. This results in a slight shift in the colour balance of the border, but the blue/yellow bias is maintained by *Penstemon heterophyllus* 'Heavenly Blue', a globe thistle (*Echinops ritro*) and *Clematis* 'Perle d'Azur', with the yellow foliage of the robinia and golden hop (*Humulus lupulus* 'Aureus') against the back wall.

UNDERSTANDING COLOUR

The colour red makes an impact in any context, but it is especially powerful when it is seen in contrast with green, its complementary colour. Red flowers, such as those of *Crocosmia* 'Lucifer', shown here arching over a clump of *Helenium* 'Moerheim Beauty', seem all the more intense when seen against a background of bright green foliage.

The Colour Wheel

Nature gives us a way in which we can arrange colours in order and establish relationships between them. This is the spectrum, which appears as the rainbow. The colours originate from different wavelengths of light and so the sequence in which they appear is immutable. When the spectrum is bent round to make a circle, it forms a colour wheel, *opposite*, which is a very useful, simple guide to the most fundamental colour relationships in the garden.

The three primary colours, red, blue and yellow, are the three essential colours from which, in theory, all other colours are constructed. This is because there are only three types of colour-sensitive cells, known as cones, in the retina of the eye – one to respond to each of the primary colours. Each of the three secondary colours, green, orange and violet, is a 'mixture' of two primaries, and lies between them on the colour wheel. Green, for instance, is perceived as a mixture of yellow and blue, and is shown half way between them. These six main colours of the rainbow are linked by infinite gradations of colour, represented here by six colours. Also missing from this diagram are black and white and the more subtle 'mixtures' of colours such as pinks and browns and greys. There are two reasons for this. Black, white and grey are inert colours, that do not react with other colours. Pinks, browns, and all the other muted colours could be plotted on a much more complex diagram, but they would obscure the simple message of the colour wheel. When using any of the more complicated 'mixtures' of colours, such as pink or lilac, be guided by its dominant component: pink, for instance, might be treated as a cool red, lilac as a muted violet.

The two most important approaches to planning colour schemes for the garden – using harmonious colours or contrasting colours – are best explained by studying the colour wheel. Harmonious colours are those that are adjacent or near-neighbours on the colour wheel. Red, orange and yellow, for instance, make a harmonious scheme together. Colours from opposite sides of the wheel form contrasting schemes. The most intense contrasts are between colours that lie directly opposite one another: red with green, blue with orange, yellow with violet. These highly contrasting pairs are called complementary colours.

As the word suggests, a complementary colour makes up for everything that its opposite colour lacks. There is a fundamental physiological relationship between the two. Stare at a bright red patch for half a minute without deflection. Then turn your eyes immediately onto a sheet of white paper in good light. You should see a phantom green patch. There is a simple explanation for this. When the eye concentrates on the original red spot, the red-sensitive cones react and soon become fatigued, so they start to underperform. The new white subject ought to stimulate all the cone cells equally, but the fatigued cones for red will transmit a false message to the brain. They now suggest to the brain that there is a shortage of red; in other words that there is more of its complementary, which is green. So the brain perceives a green phantom on the white paper.

The principle of phantom images between complementaries has a bearing on our perception of colour in the garden. The eye is constantly being affected by what it has just seen. Take the following sequence of events. First we look at a blue flower; the blue-sensitive cones are stimulated and become fatigued. Next we look at orange. The eye, tired of blue, is already perceiving its complementary – orange, so the orange appears enhanced. In other words, looking at the blue has made the orange all the more intense. The eye has been stimulated by one colour to see its complementary in the next thing it looks at. This means that the difference between the two colours is slightly exaggerated. When the two colours are adjacent and so seen together, the effect is the same and is called 'simultaneous contrast'. Since any colour stimulates the eye to see the complementary colour in its neighbour, simultaneous contrast accounts for the intense 'zing' of colour that we sometimes experience when two complementary colours, such as blue and orange, are put together. The same process also helps us to distinguish between subtle colours, and explains why groupings of plants that are only slightly different from each other in colour can be intensely pleasing. Place a blue-green hosta beside a green one, and the blue tinge pushes our perception of the green colour very slightly towards yellow-orange. In the same way a yellow-leaved hosta will make the neighbouring greens seem slightly more violet-blue.

The colour wheel also illustrates how colours fall into two distinct families. When the wheel is divided roughly into two halves as shown in the small diagram, the colours in the portion that includes the reds and oranges are the 'hot' colours. The colours on the other side of the wheel, including blues and violets, are 'cold'. When complementary colours, such as blue and orange, are put together, the two components come from opposite sides of the colour wheel and so one of them is bound to be hot and the other cold. This is broadly true of all colour contrasts, and so they always involve a hot-cold relationship. In colour harmonies, on the other hand, the components are usually relatively close in colour temperature. However, some seemingly similar colours, such as orange and pink, diverge in colour temperature. This creates a contrast disguised as a harmony, and results in a colour 'shock'.

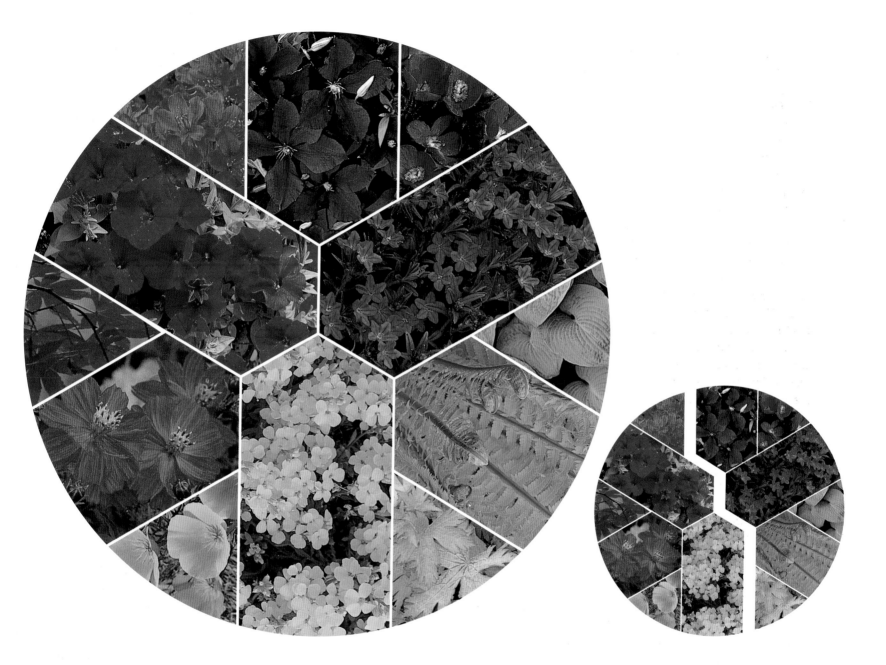

ABOVE The colour wheel is formed by rolling up the colours of the spectrum to create a circle. In this version, the three largest spokes are the three primary colours, red, yellow and blue. They are the main building blocks of colour. The three shorter spokes are the secondary colours, green, orange and violet. The six small wedge-shaped sections, the tertiaries, are transitional steps between the main colours. Each section on this diagram is illustrated by a plant and the result is a hotchpotch of colours that would be alarming if it were reproduced in a garden. The wheel is a summary of all colour relationships – and of course it is not recommended to use them all at once. The pages that follow explore ways to apply the colour wheel using a much more restricted palette in the garden.

ABOVE Divided roughly in half, the wheel falls into two distinct families of colour – 'hot' or 'warm' colours based on red and orange, and 'cold' or 'cool' colours based on blue. Green and magenta, the colours at the tips of the divisions, vary between warm and cool according to context.

Saturation

Saturation describes the intensity of a colour: a saturated colour is one in its purest form, at full strength. An unsaturated colour is weaker and less intense, as if it has been 'diluted' with white, or 'muted' with darker hues.

The plants seen here show nine different saturations of red, the lobelia in the middle being the most intense. The pink of the peony's petals (*centre right*) may be thought of as red diluted by white. Similarly, the intensity of a colour can be muted by 'muddying' it with black or other hues. The dusky foliage of the maple (*top left*) leans towards blue and is often inaccurately described as purple, but it is really a muted, unsaturated red. The dull crimson of the clematis (*top centre*) is a clearer colour but still lacks intensity.

Light can also affect a colour's saturation. Bright sun picks out the red undertones of the cosmos (*centre left*), but in a softer light the colour can appear almost black. The dogwood stems (*bottom left*) appear to be an unsaturated red because the direct sunlight has leeched their colour and cast dark shadows between the stems. Similarly, the smooth, reflective texture of the double poppies' petals (*bottom centre*) reduces the intensity of their colour.

The pattern of colour within a flower, or any variegation of foliage, also reduces the saturation of its overall colour. In the clematis, the dull crimson of the petals is further softened by the flower's paler centre. The already pale crimson of the campanula is diluted by the flower's near-white edges, which make the petals appear almost pink. Similarly, a flower's stamens, whether lighter or darker than the petals, can change the perceived intensity of the flower's colour. In the peony, the already pale pink of the flower appears even more unsaturated because of its pale stamens. However, this effect varies according to the distance from which it is seen.

For the gardener, colour saturation is a consideration when planning a scheme. Usually an intense, clear colour will stand out from its unsaturated surroundings. This is especially true of saturated reds, yellows and oranges which will always stand out from the garden's foliage framework. Unsaturated colours, on the other hand, seem to sink into the background, especially if they have blue in them. The gardener can achieve a harmonious effect by combining plants that are from the same colour family but vary in level of intensity. Flowers ranging from palest pinky white to deepest crimson, for example, are all different saturations of blue-red. When mixing plants from different colour families, it is a good idea to keep the saturation levels roughly equal. Choose a narrow range of unsaturated 'pastel' colours for a tranquil scene, or a limited range of deep, saturated colours for a rich, more sombre effect.

Maple (*Acer palmatum* Dissectum Atropurpureum Group)

Cosmos (*C. atrosanguineus*)

Dogwood (*Cornus alba* 'Sibirica')

Clematis (*C. viticella* 'Purpurea Plena Elegans') · Campanula (*C.* 'Elizabeth')

TOP ROW These three reds, tinged with blue, are unsaturated in varying degrees. Even though the maple is such a dark, muted colour, and the campanula is so pale, both have a recognizable content of red.

Lobelia (*L.* x *speciosa*) · Tree peony (*Paeonia* x *lemoinei* 'Madame Louis Henri')

MIDDLE ROW Here red is seen in its purest, fully saturated form in the lobelia, *centre*. On either side are unsaturated reds, the cosmos having some black in it, the tree peony some white.

Oriental poppy (*Papaver orientale* 'May Queen') · Poinsettia (*Euphorbia pulcherrima* 'Rosetta')

BOTTOM ROW These are unsaturated reds that lean toward yellow. The dogwood and poppies, both already somewhat unsaturated by the addition of some yellow, show the added effect that light can have in draining a colour's saturation. The poinsettia demonstrates how, with the addition of even more yellow, the new colour still retains an echo of the original red, but if you had to describe the colour you would no longer call it red.

Light and Dark Tones

Tone is a measure of brightness. It is the lightness or darkness of a thing. Every colour has its intrinsic tone. Violet, for instance, is dark in tone, and yellow is light. Tonal differences are what you see in a black and white photograph. They are perceived in the eye by separate light-sensitive cells, the rods, that only detect differences in light and dark. In dim light the rods function better than the colour-sensitive cells, the cones. This is why you can still distinguish between light and dark in the failing light of dusk, even when you can no longer tell the difference between colours.

The tonal differences between colours are very important in our garden planning. In some plant partnerships the contrast of tone affects us more than the contrast of colour. For instance, if you grow deep violet and pale yellow flowers together, such as the verbena and achillea shown *opposite above,* the strong tonal contrast between them tends to dominate the colour contrast, even though violet and yellow are complementary colours.

Putting together contrasting colours that are close in tone usually makes the the strongest effects. Complementary colours such as red and green make a powerful colour contrast. These colours are so close in tone that the difference does not show up in a black and white photograph, *opposite*. On the other hand, putting together colours like yellow and green will usually make strong tonal contrasts, even though they are not far apart in colour terms. These will show up well in a black and white photograph, *below*. You can use this test to guide your choice of plant combinations for use in dim light conditions, such as in dense shade, or in parts of the garden where you sit out in the late evening. It is a good idea to use variegated plants in shady areas, for example, because they provide interesting patterns of light and dark in a situation where the eye cannot easily distinguish colours.

White and black are the tonal extremes, and although true black flowers and foliage do not exist, there are many near-black plants available to the gardener. Extreme tonal differences can be used to create dramatic effects in the garden. For instance, a deep bottle-green hedge behind a border of pale flowers emphasizes the lightness of the flowers, while the pale flowers, in turn, make the dark

ABOVE In this masterly planting, the diversity of shapes of flowers and foliage stand out as much for their tonal differences as for their colour. This is demonstrated by the clarity of the black and white photograph, in which the topiary cone of golden privet (*Ligustrum ovalifolium* 'Aureum'), and the rims of the white-edged leaves of a variegated hosta (*H. crispula*) stand out as light shapes against the darker foliage. The yellow spires of *Ligularia* 'The Rocket' and the white flowers of *Geranium pratense* f. *albiflorum,* and white *Viola cornuta* growing with *Achillea ageratum* 'W.B.Childs' also stand out clearly in black and white. But the touches of blue – of polemonium, campanulas, and delphinium – seen against green, are colour incidents that do not translate into monochrome.

hedge seem all the darker. The drama is heightened in strong sunlight, when the tonal differences are further increased. The background seems to recede into the shadow, while the light flowers, seen in clear outline, are visually thrown forward.

Being the lightest colour in the gardener's palette, white provides a tonal contrast with almost all foliage and all but the very lightest colours among flowers. You need to use whites with care, especially those with solid or heavy shapes, because they set up such strong tonal contrasts in the garden. The eye is always drawn to the lightest tones and white flowers may eclipse the force of all but the brightest colour combinations.

RIGHT In this border, colour contrasts are cleverly combined with contrasts of tone. Violet and yellow are complementary colours. So the violet *Verbena rigida* combined with yellow *Achillea* 'Taygetea' and *Kniphofia* 'Sunningdale Yellow' make a bold colour contrast. They are also the darkest and lightest colours on the colour wheel. So they make a strong tonal contrast together too. White is the lightest colour of all, and seen in bright sunlight against heavy shadow, the white willowherb (*Epilobium angustifolium album*) makes a striking silhouette of purely tonal impact.

LEFT The impact of this hot border is the result of pure colour, with scarlet *Salvia splendens* 'Blaze of Fire' and 'Lady in Red', vermilion alonsoa, and orange-red *Helenium* 'Moerheim Beauty' and *Crocosmia* 'Lucifer' making a strident contrast with the complementary green of their foliage. In black and white, however, the contrast disappears almost entirely and the picture becomes a muddle. This is because red and green are very close in tone. Although gardeners would not expect to cater for the colour-blind, there is a lesson to be learnt from this exercise. It is always worth introducing some strong shapes and tonal contrasts into a planting by using, for instance, light, dark and patterned foliage. This tonal interest adds another layer of subtlety, and usually lasts after the colour contrasts of the flowers have gone over.

The Influence of Light

To get the greatest pleasure from your colour schemes it helps to understand the effect of changing light at different times of day, at different seasons and in different weathers. The French Impressionist painter Monet planted a 'sunset' border along the western edge of his garden at Giverny and it is still kept up to this day. Here he used a preponderance of orange and yellow flowers, such as sunflowers, tithonias and marigolds. His idea was to exploit the warm orange light of sunset, so that this border glows like the embers of a fire in evening light. If you observe the transition of the sun in the course of a full day in your own garden, you may be able to plan your colours to catch particular effects of the changing light.

At sunrise and sunset, the sun is at its lowest point in the sky. At these times, the light passes obliquely through the earth's atmosphere, receiving the most interference from dust and other particles in the air. The result is to diffuse the light and to warm it up in colour, so that we often see red skies at sunrise and sunset, and our gardens are bathed in red or orange light. The hot flower colours, reds, oranges and yellows, shine out in this light, whereas the blues, greens and violets become muted and dark because there is so little blue light for them to reflect. You can exploit the low sun at the beginning and end of the day by placing sculptures, painted garden structures, and trees with coloured bark where they will be lit dramatically by the first or last light. You can also obtain striking effects with shadows which are long at these times in summer, and for most of the day in early spring and winter.

At the middle of the day when the sun is high in the sky, light passes at right angles through the earth's atmosphere and is hardly affected by it. The sun itself has a yellowish cast but blue sky, acting as a reflector, compensates for this, so that the light at midday is close to white. The reflecting action of the blue sky is greatest in shadow, where it provides the only illumination so that, on a sunny day, the light in shadow has a blue tinge. In areas shaded at midday, the most effective colours to use are blues and violets, which show up well in blue light, and also white, which will appear pale blue in this context.

After the sun has gone down and the orange glow of sunset has

ABOVE Autumn-tinted vine leaves (*Vitis vinifera* 'Purpurea') become translucent, like stained-glass windows, in low, slanting late-season sun.

LEFT A circle of Kaufmanniana tulips reflects back the early spring sunshine. The sun is quite low in the sky in spring, giving a soft light and longish shadows. When the air is clear, the light is quite cool and has the effect of softening the intensity of yellows, which predominate in this season.

faded, the natural light becomes distinctly blue again. The eye can still make out blues for some time after reds and oranges have begun to appear black, because the blue-receptors in the eye remain sensitive in dim conditions. Whites are visible then too, so it is a good idea to plant blue and white flowers in that part of the garden where you like to sit on long summer evenings.

Climate and the strength of the prevailing light also have a bearing on the colours in your garden. On overcast days when the light is diffused and shadows are softened, our eyes can pick out the most subtle colour effects. This is why muted colours and restrained harmonies of pastel colours are most appropriate in countries furthest from the Equator where the summer sun is relatively weak and the skies frequently overcast. In hotter climates, and all the countries of the tropics, the fierce summer sun creates a harsh contrast between the sun-lit colours and their sharp blue-black shadows. Understated colour cannot compete with these powerful contrasts of light and dark. In such climates, powerful colour statements are needed, with bold, saturated colours arranged in vibrant contrasts.

Changing seasonal light affects garden colour too. In spring, the soft, cool quality of the light is kind to bright colours, preventing them from looking garish and making them look clean and fresh. In summer, the most benign light to enjoy colour is at the beginning and end of the day. At midday, sunlight is so strong and casts such dark shadows that colour is fragmented and relationships obscured. By autumn the sun is getting low in the sky and the light is again soft and flattering, especially when diffused by mists. In winter the sun casts its longest shadow, and creates its greatest dramas. It lights up garden structures and bare trunks and branches of trees and throws them into silhouette against bright snow or dark earth.

The places with the greatest seasonal changes in climate and light, also have the most variation in the year's natural cycle of plant colour. In early spring, autumn and especially in winter in these places, it is not easy to control colour because relatively few plants are performing at their peak. Be flexible at these times, and go along with the characteristic colours of the season. Spring garden colours incline to fresh yellows with clear blues and violets. Emerging leaves are more yellow than green. In autumn colours are again largely dictated by nature. Celebrate this season with glowing reds and golds of berries and falling leaves, even if these hot colours are not your choice for the rest of the year. Winter is dominated by the browns and khakis of dead perennials and the dark greens of evergreens. Any additional colour will be welcome. It does not matter at all if it hardly adds up to a colour scheme, since the function of winter colour is to cheer up the dreary expanse of damp soil, and to give hope to the gardener of more colourful times to come.

ABOVE Late evening light catches an elegant stone vase and throws it into silhouette. At this time of day, ornaments, sculptures and garden structures become most dramatic. Notice how the warm light casts a cool shadow, so that in shade the path becomes quite blue, and the pink of the rose 'Mevrouw Nathalie Nypels' looks cooler, and the blue of the catmint (*Nepeta nervosa*) is rendered more intensely blue.

Colour Distribution

Once you have settled on your colour schemes, but before you have chosen all the plants that you would like to use, it is important to think about both the shapes created by the overall habits of plants and also how you are going to place them together so that they react most effectively.

A flat sheet of a single colour could lose its initial impact and become boring in a garden. A haphazard jumble of colour, on the other hand, becomes confusing because the eye is never able to come to rest on any particular colour or relationship. At the same time, a garden in which the plants are all the same mass and shape, but in carefully composed colour schemes, would be a nightmare of monotony. So as well as deciding whether to plant in blocks, or in ribbons, or in dots and dashes of colour, you also need to think about varying shapes and sizes of your plants.

Your approach will depend upon the scale of your planting, the main point from which the planting will be seen, and on whether you opt for a single or a complex colour theme. The larger your garden, the broader the effects can be; the closer your viewpoint, the more intricate they can be. If you plant in defined blocks, individual colours will remain clearly distinguishable; if you scatter the colours, the effect will be speckled at close range, from further away the colours will merge and diffuse.

If you opt for clumps of perennial colour, try following Gertrude Jekyll's practice of planting elongated 'drifts' of plants instead of round colour blocks. Drifts of plants will interlock with their neighbours without precise lines of demarcation. One advantage of this is that when a plant is over and cut back, it will not leave an unsightly scar since adjacent drifts will soon grow into its space.

ABOVE These two plantings, by the same gardener, demonstrate two distinct approaches to presenting colour. In the border *above left*, plants with small dispersed flowers, such as potentillas and verbenas, are enmeshed with sweet williams, white achilleas and scattered penstemons. Seen close, the effect is jewel-like, the border spotted with colour like a post-impressionist painting. From a distance, the colour will fuse into a haze. In the garden *above right*, the same penstemons are planted in generous-sized drifts, with dense clumps of pinks and white lychnis underplanting the old roses, which themselves form substantial blobs of pink and mauve. Even from a distance, the broad slabs of colour are still distinguishable.

RIGHT This blue and yellow scheme includes drifts of achilleas, catmints, lupins, *Campanula lactiflora,* alchemilla and veronica that spill over onto an informal path. Plants thrive and look best if they are grown in much the same way that they occur naturally in the wild. In nature perennials tend to form clumps that expand over the years as their roots spread out from the centre; they may also spread by seeding, so that new clumps spring up some distance from the parent plant. This natural process takes years, and you do not have to rely on it in your flower borders because you can imitate nature by your method of planting. Be generous, if you can afford it, and use several plants of each variety to establish a good-sized clump at the outset.

It is often more telling to plant repeated drifts of the same plant, rather than to seek constant variety and change. Repetition of colour, provided that it is not too symmetrical and regular, can establish a rhythm in the planting that is the visual equivalent to music. Also, repetition of the same plant in drifts of different sizes is reminiscent of the natural process of propagation, and will make your plantings look more convincing.

A totally different result can be achieved by distributing single plants of one colour among clumps of other colours. In spring, for instance, individual yellow daffodils growing through mounds of blue lithodora, intensify the blue and prevent any possible monotony. In summer, too, plants with small, dispersed and brightly-coloured flowers like potentillas and geums, are invaluable for adding vitality to a planting that might otherwise appear bland.

The arrangement of shapes in a garden contributes to our appreciation of their colours. Whether you are dealing with trees or shrubs on a large scale, or with smaller climbers and perennials, the basic habits and outlines of plants, as well as their flower and leaf shapes, create outlines against which neighbouring colours react. Sometimes a variation in shape can bring interest to a passage of colour, even if the new shape is more or less the same colour. Imagine a stand of purple foxgloves, for instance, next to a rounded clump of bergamot of the same colour. The distinction in shape between the two plants is refreshing. In the border above, the variety of yellow shapes, the starbursts of broom, spikes of lupins, and discs of achilleas animates the planting. Single colour schemes depend even more on variety of shape as well as texture. This is explored in greater detail on pages 24-25.

ABOVE The dark and light patterning of these Californian hybrid irises makes the colour appear to shimmer, and look less dense than if the flowers were a flat mid tone. The variegation and jagged outlines of the thistle (*Galactites tomentosa*) give the impression of dappled sunlight. The veins on the flowers of the *Geranium malviflorum* animate their colour, too, but more subtly.

BELOW Rhododendrons have enormous flowerheads that are massed together on the shrub to make it into a mound of lumpy colour. Seen close, especially in a small garden, they can seem ungainly. A fringe of matching pink campion softens the impact and helps them to blend into the landscape.

Density, Shape and Texture

Every plant variety presents its colour in a particular way, and one challenge for the garden artist is to create a balance between the varying densities of colour, shapes, and textures of the flowers and plants that make up a scheme. There is a world of difference, for example, between the diffuse haze of colour that comes from a mass of tiny flowers like gypsophila, and solid 'blobs' of colour of flowers such as some rhododendrons, or between the clear outline and waxy surface of a lily and the intricate silhouette and brittle texture of an eryngium.

'Blobby' flowers like begonias, lilies and the large-flowered roses and clematis may supply the strongest colour accents in a bed or border. Large-flowered plants, however, can be ungainly, and a border devoted exclusively to them would be crude in the extreme. Far better to soften their effect by combining them with more delicate-looking neighbours, especially ones of the same or similar colour. Partner a pink rhododendron with pink campion, for instance, so that the rhododendron's lumpy colour appears to be dispersed through the repetition of the campion's delicate flowers. Similarly, airy sprays of white spirea will counterbalance dense white flowerheads of delphiniums.

When colour is broken up into patterns in flowers or foliage, it appears less dense. Flowers of some lilies, for example, are streaked and spotted with different colours; pansies are often blotched with contrasting colours such as yellow and violet; and flowers like fuchsias or lupins may be bicoloured. At close range these patterned flowers make a bold colour scheme in themselves. From a greater distance, the colours seem to merge, but the effect is softer and more dispersed than a flat, single colour would be.

You also need to think about the shapes and textures of flowers and foliage, because it is surprising how much these influence our experience of colour. Seen at close quarters, the star-shaped, shiny-petalled flowerhead of a daisy has a brighter effect than the rounded, matt flower of an achillea, because of its shape. The star-shape, like a sunburst, suggests energy and light, whereas a dense, double shape is relatively static and inert. The textural differences among leaves are even more marked. If you compare the velvety green leaf of *Hydrangea aspera* subsp. *sargentiana* with the shiny and brittle leaf of the common holly, you will see that although they are not very far apart in colour, their textures, and consequently the effect they have, are fundamentally different. The same observation applies to flowers too. The closer they are in colour, the more obvious are the textural differences between them. So a single colour planting can be seen as a study in contrasting textures.

RIGHT Three different flower shapes introduce variety to an all-white planting. The annual white *Dimorphotheca* 'Glistening White' has been planted with perennial *Gypsophila paniculata,* which gives a veil of tiny white flowers that counters the solid double flowers of *Achillea ptarmica* 'The Pearl'.

FAR RIGHT The bulb *Tigridia pavonia* comes in dark pink, scarlet or yellow, and you need to select the right one to make a matching companion for tender perennial *Verbena* 'Sissinghurst'. The closeness of the colour of this plant partnership enables you to enjoy their disparity of shape – like triangles seen against circles.

RIGHT The flowers of the *Eryngium alpinum* are similar in colour to those of the herbaceous *Clematis integrifolia,* and so the eye tends to concentrate upon the differences in shape and texture between them. The frilled and spiny upward-facing flowers of the one are the perfect foil for the smooth, sinuous, and nodding flowers of the other.

FAR RIGHT Wild buttercups, growing at the foot of a tree lupin (*Lupinus arboreus*), provide dots of fully saturated yellow scattered among the larger but less saturated flowers of the lupin. The relationship between size and saturation is very pleasingly balanced, as you will see if you imagine the two yellows reversed.

GARDENING WITH COLOUR

Gardening rarely gives instant results, and a gardener's artistry
will sometimes reveal itself long after planting takes place. These early spring
flowering *Crocus tommasinianus*, intermixed with *Cyclamen coum*,
have taken years to self-seed and spread and make a glorious
carpet of violet and pink.

SINGLE COLOURS

Your favourite colours will always be the best starting point for whatever schemes you choose. But before you embark on ambitious plantings, it is worth familiarizing yourself with the colour palette that is available to the gardener, and understanding the influence that each colour can have, not only on neighbouring colours, but on the overall mood of your garden.

Each of us has subliminal memories and associations for particular colours. We perceive colours differently and have different ways of describing them. However, there are a few recognized guidelines that will help you make the most of a colour's qualities – whether you use it sparingly in a mixed colour scheme or concentrate it in a single colour planting.

If you opt for a single colour planting, the way to make it most interesting is to include variations on that colour, and a variety of different shapes and textures. In an all-yellow border, for instance, use flowers that run the gamut from saffron to lemon to palest cream. For shape, use lupins and verbascums so that their tall flower spikes contrast with the flat flower heads of achilleas. Above all, make use of the wide range of yellow-green foliage plants and put together the ceramic smoothness of a hosta, say, and the filigree texture of a fern. By including white flowers, or silvery foliage, you can create an extra dimension without adding any reactive colour.

Even if you do not devote a whole section of the garden to a single colour, you can use colour to make connections between plants – to link, for instance, a yellow-flowered anthemis with the yellow stamens of a nearby lily, to connect, in turn, with the yellow variegations of an ivy. One of the delights of gardening is to create echoes of one colour that reverberate around the garden to make a satisfying whole.

RIGHT These long double yellow borders are an inspired single colour planting. A broad range of yellow flowers is used, from egg-yolk yellow phlomis to primrose lupins. The differing shapes and textures of foliage prevent the yellows from looking uniform. The approach is far from purist, and the sprinkling of white flowers and mounds of silvery foliage make the borders look cheerful and sunny, even in overcast weather. (Full planting details of this scheme are given on page 172.)

Yellows

Think of yellow and the sun comes to mind. In the garden, yellow daisies can seem like miniature suns, radiant and luminous. Even on a dull day, a drift of yellow flowers can look like a patch of sunlight. Yellow brings cheerfulness to the garden, and can lift the spirits. But remember that too much exuberance can be overpowering, and so yellow needs to be carefully controlled. Use it with discretion or it can swamp more subtle colours and set up violent contrast with other strong ones.

The effect of yellow varies according to the season. In summer the sun is high in the sky, casting dense black shadows. The combination of bright yellow with dark shadows is especially fierce, so for more gentle midsummer displays, take care not to use bright yellow plants on a large scale. In spring and autumn, with the sun low in the sky, the light is softer, moderating the intensity of pure yellow.

ABOVE The exuberance of a laburnum tunnel makes up for its short season. For ten days or so in early summer it has a ceiling hung with racemes of lemon-peel yellow flowers, with little interruption from foliage which thickens up later. Here cream and yellow wallflowers make a daring choice for underplanting. Preferring full sun, they normally flower earlier than the laburnum, but here they have been held back by the trees' shade. A yellow-leaved hosta such as *H.* 'Gold Standard' would be a longer-lived alternative underplanting, but would need watering in dry summers since the laburnums (here *L.* x *watereri* 'Vossii') would take up most of the available moisture.

ABOVE A spring planting consists of 'Golden Melody' tulips teamed with the biennial wallflowers (*Erysimum* 'Golden Bedder'). The 'golden' epithet of both plants sounds poetic, but does not really describe the buttery quality of the tulips, compared with the more powdery, sulphur-yellow of the wallflowers. Bedding schemes like this are rewarding but labour-intensive. Wallflowers are grown from seed the previous summer and planted out in the autumn at the same time as the bulbs. Tulips have a better chance of flowering again the following year if they are lifted and kept cool and dry during the summer; but if they do well in your soil, leave them in.

Swathes of brilliant yellow narcissi can look exhilarating in spring, whereas a broad expanse of the same colour in high summer can look garish. Similarly, in the autumn, softer light makes large expanses of butter-yellow foliage acceptable.

To temper an all-yellow midsummer planting, you can use plenty of unsaturated yellows. Pale yellows are less boisterous than strong ones, and lemon yellows, with their touch of green, are cooler, making more comfortable companions for other colours. Primrose-yellow and cream are the most companionable of all the family of yellows, and they associate with other colours with impunity – even with pink, which does not usually sit well with brighter yellows. Cream flowers especially have a calming influence in all colour relationships, acting like green foliage to separate colours that might otherwise fight.

For an all-yellow display in spring, too, you might include some paler, primrose-yellows, such as corylopsis, as well as some of the paler yellow brooms and creamy-yellow narcissi. These all make particularly good companions for the delicate yellow-greens of spring's fresh new foliage.

To add glittering highlights to your yellow border you can include white flowers that have only a touch of yellow in them. White marguerite daisies, for instance, have yellow centres, and some white lilies, such as *Lilium regale,* have brilliant yellow stamens. They will set up resonances with yellows elsewhere in the border. And you do not have to limit your choice to flowers. Include yellow-leaved trees and shrubs too; their effect is long lasting, and they will make the backbone of your border.

The lightening effect of yellow can be exploited elsewhere in the garden. Just as yellow stamens can brighten a red flower, so yellow flowers, introduced sparingly as dots among red and orange flowers, will add sparkle to a planting that might otherwise appear dark and heavy.

ABOVE All-yellow plantings in window boxes light up a dark courtyard in spring. Here, wallflowers in two tones of yellow combine with a cream-edged ivy that trails over and hides the container. To extend this effect over the summer you could replace the spent wallflowers with annuals such as antirrhinums in a range of yellows, or with the tender perennial daisy *Argyranthemum* 'Jamaica Primrose', combined with the trailing *Bidens ferulifolia*. To maintain densely planted containers like these, use water-retaining compounds, or else water daily, and unless you have mixed a slow-release fertilizer into the compost, remember to feed them once a week.

ABOVE Four perennials make up this densely planted group of yellow daisies within a section of a border devoted to hot colours. Two are hardy – *Rudbeckia fulgida* var. *sullivantii* 'Goldsturm', in the lower left corner, and the pale yellow marguerite (*Anthemis tinctoria* 'E.C. Buxton'), and two are tender – the small-flowered *Bidens ferulifolia* and the creamy *Osteospermum* 'Buttermilk'. Any one of them planted in a mass would make a striking yellow feature, but mixed together they have the added attraction of subtle variations of shape, texture and colour.

Yellow Foliage Effects

Another way to introduce yellow to your garden is with foliage that is yellow or else variegated with stripes or splashes of yellow. Foliage is rewarding for much longer than flowers, and in spring and autumn yellow foliage may be the dominant feature of a garden. But its effect can be very subtle. To ensure that you do not eclipse its subtlety, use only a few bright yellow flowers with it. In the same way that yellow flowers can be used to lighten a red and orange planting, so plants with yellow-patterned leaves, such as hostas and ivies, can brighten up the gloom of dark green companions in the shade. Ponds can look very dark, particularly when overhung by trees. You can brighten them up by planting their boggy margins with 'golden' grasses or with variegated plants and a few scattered flowers to give an echoing touch of yellow.

RIGHT Bowles' golden sedge dominates the grass (*Phalaris arundinacea* var. *picta*), at top left, and the aquatic *Glyceria maxima* 'Variegata' at bottom right. In the foreground are *Primula florindae*, fronds of *Osmunda regalis* and a few *Mimulus guttatus* flowers. Stately *Iris orientalis* echo the theme of yellow with creamy white, and thrive, like the other plants here, in the boggy conditions around a pond. (Full planting details of this scheme are given on page 172.)

ABOVE In spring, the yellow in the foliage of a vigorous clump of yellow-variegated (*Iris pseudacorus* 'Variegata') is picked up by the water buttercup (*Ranunculus lingua* 'Grandiflorus') and the Candelabra primulas beyond. Golden club (*Orontium aquaticum*) with its yellow snakeshead flowers, has crept to the margin of the pond, although it normally favours deeper water.

ABOVE *Lysimachia punctata* makes clumps of rather strident buttercup-yellow flowers, but here it pushes through branches of the evergreen shrub *Lonicera nitida* 'Baggesen's Gold' whose pale foliage cools down the effect. Another loosestrife, *Lysimachia nummularia* 'Aurea', makes useful groundcover – it has a creeping habit with yellow-green foliage and bright yellow flowers.

ABOVE In this unusual combination for a yellow border in shade, the spiky, pale yellow flowers of *Cestrum parqui* are enhanced by combining them with the brittle-looking foliage of a golden yew trained and pruned to edge the border.

Bright Yellows

SPRING

Aurinia saxatilis (syn. *Alyssum saxatile*) Evergreen perennial that forms a dense mat of small brilliant yellow flowers. **'Citrina'** with paler flowers looks good trailing from a raised bed or rock garden. Prefers sun. H 23cm (9in) S 30cm (12in) Z3

Caltha palustris KINGCUP Perennial like a giant buttercup, for pond margins and boggy ground in full sun. H and S 60cm (24in) Z3

Corydalis lutea Evergreen perennial that will continue to flower through the summer. It comes with racemes of tubular flowers with short spurs, and blue-green filigree foliage. Tolerates sun and partial shade. H and S 30cm (12in) Z5 [ill.p.136]

Crocus x luteus 'Golden Yellow' Corm with robust goblet-shaped flowers that does best in sun. H 10cm (4in) S 8cm (3in). Z4

Doronicum LEOPARD'S BANE Late spring flowering perennial with heart-shaped leaves. It has large daisy-like flowers on long stems. Tolerates sun or shade. [ill.p.141] Good varieties include **D. x excelsum** 'Harpur Crewe' and **D. orientale** 'Magnificum'. H 90cm (3ft) S 60cm (2ft) Z4

Eranthis hyemalis WINTER ACONITE Tuberous perennial with bright yellow flowers, borne close to the ground. Frilled foliage follows, and dies back in summer. Prefers partial shade and humus-rich soil. H and S 10cm (4in) Z5

Erysimum cheiri 'Golden Bedder' WALLFLOWER Short-lived perennial usually treated as a biennial. Single colour selections are available, or mixtures from deep cerise to pale primrose. Requires sun. H and S 30cm (12in) Z7 [ill.p.30]

Erythronium 'Pagoda' Tuberous perennial that produces pendant lily-like flowers, up to twelve on a stem, with broad, mottled leaves. Requires partial shade and humus-rich soil that is protected from drying out during summer. H 35cm (14in) S 20cm (8in) Z5 [ill.p.125]

Forsythia Shrub whose bare stems are covered with brilliant star-like flowers before the leaves open. Good varieties include **F. x intermedia** H 1.5m (5ft) S 2.4m (8ft) Z6. **F. suspensa** has paler flowers. H and S 2m (6ft 6in) but higher when trained against a wall. Best in sun Z6

Fritillaria imperialis 'Maxima Lutea' CROWN IMPERIAL Bulb whose crown of hanging, bell-like flowers are held on a tall, erect stem. Tolerates sun or partial shade. H 1.5m (5ft) S 30cm (12in) Z5

Lysichiton americanus SKUNK CABBAGE Perennial whose large flower spathes, which have an unattractive smell, appear before the foliage. Later, broad, paddle-shaped leaves are a feature. Needs boggy ground. Prefers full sun but will tolerate partial shade. H 90cm (3ft) S 75cm (30in) Z6

Mahonia aquifolium Evergreen shrub with tight-packed sweet-smelling flowerheads that precede the bunches of blue berries that appear in summer. Tolerates shade or partial shade. H and S 1.5m (5ft) Z5

Narcissus DAFFODIL The yellow trumpets of this popular bulb are an essential herald of spring. Naturalizes best in ground that does not dry out. Prefers sun or partial shade. Good early flowering varieties include the Cyclamineus 'February Gold' H 32cm (13in) and 'Peeping Tom' H 45cm (18in) Z5; and the shorter 'Tête-à-Tête' H 25cm (10in) Z4. Good later flowering varieties include 'Yellow Cheerfulness' JONQUIL with double, scented flowers. H 40cm (16in) Z4

Rhododendron luteum Deciduous shrub with sticky buds and broad heads of sweetly scented tubular flowers. Needs neutral to acid soil, and prefers light shade. H and S 2.4m (8ft) Z5

Ribes odoratum BUFFALO CURRANT Shrub whose starry yellow flowers, borne along the arching stems, have the spicy scent of cloves. Does well against a sunny wall. H and S 1.8m (6ft) Z5

Trollius europaeus GLOBE FLOWER Perennial with rounded, curved flowers like giant buttercups, and graceful divided foliage. Tolerates sun or shade, but requires moist soil. H 60cm (24in) S 45cm (18in) Z4

Tulipa TULIP Bulb that appreciates summer baking. Good cultivars include early flowering 'Bellona' H 30cm (12in) S 20cm (8in) Z4; 'Golden Melody' H 30cm (12in) S 20cm (8in) Z4 [ill.p.30]; and 'West Point' H 50cm (20in) S 25cm (10in) Z4 [ill.p.169]

Uvularia grandiflora Rhizomatous perennial with graceful pendant flowers on long stems that appear among the young foliage. Requires peaty soil in partial shade. H 60cm (24in) S 30cm (12in) Z5

SUMMER

Achillea Perennial with flat, plate-shaped flowerheads that make a welcome counterpoint to the predominantly vertical emphasis in borders, with the added bonus of fern-like foliage. Needs sun and tolerates dry conditions. Good varieties include  'Coronation Gold' H 90cm (3ft) S 60cm (2ft) Z4; and **A. filipendulina** 'Gold Plate' H 1.2m (4ft) S 60cm (2ft) Z4 [ill.pp.157, 180]

Allium moly ORNAMENTAL ONION Bulb with good clear yellow flowerheads, and grass-like leaves. Will spread into clumps in favoured open sunny position with well-drained soil. H 35cm (14in) S 12cm (5in) Z3 [ill.p.183]

Anthemis tinctoria DYER'S CHAMOMILE Evergreen perennial with brilliant yellow daisy-like flowers, and feathered leaves. Will keep flowering if dead-headed regularly. Likes a sunny, open situation. H and S 90cm (3ft) Z4 [ill.p.181]

Bidens ferulifolia A trailing yellow perennial daisy, with broad, bright yellow florets and narrow leaves. Tender, but ideal for container plantings. H 75cm (30in) S 90cm (3ft) Z9 [ill.pp.31,177]

Buphthalmum salicifolium OXEYE Perennial giving masses of daisy-like flowers with narrow florets. Spreads into clumps that may need staking. Prefers sun. H 60cm (24in) S 90cm (3ft) Z4

Cassia artemisioides WORMWOOD SENNA Evergreen shrub with spikes of cup-shaped flowers and divided leaves, covered with white down. Frost tender, so suitable for a conservatory. Requires sun. H and S 1.8m (6ft) Z10

Eranthis hyemalis

Fritillaria imperialis 'Maxima Lutea'

Narcissus 'February Gold'

Uvularia grandiflora

Allium moly

Clematis

Climbing or scrambling plants that tolerate sun or partial shade but need a cool root run. Good late-summer flowering varieties include climbers '**Bill Mackenzie**', which has nodding bell-shaped flowers with upturned tips to the sepals, followed by fluffy round seedheads, H and S 7m (22ft) Z6; and *C. tangutica*, which has smaller, daintier flowers and similar seedheads, H and S 4.6m (15ft) Z6.

Coreopsis verticillata TICKSEED

Perennial with a mass of bright, star-shaped flowers and finely divided foliage. Requires sun. H 60cm (24in) S 30cm (12in) Z3

Crocosmia MONTBRETIA

Corm with sprays of trumpet-shaped flowers and sword-shaped leaves. Good yellow varieties include '**Golden Fleece**' (syn. 'Citronella') [ill.p.163]. Prefers sun. H 75cm (30in) S 20cm (8in) Z6

Fremontodendron californicum FLANNEL FLOWER Evergreen or semi-evergreen shrub bearing large, bright, saucer-shaped . Best grown against a sunny, sheltered wall in not over-rich soil. H 6m (20ft) S 3.7m (12ft) Z9

Genista aetnensis MOUNT ETNA BROOM Bright pea-like flowers on the arching branches of this shrub give an explosion of colour. Best in sun, in not over-rich soil. H 7.5m (25ft) S 9m (30ft) Z8

Glaucium flavum HORNED POPPY

Perennial with poppy flowers, opening like crinkled tissue paper, and light blue-green foliage. Prefers sun. H 60cm (2ft) S 45cm (18in) Z5

Helenium SNEEZEWEED

Perennial with robust sprays of flat flowers that cover the plant in late summer. [ill.pp.177,180] '**Butterpat**' is a good variety. Requires sun. H 90cm (3ft) S 60cm (2ft) Z4

Helianthus SUNFLOWER

Annual *H. annuus* is the archetypal sunflower, with whorls of seeds at the centre, rimmed with curling yellow florets. H 3m (10ft) S 45cm (18in). Perennial *H. salicifolius* WILLOW LEAVED SUNFLOWER has relatively small daisy-like flowers on very tall stems. H 2.1m (7ft) S 60cm (2ft) Both require full sun Z6

Hemerocallis DAYLILY

Grassy-leaved perennial whose exquisite lily-shaped flowers last only a day but appear in succession. Good varieties include graceful *H. lilio-asphodelus*, one of the earliest to flower; '**Marion Vaughn**' [ill.p.181]; and '**Stella de Oro**' [ill. p.157]. Best in full sun. H and S 90cm (3ft) Z4

Hypericum

Shrub bearing clear yellow flowers with prominent stamens. Tolerates sun or partial shade. Good varieties include *H. calycinum* ROSE OF SHARON,

which is tolerant of drought and poor soil and makes a good spreading groundcover, H 60cm (2ft) S 1.2m (4ft) Z6; and *H. x inodorum* '**Elstead**' which has bright red fruit, H and S 90cm (3ft) Z7

Inula magnifica

Perennial with daisy-like flowers, the size of tea-plates, above broad, hairy leaves. Makes huge clumps in damp ground in sun. H 1.8m (6ft) S 90cm (3ft) Z4

Iris

Rhizomatous perennials. Good tall bearded irises that do best in sun include '**Canary Bird**' [ill.p.40] and '**Kent Pride**' [ill.p.125]. Both H 90cm (3ft) S 45cm (18in) Z4. *I. pseudacorus* YELLOW FLAG IRIS is good for waterside planting and requires partial shade. H 1.2m (4ft) S 45cm (18in) Z5 [ill.p.32]

Isatis tinctoria WOAD

Biennial producing tiny flowers in diffuse sprays. Needs sun. H 1.2m (4ft) S 45cm (30in) Z7

Kniphofia citrina

A yellow variety of the familiar perennial with poker-like flowers. Requires sun and moist soil. H 90cm (3ft) S 45cm (18in) Z8

Laburnum x watereri '**Vossii**'

Tree that produces graceful hanging racemes of pea-like flowers. Amenable to training, it looks marvellous bent to form an arch. Does best in sun. H 9m (30ft) S 7.6m (25ft) Z5 [ill.pp.30,139]

Ligularia przewalskii

Perennial with tall pointed spikes of small flowers that appear above elegant finely cut foliage. [ill.p.178]. '**The Rocket**' is a selected hybrid with larger flowers [ill.pp.18,177]. Tolerates sun or partial shade, and requires moist soil. H 1.5m (5ft) S 90cm (3ft) Z4

Lilium LILY

Good yellow cultivars of this bulb that does best in sun include the **Citronella Group** with pendant spotted turkscap flowers, H 90cm (3ft) [ill.p.122]; '**Connecticut King**' with radiant upward-facing flowers, H 90cm (3ft); and the **Golden Splendour Group** with trumpet-shaped flowers, H 1.5m (5ft). All Z4

Limnanthes douglasii POACHED EGG PLANT Annual that becomes a cheerful mass of brilliant egg yolk yellow flowers edged with white, which may self-seed in a sunny spot. Requires sun. H 30cm (12in) S 40 cm (15in) [ill.pp.167,179]

Lysimachia punctata LOOSESTRIFE

Perennial with spikes of vivid yellow flowers. It forms clumps and may be invasive. Requires sun or partial shade and moist soil. H 75cm (30in) S 60cm (2ft) Z4 [ill.pp.32,180]

Meconopsis cambrica WELSH POPPY

Perennial poppy that seeds itself liberally. Requires shade and moist soil. H 45cm (18in) S 30cm (12in) Z6 [ill.pp.136,183]

Oenothera macrocarpa (syn. *O. missouriensis*) EVENING PRIMROSE

Perennial producing large funnel-shaped flowers that open in the evening followed by large seed-pods. Requires sun and prefers sandy soil. H 25cm (10in) S 40cm (16in) Z5

Orontium aquaticum GOLDEN CLUB

Perennial. A floating, deep-water plant, that also grows at pond margins. Produces curious pointed flowers, yellow at their tip, that look like snakes' heads. S 60cm (24in) Z7 [ill.p.32]

Phlomis

P. fruticosa JERUSALEM SAGE is an evergreen shrub with sage-like grey-green foliage and whorls of rich yellow flowers followed by attractive pepperpot-shaped seedheads. Requires sun. H and S 1.2m (4ft) Z8 [ill.pp.162,169]. *P. russeliana* is an evergreen perennial with similar qualities. H 90cm (3ft) S 60cm (2ft) Z4

Piptanthus nepalensis (syn. *P. laburnifolius*) Semi-evergreen shrub that produces racemes of pea-like yellow flowers among attractive leaves that are divided into three leaflets. Requires sun and winter protection in cold areas. H 3m (10ft) S 1.8m (6ft) Z8 [ill.p.174, foliage only]

Potentilla fruticosa '**Elizabeth**'

A compact rounded shrub, with small saucer-shaped flowers among the neat, divided leaves. Requires full sun. H 90cm (3ft) S 1.5m (5ft) Z3 [ill.p.178]

Clematis 'Bill Mackenzie'

Glaucium flavum

Iris pseudacorus

Lilium 'Connecticut King'

Phlomis fruticosa

Ranunculus lingua 'Grandiflorus'
GREATER SPEARWORT A tall
perennial buttercup for pond
margins or a bog-garden.
H 90cm (3ft) S 30cm (1ft) Z4
[ill.p.32]

Rosa ROSE
A good climbing variety is
'Golden Showers', which has
clusters of vivid yellow semi-
double flowers in succession.
H 2m (7ft) S 2.1m (6ft6in) Z5.
Good shrub roses include
'Graham Thomas', a fine yellow
'English' rose, H 1.2m (4ft)
S 1.5m (5ft) Z5 [ill.pp.141,172];
and *R. xanthina* 'Canary Bird'
with small single flowers
appearing early on arching
stems, and small fern-like leaves,
H and S 2.1m (7ft) Z5

Rudbeckia BLACK-EYED SUSAN
Perennial with yellow daisy-like
flowers that appear in late
summer and have dark, cone-
shaped centres. Requires sun or
partial shade. Good varieties
include *R. fulgida* var. *sullivantii*
'Goldsturm' H and S 90cm (3ft)
Z4 [ill.pp.31,177]; and
R. nitida 'Herbstsonne', a good
back-of-border plant, H 2.1m
(7ft) S 75cm (30in) Z5

Sedum acre STONECROP
A mat-forming succulent that
readily colonizes stone walls and
screes, in full sun. H 5cm (2in)
S indefinite Z5 [ill.p.172]

x *Solidaster luteus*
Perennial, the result of crossing
an *Aster* with a *Solidago,* with
sprays of small daisy-like flowers.
x *S.* 'Lemore' is a good variety
with plumes of tiny yellow
flowers late in summer; it forms
large clumps that may become
invasive. Enjoys sun or shade.
H 60cm (2ft) S 75cm (30in) Z4
[ill.p.139]

Verbascum 'Cotswold Queen'
MULLEIN Perennial that sends up
spikes of deep yellow flowers
from a rosette of broad mid-
green leaves. Prefers sun but will
tolerate shade. H 1.2m (4ft)
S 60cm (2ft) Z5 [ill.p.125]

AUTUMN FOLIAGE

*Autumn foliage can be pure yellow
with no trace of green. For 'yellow'
foliage see yellow-greens on p. 86*

Acer cappadocicum CAUCASIAN
MAPLE A stately tree, whose
lobed leaves turn butter-yellow
in autumn. Tolerates neutral to
acid soil and sun or partial
shade. H 20m (70ft) S 15m
(50ft) Z6

Ginkgo biloba MAIDENHAIR TREE
The fan-shaped leaves of this
slow-growing tree turn yellow in
autumn. Requires sun or partial
shade. H 30m (100ft) S 7.6m
(25ft) Z4 [ill. (in spring) p.136]

WINTER

Hamamelis mollis CHINESE WITCH
HAZEL Shrub with sweet-smelling
flowers, curiously shaped like
twisted wires, that appear on
bare branches in mid-winter.
Requires sun or partial shade
and peaty, acid soil. H and S
3.7m (12ft) Z6

Jasminum nudiflorum WINTER
JASMINE Usually trained as a
wall-shrub. In mild weather
through the winter waxy, yellow
flowers open on bare arching
stems. Requires full sun. H and S
3m (10ft) Z6

Mahonia x *media* 'Charity'
Evergreen shrub with clusters of
sweet-scented yellow flowers,
held above dark green spiny
foliage. Prefers shade. H 4m
(12ft) S 3m (10ft) Z6

STEMS

Cornus stolonifera 'Flaviramea'
DOGWOOD Shrub whose bare
young stems are yellow; cut
them back to near ground level
in spring to stimulate new
growth. Prefers sun. H 1.8m
(6ft) S 4m (12ft) Z2

Pale Yellows

SPRING

Corylopsis pauciflora BUTTERCUP
WITCH HAZEL Shrub with small,
fragrant bell-shaped flowers that
hang from spreading branches
before the leaves appear. Prefers
acid soil in partial shade. H 1.8m
(6ft) S 2.4m (8ft) Z6

Cytisus x *praecox* 'Warminster'
WARMINSTER BROOM Pale, lemon-
yellow pea-like flowers cover the
shrub in spring. Requires full sun
and soil that is not over-rich.
H and S 1.5m (5ft) Z5 [ill.p.179]

Erysimum cheiri WALLFLOWER
Short-lived perennial usually
treated as a biennial. Prefers sun.
[ill.pp.30,31,167,169]. Good
cultivars include 'Moonlight'
H 45cm (18in) S 30cm (12in);
and 'Primrose Bedder' H and S
40cm (15in)

Narcissus DAFFODIL
Good miniature varieties of this
bulb that have clusters of
delicate-looking trumpets
include 'Hawera' H 20cm (8in)
Z5 [ill.p.141]; and 'Jack Snipe'
H 23cm (9in) Z5

Primula
Perennial with flowers that rise
from a rosette of oval leaves.
Prefers sun or partial shade and
moist, peaty soil. *P. florindae*
GIANT COWSLIP is sweet-scented.
H 90cm (3ft) S 60cm (2ft) Z6
[ill.p.32]. *P. veris* COWSLIP has
heads of tubular flowers. H and S
20cm (8in) Z5. *P. vulgaris*
PRIMROSE has flat flowers, borne
singly. H and S 20cm (8in) Z5
[ill.p.136]

Tellima grandiflora FRINGECUPS
Semi-evergreen perennial with
spires of small cream bell-shaped
flowers, above heart-shaped
hairy leaves. Requires a cool
situation in partial shade. H and
S 60cm (24in) Z4 [ill.pp.71,139]

Tulipa TULIP
Bulb that appreciates summer
baking. Good varieties include
T. acuminata, with twisted, pale
yellow petals rimmed with red,
H 45cm (18in) S 23cm (9in) Z5;
T. kaufmanniana WATERLILY TULIP,
which is very early flowering,
H 35cm (14in) S 20cm (8in) Z5;
and *T. tarda*, which is very short
stemmed, and opens out into a
star-shape in full sun, H and S
15cm (6in) Z5 [ill.p.149]

SUMMER

Achillea 'Moonshine'
Perennial whose flowerheads are
flat disks of primrose yellow
which rise above feathery grey-
green foliage. Prefers sun.
H 60cm (24in) S 50cm (20in) Z4
[ill.p.179]

Aconitum MONKSHOOD
Perennial with poisonous
tuberous roots that prefers sun,
but tolerates some shade.
'Ivorine' has spikes of helmet-
shaped, creamy yellow flowers,
and elegantly divided leaves,
H 1.2m (4ft) S 60cm (2ft) Z5
[ill.p.181]; *A. lycoctonum* (syn.
A. vulparia) WOLFSBANE is darker
and shorter.

Anthemis tinctoria 'E.C. Buxton'
YELLOW CHAMOMILE Perhaps the
best choice for a primrose-
yellow daisy-like flower. It also
has fine, feathery foliage. Does
best in sun. H and S 90cm (3ft)
Z4 [ill.pp.31,157]

Rudbeckia nitida 'Herbstonne'

Acer cappadocicum

Cornus stolonifera 'Flaviramea'

Narcissus 'Jack Snipe'

Anthemis tinctoria 'E.C.Buxton'

Antirrhinum SNAPDRAGON
Seed for this annual is available for single colours, such as pale yellow, in most of the series, such as **Coronette** or **Monarch**. Prefers sun. H 45cm (18in) S 30cm (12in) [ill.p.139]

Asphodeline lutea JACOB'S ROD
Perennial rhizome with star-shaped flowers on tall spikes that grow from a fringe of spiky grey-green leaves. Prefers sun. H 1.2m (4ft) S 90cm (3ft) Z6

Cephalaria gigantea GIANT SCABIOUS
Perennial whose sprays of pin-cushion-shaped flowers are held high above the jagged-edged leaves. Prefers sun. H 1.8m (6ft) S 1.2m (4ft) Z3 [ill.p.181]

Clematis rehderiana
Climber producing clusters of little bell-shaped flowers that give an exquisite late-season scent. H and S 4.6m (15ft) Z6

Dietes bicolor
Evergreen perennial. The flat, creamy yellow flowers have brown blotches at the base of the petals. Narrow grass-like leaves. Prefers sun. H 90cm (3ft) S 60cm (2ft) Z9

Digitalis grandiflora YELLOW FOXGLOVE Perennial with spikes of soft, tubular flowers that grow from a rosette of smooth oblong leaves. Best in partial shade and moist soil. H 90cm (3ft) S 30cm (12in) Z4

Gentiana lutea GREAT YELLOW GENTIAN Perennial with starry flowers arranged in whorls

around tall, sturdy spikes above tufts of large oval leaves. Prefers sun or partial shade and moist, neutral to acid soil. H 1.2m (4ft) S 60cm (2ft) Z5

Helianthemum 'Wisley Primrose' ROCK ROSE Evergreen shrub whose little saucer-shaped flowers last only a day, but they are produced in succession over several weeks to give a mound of colour. Best in full sun. H 45cm (18in) S 60cm (24in) Z6

Helichrysum 'Schweffellicht'
Perennial that makes clumps of small, tufty flowers, which dry well when picked, and silvery foliage. Prefers sun. H 60cm (24in) S 30cm (12in) Z5

Hemerocallis citrina DAYLILY
Perennial with flowers that open in the evening. Prefers full sun and moist soil. Slug and snail control is essential. H and S 75cm (30in) Z4

Hypericum olympicum 'Citrinum'
Open, creamy-yellow flowers with darker yellow stamens cover the compact shrub through the summer. Prefers full sun. H and S 30cm (12in) Z6

Kniphofia 'Little Maid'
Perennial with poker-shaped spikes of creamy-yellow tubular flowers that grow out of clumps of narrow, grass-like leaves. Prefers sun. H 60cm (24in) S 45cm (18in) Z5

Lilium monadelphum (syn. *L. szovitsianum*) CAUCASIAN LILY
Bulb with exquisite large

pendant flowers, with crimson tips to the curving petals. Prefers sun. H 1m (3ft3in) S 30cm (12in) Z5

Lonicera japonica 'Halliana'
JAPANESE HONEYSUCKLE One of the best honeysuckles for scent, this evergreen climber has flowers that open cream but mature to pale straw-yellow. Tolerates sun or partial shade. H and S 10m (30ft) Z5

Lupinus LUPIN
L. arboreus TREE LUPIN is a quick growing but short-lived shrub with spikes of fragrant flowers. H 8ft (2.4m) S 6ft (1.8m) Z4 [ill.pp.6,25,168]. **'Chandelier'** is a perennial with spires of pea-like flowers above cut foliage, which is shaped like an open fan. H 1.2m (4ft) S 60cm (2ft) Z3 [ill.pp.141,172]. Both prefer sun.

Nepeta govaniana
Perennial producing sprays of small, hooded creamy-yellow flowers with a touch of brighter yellow on the lip, useful for a soft haze of yellow. Prefers sun and moist soil. H 90cm (3ft) S 60cm (2ft) Z5 [ill.p.157]

Oenothera biennis EVENING PRIMROSE Perennial with delicate, saucer-shaped flowers that open in succession in the evening, and fade to pale pink by the following day. Prefers full sun and sandy soil. H 1.5m (5ft) S 20cm (8in) Z4 [ill.p.180]

Osteospermum 'Buttermilk'
Tender in all but the most

benign climates, this evergreen perennial daisy is useful for summer bedding and container plantings. Best in sun. H 60cm (24in) S 30cm (12in) Z9 [ill.p.31]

Phygelius aequalis 'Yellow Trumpet' Evergreen or semi-evergreen sub-shrub that produces clusters of hanging, tubular flowers in a sheltered situation. Prefers sun H and S 1.2m (4ft) Z8 [ill.p.167]

Potentilla recta var. *sulphurea*
Perennial with cup-shaped flowers in loose clusters, and lobed leaves like those of a strawberry. Prefers sun. H to 45cm (18in) S 60cm (24in) Z4 [ill.p.172]

Rosa ROSE
Good climbing varieties include **'Albéric Barbier'** which is semi-evergreen and will tolerate a shady wall, H 5m (15ft) S 3m (10ft) Z7; **R. banksiae** 'Lutea' BANKSIAN ROSE which has clusters of creamy yellow double flowers like frilly buttons, is thornless, and enjoys the shelter of a warm wall, H and S 9m (30ft) Z9; and **'Mermaid'** which has broad, single flowers and a slightly stiff habit and so looks best trained against a wall, H and S 2.4m (8ft) Z7. Good shrub roses include **'Golden Wings'** which has exquisite pale yellow single flowers with bright yellow stamens, repeating throughout the summer, H 1.5m (5ft) S 90cm (3ft) Z7; and **R. xanthina**

f. hugonis H 2.4m (8ft) S 3.7m (12ft) Z5

Santolina pinnata subsp. *neapolitana* Evergreen shrub that produces small primrose-yellow flowers above feathery silvery-green foliage. May be shaped to make a low hedge. Prefers sun. H 75cm (30in) S 90cm (3ft) Z7 [ill.pp.176,178]

Sisyrinchium striatum
Semi-evergreen perennial with towers of small flowers that emerge from tufts of sword-shaped leaves. Prefers sun. H 60cm (24in) S 30cm (12in) Z8 [ill.p.167]

Verbascum 'Gainsborough'
MULLEIN Semi-evergreen perennial with branching spikes of cupped flowers that make a wonderful frothy mass of creamy yellow. Tolerates shade but prefers an open sunny site. H 1.2m (4ft) S 60cm (2ft) Z5 [ill.pp.141,157]

WINTER

Clematis cirrhosa var. *balearica*
Evergreen climber whose nodding down-turned flowers have crimson spots towards their throats. H and S 3m (10ft) Z7

Hamamelis x *intermedia* 'Pallida'
WITCH HAZEL Shrub with deliciously scented spiky flowers that open on bare branches. Tolerates sun or partial shade and is best in peaty, acid soil. H and S 3.7m (12ft) Z5

Clematis rehderiana

Kniphofia 'Little Maid'

Lilium monadelphum

Rosa banksiae 'Lutea'

Clematis cirrhosa var. *balearica*

ABOVE The sun in late summer lights up the peeling bark of *Acer griseum* as if it was on fire. The same light gives an orange cast to the scarlet flowers of *Crocosmia* 'Lucifer'. The edges of the rodgersia foliage at the foot of the tree offer an echo of brownish orange. *Acer griseum* is a fine tree in all seasons, but is especially useful in winter when its mahogany trunk and branches, with their peeling orange skins, brings scarce colour to the garden.

Oranges

Orange is a demanding, attention-grabbing colour. It can be difficult to place because it reacts so fiercely with other colours, harmonizing only with orange-red and yellow, or with unsaturated versions of itself, such as bronze and ivory. Some gardeners banish it from their gardens altogether, but if you crave strong colour, you will love orange for its richness and intensity.

Falling between red and yellow on the colour wheel (see page 15), pure orange is at the core of the 'hot' group of colours. The most obvious way to use it is with other hot colours. For a cheerful hot splash in spring, plant orange tulips with red and yellow ones. A bold, hot planting of oranges with reds and yellows more than holds its own in midsummer, especially in strong, bright sunlight. Try vivid orange rock roses with glitzy orange alstroemerias, orange daisies and Californian poppies. For late summer there is a wealth of orange flowers available, with perennial crocosmias, kniphofias and dahlias, combined with annual marigolds and nasturtiums. Later still, orange takes its place with reds and yellows in the autumn foliage of maples, fothergilla and euonymus.

A way to moderate the intensity of orange flowers is to partner them with bronze or cream. There are very few bronze flowers – *Viola* 'Irish Molly' is one example – but there are several foliage plants, including heucheras, phormiums, cotinus, cordyline and fennel that make excellent bronze or bronze-red foliage companions. Take account, too, of the interesting mahogany-orange bark of trees such as the paperbark maple (*Acer griseum*), or the strawberry tree (*Arbutus* x *andrachnoides*), which can contribute to orange plantings. Orange fruit are worth considering too, especially those of the orange tree itself, although in temperate regions these can only be grown outside in tubs which are moved indoors in winter. In some Italian gardens, orange trees in terracotta pots supply the only stab of bright colour among formal hedging and statuary.

Because orange is so dominant, it is easier, especially in a small garden, to use it as an isolated patch of colour, rather than for a complete border, where it could quickly become overpowering. You could also limit orange to a container planting. Because of its harmonizing colour, a simple terracotta pot would make a good base for a sequence of orange and bronze plantings. Begin in spring with orange tulips, such as 'Generaal de Wet', combined with orange wallflowers. For summer you could replace these with orange gazanias and trailing nasturtiums, arranged round a central rosette of red-bronze *Cordyline australis*. These plantings would be all the more intense in a blue ceramic pot, since orange and blue are complementary colours and enhance each other to maximum effect.

LEFT ABOVE The colour of the orange tulips is so intense that, even planted 45cm/18in apart, they stand out vividly against the green of the box parterre. This sparse planting is in the style of the seventeenth century when tulip bulbs were rare and expensive.

LEFT BELOW The orange-flowered *Helianthemum* 'Fire Dragon', the orange *Alstroemeria aurea* and the daisy-flowered *Anthemis sancti-johannis* have been assembled round a stone trough. An all-orange scheme like this is stimulating in a small corner of the garden, like this, but would be overpowering in a larger area.

BELOW The foliage of bronze fennel (*Foeniculum vulgare* 'Purpureum') gives support to an orange variety of oriental poppy (*Papaver orientale*) which would otherwise need staking. Its solid blob of colour contrasts with the more diffuse flowerheads of *Euphorbia griffithii* 'Fireglow'. The sword-shaped foliage is *Crocosmia masoniorum*, which will contribute its orange flowers later.

Pale Orange and Apricot

Pale orange and apricot are unsaturated versions of their parent colour, and share some of the same properties. Delicate and warm, they bridge the divide between pinks and yellows, and they translate into flowers of exquisite beauty, often naturally producing soft harmonies within the same flower. The hybrid musk rose 'Penelope', for instance, has buds of pale orange which lighten to apricot as they open, then fade to cream. Certain strains of Candelabra primulas run the whole gamut from pale orange to warm pink, with such diversity in adjacent, or even the same plant, that they hardly need companions.

These warm colours look good with closely-related tints of pale yellow and yellow-pink, and with muted russets and bronzes. However, they are difficult to place with other colours, especially with cool blue-pinks, because the warm and cool elements fight one another. Instead, it is a good idea to limit them to plantings restricted almost to a single colour. Choose one particular pale orange plant, and build up a collection of flowers around it, perhaps based on colour echoes. You can exploit the orange stamens of a lily, for instance, to make a link with the whiskers on the fall of a bearded iris.

Alternatively, flatter and subdue apricot by surrounding it with creams, pale yellows and the yellow-greens of foliage. Try pale amber irises with primrose-yellow ones, and combine them with lime-green euphorbias and the foliage of golden hop.

ABOVE The rose 'Penelope' is partnered here with a creamy hybrid of the common foxglove (*Digitalis purpurea*). The pale orange buds of the rose and its coppery red stems are concentrated versions of colours that appear in a faded form in the mature flowers. The deep pink foxglove is a wild seedling.

ABOVE A clump of the yellow turkscap lily (*Lilium pyrenaicum*) with bright orange stamens, is teamed with *Iris* 'Canary Bird' which has an orange beard. This lily is one of the earliest to flower. A good choice for later in the summer is the taller *Lilium x testaceum*, which has apricot flowers and bright orange stamens.

ABOVE The wispy buff-coloured flowers of a grass and the 'Bright Star' lily, with its pale, orange-throated cream trumpets, soften the contrast between the oranges and yellows of daylilies. At the front of the border is a clump of the annual African daisy (*Lonas annua*) which has disk-shaped flowerheads, like a small achillea.

RIGHT The muted ginger-orange flowers of the clump of irises in the foreground have yellow centres that make a link with the more distant pale yellow irises and the yellow-green flowerheads of the euphorbias and the foliage beyond. Tall bearded irises like these will nearly always dominate a scheme because they present large blobs of rich colour, but they have a short flowering period – two weeks at most – so do not rely on them as the backbone for a colour scheme.

RIGHT In boggy ground beside a stream, Candelabra primulas stretch as far as the eye can see. These are Inshriach Hybrids, which have enough natural variation to produce their own harmonizing scheme of pale orange, salmon and amber-yellow. They have spread themselves by seed over the years, and colonized the waterside. The tall perennial St Bruno's lily (*Paradisea liliastrum*) was planted higher up the bank because it needs a well-drained soil, and it is spreading too.

Oranges

SPRING

Aquilegia canadensis CANADIAN COLUMBINE Perennial with bicoloured flowers, yellow at the centre with vermilion spurs, that look orange at a distance. Prefers an open sunny site. H 60cm (24in) S 30cm (12in) Z4

Erysimum cheiri WALLFLOWER Evergreen perennial, best treated as a biennial. Requires an open sunny situation. H to 60cm (24in) S 38cm (14in) Z7 [ill.pp.132,178,179]

Fritillaria imperialis CROWN IMPERIAL Bulb with a ring of bell-like flowers, orange or yellow, topped by a fringe of green bracts suspended on a tall stem. Plant the bulbs on their sides on a bed of sand, to prevent them rotting from damp. Tolerates full sun or partial shade and grows best in soil that dries out slightly in summer. H 1.5m (5ft) S 30cm (12in) Z5

Rhododendron kaempferi Semi-evergreen shrub with clusters of funnel-shaped flowers that vary from orange through apricot to biscuit-colour. Needs acid soil. Best in dappled shade. H and S 2.4m (8ft) Z5 [ill.p.9]

Trollius chinensis '**Golden Queen**' GLOBEFLOWER Perennial with buttercup-like flowers that are uniformly orange with prominant stamens. Lovely cut foliage. Requires moist soil. H 75cm (30in) S 35cm (15in) Z4

Tulipa TULIP Sun-loving bulbs that appreciate summer baking. Good varieties include graceful ***T. clusiana*** var. ***chrysantha*** (syn. *T. aitchisonii*) LADY TULIP H 30cm (12in) S to 20cm (8in) Z6. *T.* '**Generaal de Wet**' is the best of the plain and simple orange tulips. H 45cm (18in) S 23cm (9in) Z4

SUMMER

Alstroemeria aurea (syn. *A. aurantiaca*) PERUVIAN LILY Perennial with large flowerheads composed of small lily-like flowers that are bright orange, streaked with crimson. Prefers sun and a sheltered site. H and S 90cm (3ft) Z7 [ill.p.39]

Asclepias tuberosa BUTTERFLY WEED Perennial with small upright, crown-shaped flowers arranged in clusters, and narrow lance-shaped leaves. Requires sun and a humus-rich, peaty soil. H 75cm (30in) S 45cm (18in) Z4

Calendula officinalis POT MARIGOLD Annual producing a succession of daisy-like flowers through the summer, and thriving on the poorest of soils. Double-flowered mixtures include **Art Shades** and **Fiesta Gitana**. Needs sun. H and S 30cm (12in)

Crocosmia MONTBRETIA Corm with flowers held on arching sprays above broad sword-shaped leaves. Thrives in a sunny, open situation. Good varieties include **C. masoniorum** H 1.5m (5ft) S 45cm (18in) Z7 [ill.pp.122,177]. **C.** '**Star of the East**' has larger, more open flowers on a smaller plant, giving a more concentrated stab of colour. H 90cm (3ft) S 23cm (9in) Z6 [ill.p.177]

Dahlia Countless varieties of this late flowering tuberous perennial are available, ranging from the small-flowered orange species ***D. coccinea*** to Cactus with double spiky flowers, Pompons with small spherical flowers, and singles. All require sun, and the tubers storing in frost-free conditions for the winter. Good varieties include '**Jescot Julie**' H 90cm (3ft) S 60cm (2ft) Z9

Eschscholzia californica CALIFORNIAN POPPY Annual producing single, vivid orange flowers that open in the sun, and feathery blue-green foliage. Requires sun and tolerates poor soil. H 30cm (12in) S 15cm (6in)

Euphorbia griffithii '**Fireglow**' Perennial with glowing orange flowerheads above short, narrow leaves with red midribs. Much used but can be invasive. Tolerates sun or partial shade and requires moist soil. H 90cm (3ft) S 50cm (20in) Z4 [ill.p.39]. *E.* '**Dixter**' is similar, but with rusty-red leaves [ill.pp.125,178, 179]

Geum AVENS Perennials that interweave well with others at the front of a border. Need sun and moist soil. Good varieties include '**Borisii**' with single orange flowers with brilliant yellow stamens; and '**Fire Opal**' with double bronze-red flowers [ill.p.133]. H and S 12in (30cm) Z4

Helenium SNEEZEWEED The wild species of this perennial has sprays of yellow daisy-like flowers, but a good garden variety is ***H. autumnale*** which has orange flowers [ill.p.144]. '**Wyndley**' has deep yellow flowers flecked with orange [ill.p.177]. Requires full sun. H to 1.5m (5ft) S 60cm (2ft) Z4

Helianthemum ROCK ROSE Good orange varieties of this evergreen shrub, such as '**Ben Hope**' and '**Ben More**', make compact mounds of colour from countless small flowers packed tight among small blue-green leaves. Requires full sun. H to 45cm (18in) S 60cm (24in) Z6 [ill.pp.39,178]

Hemerocallis DAYLILY Perennial with long arching leaves, and a daily successsion of flowers. Good varieties include ***H. fulva***, and ***H. f.*** '**Kwanso Variegata**'. Requires sun and most soil. H and S 90cm (3ft) Z4

Ipomoea lobata (syn. *Mina lobata*) SPANISH FLAG Annual climber with tubular flowers that are bright red in bud, fading to orange as they open, and then to cream. Clusters have flowers at each stage, giving a jazzy multicolour effect. Attractive leaves with three lobes. Requires sun and moist soil. H and S 3m (10ft)

Iris Tall bearded irises flower best when their rhizomes are on the surface of the soil and bake in full sun [ill.p.41]. Muted orange and brown varieties include '**Olympic Torch**' and '**Autumn Leaves**' H 90cm (3ft) S 40cm (15in) Z4

Ligularia dentata '**Desdemona**' Perennial with clusters of vivid orange daisy-shaped flowers that make an intense contrast with the dark green leaves, which are purple-red beneath. Tolerates sun or partial shade. Requires moist soil. H 1.2m (4ft) S 60cm (2ft) Z4

Lilium LILY Bulb. '**Enchantment**' has clusters of upward-facing flowers, with black markings. H 3ft (90cm) Z5. Late-summer flowering ***L. henryi*** has pale orange turkscap flowers, and flourishes in limey soil. H 90cm (3ft) Z4 [ill.p.132]. ***L. pardalinum*** LEOPARD LILY has erect stems bearing hanging turkscap flowers, vermilion above, orange below with red spots. H 1.8m (6ft) Z5

Lonicera* x *tellmanniana HONEYSUCKLE What this climber lacks in scent it makes up in its vivid yellow-orange colour.

Trollius chinensis

Tulipa 'Generaal de Wet'

Eschscholzia californica

Hemerocallis fulva 'Kwanso Variegata'

Lonicera x *tellmanniana*

Tolerates sun or partial shade. H and S 5m (15ft) Z6

Mimulus aurantiacus MONKEY MUSK A useful shrub for a container. It produces a succession of trumpet-shaped flowers, which vary in colour from peach to red-orange, through the summer. Requires sun and moist soil. H and S 1.5m (5ft) Z9

Rudbeckia hirta CONE FLOWER Perennial, grown as an annual, with daisy-like flowers with cone-shaped black centres produced through the summer. The leaves and stems are hairy. *R.h.* 'Marmalade' is a good orange variety. Tolerates sun or shade and needs moist soil. H 45cm (18in) S 30cm (1ft) Z7

Solanum pyracanthum Shrubby perennial grown for its blue-violet flowers, like those of a potato, and for the orange spines along its stems. Requires full sun. H and S 90cm (3ft) Z10 [ill.p.134]

Tagetes MARIGOLD Stubby, low-growing annual for the front of a border or as a colourful edging to a path. Flowers right through the summer. Requires sun. Good varieties include 'Disco Orange' and 'Star Fire' H and S 30cm (12in); and 'Tangerine Gem' which has single flowers of an intense all-over orange, H 20cm (8in) S 30cm (12in) [ill.p.134]

Tithonia rotundifolia MEXICAN SUNFLOWER Annual with deep orange daisy-like flowers with paler orange centres, on tapering tubular flower-stalks. Requires sun. H 1.5m (5ft) S 60cm (2ft)

Tropaeolum majus NASTURTIUM Annual with brilliant orange trumpet-shaped flowers with spurs borne among aromatic rounded leaves. Trailing varieties are available for hanging baskets, and more compact ones, with upturned flowers, for borders. Requires sun. Trailing varieties: H and S 1.5m (5ft), others H and S 60cm (2ft) [ill.pp.163,173]

AUTUMN

Kniphofia TORCH LILY Perennial producing dramatic spikes of flowers, like large candle flames, on long stems. *K. caulescens* has stout, tight-packed tapering flowerheads, with orange buds, opening to yellow. H 1.5m (5ft) S 1.2m (4ft) Z6. *K. triangularis* has looser flower-heads, uniformly orange, and narrow, grass-like leaves. H 1m (3ft3in) S 75cm (30in) Z6. Needs sun and moist soil.

Physalis alkekengi CHINESE LANTERN The sepals that frame the tiny white flowers of this perennial in summer, expand into bright orange bladders which enclose the fruits in fall. Tolerates sun or partial shade. H 45cm (18in) S 30cm (12in) Z5

BERRIES

Malus 'John Downie' CRAB APPLE Tree that prefers full sun but tolerates shade and any except waterlogged soil. H 9m (30ft) S 7m (20ft) Z4

Pyracantha FIRETHORN Shrub that tolerates sun or partial shade and needs a sheltered site and is effective trained against a wall. 'Orange Glow' has clusters of small berries that cover the plant in such profusion that the leaves become almost invisible. H 4.6m (15ft) S 3m (10ft) Z7

WINTER

STEMS

Salix alba var. *vitellina* 'Britzensis' (syn. *S.a.*'Chermesina') WHITE WILLOW Tree that prefers full sun and tolerates any soil but very dry. H 24m (80ft) S 9m (30ft), but H 2.4m (8ft) when coppiced annually Z2

Apricots

SPRING

Acer pseudoplatanus 'Brilliantissimum' SYCAMORE The young leaves of this tree are the colour of boiled shrimps for a few weeks in spring, before they fade to dull yellow and then turn green. H and S 6m (20ft) Z5

Tulipa 'Apricot Beauty' TULIP A reliable and early flowering bulb, apricot at the base and cream around the edges of the petals. Tolerates full sun or light shade. H 50cm (20in) S 23cm (9in) Z4

SUMMER

Crocosmia 'Solfaterre' MONTBRETIA Corm with spikes of apricot flowers that make a unity with the khaki-coloured spear-shaped leaves. Requires an open, sunny site. H 60cm (2ft) S 23cm (9in) Z7

Diascia 'Salmon Supreme' Perennial with loose spikes of small pale apricot flowers, useful for edging beds. Requires sun and humus-rich soil. H 30cm (12in) S 45cm (18in) Z8

Digitalis purpurea 'Sutton's Apricot' FOXGLOVE Biennial with spires of tubular pale apricot flowers. Prefers partial shade and moist soil. H 1.5m (5ft) S 60cm (2ft) Z3 [ill.pp.57,175]

Lilium LILY Good varieties of this sun-loving bulb include 'Bright Star' with downward-facing flowers with swept-back petals marked with central apricot-yellow streaks, H 1.5m (5ft) S 30cm (12in) Z5 [ill.p.40]; *L. x testaceum* NANKEEN LILY has waxy flowers, creamy apricot in colour, with vivid orange stamens, H 1.5m (5ft) S 30cm (12in) Z5

Potentilla fruticosa 'Daydawn' Shrub with small, open flowers of delicate apricot, merging into the yellow centre. They appear in succession on the bushy plant through the summer months. Requires shading from the hottest sun. H 90cm (3ft) S 1.2m (4ft) Z3

Rosa ROSE Most roses require an open, sunny site and moist soil. Good climbing varieties include 'Gloire de Dijon' with large double 'cabbage-shaped' flowers that are gingery-apricot in bud, and fade to cream with age. H and S 3.7m (12ft) Z6. Good shrub varieties include 'Buff Beauty' with flowers that are apricot in bud and when young, becoming creamy yellow as they fade, H and S 2.4m (8ft) Z6; 'Chicago Peace' with touches of pink and cream overlying a base colour of apricot, H 1.2m (4ft) S 90cm (3ft) Z7; 'Penelope' with pale apricot-pink flowers, H and S 1.5m (5ft) Z6 [ill.p.40]; and *R. x odorata* 'Mutabilis' with floppy single flowers that are variable in colour, opening apricot and fading to pink and later crimson, all visible together on one plant, H and S 2.4m (8ft) Z7

Verbena 'Peaches and Cream' Perennial with rounded flowerheads that have some orange flowers and some creamy yellow, giving an overall apricot effect. Requires sun. H 45cm (18in) S 30cm (12in) Z9

Tithonia rotundifolia

Physalis alkekengi

Pyracantha 'Orange Glow'

Lilium x *testaceum*

Rosa 'Buff Beauty'

ABOVE This skilful summer planting combines *Dahlia* 'Bishop of Llandaff' with matching *Pelargonium* 'Paul Crampel'. It works without being overpowering, not only because the flowers are evenly spaced among the abundant foliage, but also because of the introduction of the light green tobacco plants (*Nicotiana* x *sanderae* 'Lime Green'). The colour match between the foliage of the dahlia and the paintwork of the chair is a brilliant touch.

Reds

Red stands for danger. Red lights and red flags are supposed to stop us in our tracks. We are said to 'see red' when we are angry and to 'paint the town red' when we have a wild night out. Our feelings for red are also coloured by its association with blood. Blood itself can stand for injury and pain, but also for passion. All these subliminal memories affect us when we see red in the garden.

Artists know how to play on the potency of red, perhaps using just a dab of this colour to draw the eye into a picture. It has the same effect in a garden where a few vibrant red flowers – poppies for instance – will attract attention like fireworks in a night sky. Red flowers are nearly always seen against contrasting green foliage. Used in profusion, pure red flowers will dominate everything around them. But as an occasional touch of brilliant colour, red flowers can give weight to a planting, spicing up neighbouring colours that might otherwise appear insipid. The most useful plants in this respect are those with small and scattered red flowers, like geums, heucheras, verbenas and potentillas, that can punctuate a multicolour planting with small dots of red and brighten up adjacent colours without swamping them.

Broadly, there are two families of reds. The scarlets and vermilions verge towards the yellow section of the colour wheel, whereas the crimsons, with a touch of blue in them, are on the cooler, violet side. Unlike most other colours, reds are only truly red in their saturated form. When red pigments are diluted with other colours, the result assumes a different character altogether. Red with yellow becomes orange; red with blue becomes purple; and mixtures of red with white make pink. You need to be careful when using these derivatives of red in the garden: they do not all sit happily together. Hot, vermilion 'letterbox' red has an especially uneasy relationship with any pink. This combination may be exploited in small doses, but is jarring on a large scale.

So-called 'red' foliage, like that of the copper beech and the castor-oil plant, contains green chlorophyll, which overlies the red pigment to produce a near-black shade. In some lights this can look purple, and it has a cooling effect in the company of red flowers. Associations of red flowers and near-black foliage can look suprisingly gloomy *en masse*, and are best kept as dramatic incidents. Otherwise it is good idea to use some bright green foliage or lighter flowers to alleviate the dark tones. For a more cheerful scheme, for instance, you could introduce some red flowers with bright yellow stamens, from among the dahlias perhaps, or else include some orangey-red flowers, like nasturtiums, red valerian, annual alonsoa or the tender perennial, arctotis.

ABOVE Silky red poppies accompany the rose 'Frensham', the near-black sweet william (*Dianthus barbatus* Nigrescens Group) and the dark red snapdragon with deep red foliage (*Antirrhinum* 'Black Prince'). A few flower spikes of *Salvia elegans* are slightly obscured by foliage towards the back. In all-red plantings like this, bright green foliage like that of the annual poppy lightens up the effect and balances the dusky reds of the underplanting which are exciting but need contrast to show them up.

ABOVE In one of a pair of red borders, a clump of *Lobelia* 'Cherry Ripe' grows through a fringe of *Potentilla atrosanguinea* 'Gibson's Scarlet' with two scarlet dahlias mingling behind. The smoky leaves of the left-hand *Dahlia* 'Bishop of Llandaff' are echoed by the background foliage of purple cob-nut (*Corylus maxima* 'Purpurea'). Elsewhere in this border, the dark reds are relieved by incidents of deep blue, from delphiniums and aconitums, and of orange from lilies and daylilies.

Red Borders

The best plants for a long lasting all-red border will include those that flower non-stop from mid-summer to autumn, as well as some to provide foliage interest throughout this period. Many of these are tender perennials or annuals, which means that they will need planting out afresh each year. Although this is labour intensive, it gives flexibility and opportunities to experiment with different combinations.

The flower colours in an all-red border need to be fully saturated reds. You can choose hot reds, such as scarlets and vermilions, or cooler, darker, crimsons. Mixing scarlets and crimsons gives a vibrancy of colour which is stimulating, but falls short of the 'colour shock' that comes from putting scarlets and pinks together. As for foliage, you can choose plants with harmonizing deep red leaves, or those with contrasting and lighter, green leaves.

LEFT This border in which red flowers and foliage reach a crescendo in late summer, gives an overall impression of deep, resonant colour, with hot, scarlet highlights in a relatively cool setting of crimsons and purples. The inky dahlia foliage is echoed by that of the purple-leaved shrubs that comprise the backdrop, and by the sedum and dark-leaved beet at the front. The crimson-variegated *Iresine herbstii* leaves lighten up the sobriety of the foliage. (Full planting details of this scheme are given on page 173.)

RIGHT Roses, *Lychnis chalcedonica* and arctotis form the backbone of this glowing planting in which the predominantly lighter, vermilion red flowers make a link with the dulled terracotta-red brick wall behind them. Note how much the foliage influences the effect – the pale green leaves of the red opium poppy lighten the mood, and make a contrast with the sombre leaves of the neighbouring dahlia. (Full planting details of this scheme are given on page 173.)

Deep Plum Reds

Muted forms of red make subtler plantings than bright reds. Flowers of deep plum or garnet are especially desirable, and make near-matching partnerships with the foliage of some prunus, berberis and cotinus. They also make gentle contrasts with the greens of normal foliage, and combine comfortably with pinks. In this respect they are much more peaceable in mixed colour borders than the more ostentatious scarlets.

Because its colour is so dense, deep red foliage can be gloomy on its own. But it adds rich depths of colour when it is interspersed with bright green or silver foliage. Coloured foliage needs to be used with discretion. In gardens where all the trees and shrubs are plum- or yellow-leaved, the eye yearns for the calming influence of green.

ABOVE Flowering together in late summer against a wall, the single-flowered *Clematis* 'Ville de Lyon' and the double *C. viticella* 'Purpurea Plena Elegans' offer approximately the same plum-red hue in quite different flower forms.

FAR LEFT A deep plum bearded iris has been perfectly colour matched with an oriental poppy (*Papaver orientale* 'Patty's Plum'). The dusky *Cotinus coggygria* 'Royal Purple' that forms the backdrop picks up the darker shades of the iris falls, and the black centres of the poppies.

LEFT Well placed between two red-leaved shrubs, *Astrantia major* 'Hadspen Blood' stands out brightly against the background *Berberis* x *ottawensis* 'Superba', and makes a close colour match with the young leaves of the dwarf *Berberis thunbergii* 'Atropurpurea Nana' in the foreground.

Scarlets and Vermilions

SPRING

Tulipa TULIP
Bulb that tolerates sun or partial shade and appreciates summer baking. Bold scarlet tulips look inviting in containers beside a front door. Good varieties include 'Plaisir' H 20cm (8in) S 25cm (10in) Z4; *T. praestans* H 45cm (18in) S 23cm (9in) Z5 [ill.p.5]; and 'Red Shine' which is Lily-flowered and blooms late and for a long period, H 60cm (24in) S 35cm (10in) Z4

SUMMER

Arctotis x *hybrida* 'Flame'(syn. x Venidioarctotis) AFRICAN DAISY A graceful annual daisy which only opens in full sun. Available in several colours; the vermilion one verges towards soft tangerine. Requires sun. H 50cm (20in) S 40cm (16in) Z10 [ill.p.173]

Canna indica INDIAN SHOT\CANNA LILY Rhizome that makes an exotic centrepiece for a large container or a bedding scheme, with huge translucent leaves and folded scarlet flowers. *C. i.* 'Purpurea' has deep red foliage. Requires sun and moist, rich soil. H 2m (6ft6in) S 90cm (3ft) Z9

Crocosmia 'Lucifer' MONTBRETIA
Corm with arching sprays of vivid scarlet flowers and bright, spear-shaped foliage that make this a staple for an all-red border. Best in an open, sunny situation. H 1m (3ft3in) S 40cm (15in) Z5 [ill.pp.13,19,38,122]

Dahlia 'Bishop of Llandaff'
Tuberous perennial whose single scarlet flowers have lightening yellow centres. Grown as much for its liquorice-coloured foliage. Requires sun. H and S 90cm (3ft) Z9 [ill.pp.44,173,177]

Geum 'Mrs J. Bradshaw' AVENS
Perennial with small double flowers on longish stems that provide dots of strong colour at the front of the border. Requires sun and moist soil. H 80cm (2ft8in) S 45cm (18in) Z5

Helenium SNEEZEWEED
A good red variety of this perennial is 'Moerheim Beauty'. Requires full sun. H to 1.5m (5ft) S 60cm (2ft) Z4 [ill.pp.13,19]

Hemerocallis 'Stafford' DAYLILY
Perennial with a daily succession of flowers of a deep copper red, with long arching leaves. Requires full sun and moist soil. H and S 90cm (3ft) Z4

Lobelia cardinalis CARDINAL FLOWER
Perennial with tall spikes of vivid scarlet flowers that tolerates sun or partial shade in moist soil, even in boggy ground beside a pond. H 1m (3ft3in) S 30cm (12in) Z3 [ill.pp.45,177].
L. 'Queen Victoria' has deep red, near-black foliage. H 1m (3ft3in) S 30cm (12in) Z6 [ill.p.80]

Lychnis chalcedonica MALTESE CROSS Perennial with star-shaped flowers that are massed in compact rounded flowerheads on tall stems, giving brilliant blobs of vermilion for the 'hot' border. Requires sun. H 1.2m (4ft) S 45cm (18in) Z4 [ill.p.173]

Papaver POPPY
Annual *P. commutatum* 'Lady Bird' has a black blotch at the base of the scarlet petals. H and S 45cm (18in). Perennial *P. orientale* ORIENTAL POPPY has flowers that open like crumpled tissue paper, their brilliance eclipsing all but the brightest companions. H and S 90cm (3ft) Z4. [ill.p.8] A good deep red variety is *P. o.* 'Beauty of Livermere' [ill.p.167]. All do best in full sun.

Pelargonium GERANIUM
Evergreen perennial, sometimes treated as an annual. A house, porch or conservatory plant that will thrive outside in full sun in summer, in containers or borders that are not damp. Countless varieties are available, with scarlet, crimson, pink, salmon or white flowers, some with patterned foliage. Among the best with red flowers is 'Paul Crampel' H and S 45cm (18in) Z9 [ill.pp.44,128]

Penstemon
Semi-evergreen perennials that make clumps of flowers lasting over a long period. Good varieties include *P. barbatus* with spikes of slender tubular flowers Z4. 'Flame' Z9, 'Rubicundus' Z9 and 'Schoenholzeri' Z6 have broader flowers giving a brighter splash of colour. H up to 90cm (3ft) S 60cm (2ft) All do best in sun.

Potentilla atrosanguinea 'Gibson's Scarlet' Perennial with clusters of flowers of the most vivid red, contrasting with the intense green of the strawberry-like leaves. Tolerates full sun, but is best in partial shade for the most vibrant colour. H and S 45cm (18in) Z5 [ill.p.45]

Rosa ROSE
Good climbing roses include 'Dublin Bay' H and S 2.1m (7ft) Z6; 'Parkdirektor Riggers' H and S 3.7m (12ft) Z6 [ill.p.173]. Good shrub roses include *R. moyesii* which has the double interest of single scarlet flowers and brilliant red hips, seen against yellowing foliage in the autumn. H 4m (13ft) S 3m (10ft) Z5

Salvia SAGE
The sub-shrub *S. fulgens* has racemes of scarlet flowers on crimson-red stems borne above slightly hairy leaves. H and S 75cm (30in) Z9. The evergreen shrub *S. microphylla* (syn. *S. grahamii*) has rounded and lipped scarlet flowers. H and S 1.2m (4ft) Z9 [ill.p.183].
S. splendens SCARLET SAGE, a perennial sub-shrub grown as an annual, is sometimes mocked as the archetypal bedding plant, but undeservedly, as it can provide a useful flash of scarlet at the front of a border if sensitively used. Good cultivars include *S.s.* 'Blaze of Fire' and 'Lady in Red'. H and S 30cm (12in) Z10 [ill.p.19]

Tropaeolum speciosum
Rhizomatous climber with clusters of spurred, scarlet flowers that hang like curtains from supporting plants or structures. Requires sun, but roots must be shaded. H and S 3m (10ft) Z7 [ill.p.128]

Verbena
Annual or perennial that is useful for the front of a red border, or as a cascade of colour from the edge of a container. Good varieties with rounded clusters of tiny scarlet flowers include 'Lawrence Johnston' [ill.p.173], and 'Nero' [ill.p.144]. Both require sun. H 30cm (12in) S 60cm (2ft) Z10

Zauschneria californica (syns. *Epilobium californicum, E. canum*) Perennial sub-shrub with dainty tubular vermilion flowers that cover the plant for several weeks in late summer. Requires sun. H 45cm (18in) S 75cm (30in) Z8

Zinnia
Annual with bold and generous-sized daisy flowers to add zest to a summer border. Requires sun. H 60cm (2ft) S 30cm (12in)

Tulipa 'Red Shine'

Hemerocallis 'Stafford'

Papaver commutatum 'Lady Bird'

Salvia fulgens

Zauschneria californica

AUTUMN

Schizostylis coccinea KAFFIR LILY
Rhizome with graceful vase-shaped flowers and narrow leaves. Requires sun and moist soil. H 60cm (24in) S 30cm (12in) Z6

FOLIAGE

Acer MAPLE
A. palmatum JAPANESE MAPLE has seven-lobed leaves that turn scarlet for a week or two before falling. H and S 6m (20ft) Z6 [ill.p.129]. **A. p. 'Osakazuki'** has leaves that turn bright scarlet. H and S 4.5m (15ft). **A. japonicum 'Aconitifolium'** has delicately cut leaves that turn red and yellow. H and S 7m (22ft) Z6. **A. rubrum** H 18m (60ft) S 11m (36ft) Z3. They tolerate sun and partial shade in neutral to acid soil.

Liquidambar styraciflua
Tree with brilliant red and yellow autumn colours. Requires sun and moist soil. H 22.5m (75ft) S 12m (40ft) Z5

Parthenocissus quinquefolia
VIRGINIA CREEPER Climber that is capable of covering complete buildings, making them glow crimson for a short season. Requires sun or partial shade. H and S 15m (50ft) Z4 [ill.p.129]

Vitis coignetiae CRIMSON GLORY VINE Climber with large heart-shaped leaves, up to 30cm (1ft) wide, that take on crimson to orange tints. Tolerates sun or partial shade. Prefers chalky soil. H and S 15m (50ft) Z5 [ill.p.129]

WINTER

BARK

Cornus alba 'Sibirica' SIBERIAN DOGWOOD Shrub that needs pruning back in spring to within 30cm (1ft) of ground level, to en-courage young shoots; these have brilliant scarlet bark, but it is less colourful on older growth. Tolerates sun and partial shade. H and S 2m (6ft6in) Z3 [ill.pp.16,170]

Crimsons and Deep Reds

SPRING

Paeonia officinalis 'Rubra Plena' PEONY Perennial cottage garden favourite that survives in the same garden for generations. To increase it, divide the tubers, but it may take two or three years to recover. Prefers sun but will tolerate light shade in rich soil. H and S 75cm (30in) Z3 [ill.p.183]

SUMMER

Centranthus ruber RED VALERIAN Perennial that remains in flower for much of the summer, and will regenerate if you cut it back. Self-seeding, and a survivor in the most unlikely places. There are pink and white varieties too. Requires sun and thrives in an exposed situation and poor, alkaline soil. H 75cm (30in) S 60cm (24ft) Z5 [ill.p.131]

Clematis
Good climbing varieties include **'Ville de Lyon'** which has crimson flowers, with cream-coloured anthers [ill.p.48]; and **C. viticella 'Purpurea Plena Elegans'** which has muted crimson flowers like stuffed velvet buttons [ill.pp.17, 48]. Both tolerate shade or full sun but need their roots shaded. H and S 3m (10ft) Z6

Dianthus barbatus SWEET WILLIAM
Each flowerhead of this biennial is like a bouquet, and each flower throbs with concentric rings of colour. Requires an open, sunny situation in slightly alkaline soil. H 75cm (30in) S 30cm (12in) Z4 [ill.pp.75,113]

Monarda BERGAMOT
Perennial whose rounded whorls of hooded crimson-red flowers have an overall jagged appearance that makes the plant useful as a softening influence in an all-red border, breaking up the hard edges of adjacent plants. Requires sun and moist soil. Good varieties include **'Cambridge Scarlet'** H 1m (3ft3in) S 45cm (18in) Z4 [ill.p.177]; **M. didyma** H 90cm (3ft) S 45cm (18in) Z4; and **'Mrs Perry'** H 50cm (20in) S 45cm (18in) Z4 [ill.p.173]

Penstemon 'Garnet'
One of the most popular varieties of the semi-evergreen perennials that make clumps of flowers lasting over a long period. Requires full sun. H 75cm (30in) S 60cm (2ft) Z6 [ill.p.175]

Rosa ROSE
Most need an open, sunny site with moist soil. Good climbing roses include the dusky crimson and deeply scented **'Guinée'** H 5m (15ft) Z6. Good shrub roses include **'Dusky Maiden'** with clusters of semi-double flowers of deply shaded scarlet, H 1.2m (54t) S 1.5m (5ft) Z5 [ill.p.6]; **'Frensham'** which is cluster-flowered and deep red, H 1.2m (4ft) S 75cm (30in) Z6 [ill.pp.45,166]; and **'Tuscany Superb'** which is a Gallica rose, double in form and velvety crimson in colour, H and S 1.1m (3ft6in) Z5

Deep Plum and Smoky Reds

SPRING

Helleborus orientalis LENTEN ROSE
Evergreen perennial with many flower colours available, from yellow-green to spotted pink, the most desirable are the dusky reds, and near-blacks. Requires partial shade and moisture-retentive soil. H and S 45cm (18in) Z4

Tulipa 'Queen of Night' TULIP
Bulb that produces single late-flowering tulips of a deep velvety purple. Requires a sunny situation. H 60cm (2ft) S 23cm (9in) Z4 [ill.pp.10,149,169]

SUMMER

Antirrhinum 'Black Prince'
SNAPDRAGON Annual whose flowers are so dark that there is only a glint of red in good light. Requires sun. H 45cm (18in) S 30cm (12in) [ill.pp.45,131]

Astrantia major 'Hadspen Blood'
Perennial with a familiar crown-shaped flower, but a deep muddied red. Tolerates sun or partial shade. H 60cm (24in) S 45cm (18in) Z4 [ill.p.48]

Cosmos atrosanguineus CHOCOLATE COSMOS Tuberous perennial whose near-black flowers are coppery red in good light, and smell of chocolate. Requires sun and moist soil. H 60cm (24in) S 45cm (18in) Z8 [ill.p.16]

Dianthus barbatus Nigrescens Group SWEET WILLIAM Biennial whose flowers and foliage create a black shadow towards the front of the all-red border. Requires an open, sunny situation in slightly alkaline soil. H 75cm (30in) S 30cm (12in) Z4 [ill.pp.45,119,131,173]

Geranium phaeum MOURNING WIDOW Perennial with exquisite

Acer palmatum 'Osakazuki'

Centranthus ruber

Monarda 'Cambridge Scarlet'

Rosa 'Tuscany Superb'

Geranium phaeum

translucent small black flowers that glow deep purple with the light behind them. Requires shade and any but waterlogged soil. H 75cm (30in) S 45cm (18in) Z4 [ill.p.183]

Knautia macedonica
Star performing perennial that produces a succession of small dark-shaded crimson flowers throughout the summer. Requires sun. H 75cm (30in) S 60cm (2ft) Z5 [ill.pp.164,183]

Rosa ROSE
Requires an open, sunny site and a moist soil. Good shrub roses include the dusky crimson **'Cardinal de Richelieu'** H 1.2m (4ft) S 90cm (3ft) Z5; and **'Nuits de Young'** H 1.2m (4ft) S 90cm (3ft) Z5

Viola **'Molly Sanderson'** PANSY
The deepest black viola, but **'Bowles' Black'** is a good second choice. H and S 25cm (10in) Z4

FOLIAGE

Acer MAPLE
Shrubs and trees that require sun or partial shade in neutral to acid soil. *A. palmatum* Dissectum **Atropurpureum Group** JAPANESE MAPLE Very slow-growing, it produces a mound of finely cut leaves that reach to the ground. H 1.5m (5ft) S 2.4m (8ft) Z6 [ill.p.16]. *A. platanoides* **'Crimson King'** NORWAY MAPLE is a good specimen tree with dark purple-red foliage. H 15m (50ft) S 10m (33ft) Z3 [ill.p.177]

Anthriscus sylvestris **'Ravenswing'** COW PARSLEY Perennial that would be regarded as a wild flower, if not a weed, were it not for its lovely deep red-black divided foliage, which makes a strong tonal contrast with its own diaphanous white flowers. H 90cm (3ft) S 60cm (2ft) Z5

Atriplex hortensis var. *rubra* RED MOUNTAIN SPINACH Annual with useful plum-red foliage. Requires full sun. Grows well in coastal situations. H 1.2m (4ft) S 30cm (1ft) [ill.pp.131,184]

Berberis thunbergii f. *atropurpurea*
A useful but unostentatious shrub, small-leaved and amenable to pruning so that it can be used as a hedge. Tolerates sun or partial shade and thrives in any except waterlogged soil. H 2.4m (8ft) S 3m (10ft) Z5 [ill.pp.48,131,177]. *B. t.* 'A. Nana' is a dwarf variety. H and S 60cm (2ft) [ill.pp.148,178]

Beta vulgaris **'Bull's Blood'** BEETROOT Dark-leaved varieties of annual make useful foliage plants for the front of an all-red border. H 25cm (10in) S 15cm (6in) [ill.pp.131,173]

Cercis canadensis **'Forest Pansy'**
One of the loveliest small trees, with plum-coloured heart-shaped leaves. Requires full sun. H and S 3.7m (12ft) Z4 [ill.p.130]

Cimicifuga simplex **Atropurpurea Group** BUGBANE Perennial with

lovely dark red cut-leaf foliage followed by plumes of white flowers in late summer, that requires light shade and moist soil. H 1.2m (4ft) S 60cm (2ft) Z4 [ill.p.81]

Cordyline australis **'Purpurea'** NEW ZEALAND CABBAGE PALM Evergreen shrub or tree that produces a sheaf of leathery purple foliage. Useful architectural plant to make a centrepiece in a container. Size in a container: H and S 1m (3ft3in) Z9 [ill.p.80]

Corylus maxima **'Purpurea'** HAZEL
Vigorous shrub, good as a dark background, but needs to be coppiced to keep it within bounds. Tolerates sun or partial shade. H 6m (20ft) S 5m (15ft) Z5 [ill.pp.45,173,178]

Cotinus coggygria **'Royal Purple'** SMOKE TREE Shrub with deepest plum-red foliage, fading to a translucent red in autumn. For the largest leaves and to contain the plant, prune back to the base in spring, but this will eliminate the feathery flowers that create a 'smoke' over the mature shrub in summer. H and S 5m (15ft) Z5 [ill.p.147]

Euphorbia dulcis **'Chameleon'**
Semi-evergreen perennial with foliage and flowers in variable shades of khaki, purple and near-black. Tolerates sun or partial shade in moist soil. H and S 75cm (30in) Z4

Heuchera micrantha var. *diversifolia* **'Palace Purple'**

Perennial that makes clumps of crinkled, heart-shaped leaves of deepest plum red; they are shiny and so reflect the light. Puts up diffuse sprays of small white flowers. H and S 45cm (18in) Z4 [ill.p.177]

Iresine herbstii BEEFSTEAK PLANT
A tender foliage perennial with tints of deep purple melding into pinks. Requires bright light for good leaf colour, and loamy soil. H 60cm (2ft) S 45cm (18in) Z9 [ill.p.173]

Ocimum basilicum var. *purpurascens* PURPLE BASIL A tender culinary herb with purple-tinged foliage, used as an ornamental in containers. Requires sun. H 40cm (15in) S 30cm (12in) [ill.p.119]

Ophiopogon planiscapus **'Nigrescens'** Evergreen perennial producing clumps of grass-like foliage which is dark green at the base and shiny black elsewhere. Best in partial shade. H and S 20cm (8in) Z6

Perilla frutescens rubra
Annual with deep red-purple serrated leaves. Pinch out the shoots of the young plants to make them bushy. Requires sun. H 60cm (2ft) S 30cm (1ft)

Prunus cerasifera CHERRY PLUM
Tree whose small white flowers are among the first of spring, but which is also grown for its dark purple foliage. Useful hedging plant. Requires full sun and any but waterlogged soil.

Good varieties include *P.c.* **'Nigra'** H and S 10m (30ft) Z4 [ill.p.178]; and *P.c.* **'Pissardii'** H and S 10m (30ft) Z3 [ill.p.181]

Ricinus communis CASTOR OIL PLANT
The dark-leaved varieties of this evergreen shrub, usually grown as an annual, provide bold and exotic foliage. The leaves are large and deeply cut. Spiky red seedpods follow the small red flowers in late summer. Requires sun. H 1.5m (5ft) S 90cm (3ft) Z9 [ill.pp.173,177]

Sambucus nigra **'Guincho Purple'** PURPLE ELDER Tree with divided purple leaves that make a contrast with the flattened cream-coloured flowerheads. Requires sun and moist soil. H and S 6m (20ft) Z6 [ill.p.57]

Veratrum nigrum BLACK FALSE HELLEBORE Perennial grown for its fluted oval leaves, and also for its tall spires of tight-packed flowers that are such a dark red they are almost black. Requires partial shade and moist soil. H 1.8m (6ft) S 90cm (3ft) Z4

AUTUMN

Sedum telephium subsp. *maximum* **'Atropurpureum'**
Perennial whose succulent purple foliage glows red in autumn, when the small deep red-pink flowerheads mature. Requires sun. H 60cm (24in) S 45cm (18in) Z4 [ill.p.173]

Viola 'Bowles' Black'

Anthriscus sylvestris 'Ravenswing'

Euphorbia dulcis 'Chameleon'

Heuchera micrantha var. *diversifolia* 'Palace Purple'

Sedum telephium subsp. *maximum* 'Atropurpureum'

Pinks

Pinks make up a huge family of colours. They range from vivid magenta to palest blush pink. Pinks do not feature on the colour wheel because they are more complex mixtures of colours than the rainbow hues that do appear there. However the constituent colours of the various different pinks follow the same principles that the colour wheel demonstrates. We can think of pink as a red with a bias towards either yellow or blue and diluted with a varying proportion of white. Colours derived from crimson-reds make the cool blue-pinks (see pages 54-55). Those derived from orange-reds make warm, peachy pinks (see pages 56-57). In general it is a good idea to keep the two families of pinks apart. If they are put together, the eye detects the contrast between the blue element of the cool pink and the yellow element of the warm one. The results can be jarring.

The differences between pinks can be very subtle, and they sometimes seem to change their allegiances according to the context in which they are seen. A pink opium poppy, for instance, looks like a warm intruder in a cool border of blue catmints and violet-blue salvias; the same poppy will appear cool pink if it pops up in a bed of red roses. Changing light also nudges these chameleon pinks from warm to cool. The yellow light of sunset makes them look warm; but as soon as the sun goes down, the same pinks will appear cool or bluish.

An all-pink planting is feasible on any scale, whether it is to occupy a complete woodland or merely a single container. On a small scale, repetition of a single plant can be effective, but over large areas a uniform pink planting could look sweet and cloying. For ambitious plantings you need to draw upon the great diversity of pinks and use plants of different habits and flowers of different shapes. It can be effective to use drifts of different strengths of pinks, derived from varieties of the same plant. On a small scale you could use dianthus ('pinks') or verbenas; for larger areas, tulips or azaleas.

Pink flowers form successful partnerships with whites, but, despite their red content, pinks do not combine well with pure reds. This is because the white that is in pink cools down its red content. When this cooled-down red encounters a pure, hot red there is a hot-cool reaction which is disturbing. With deeper pinks like magenta, this reaction is extreme, and the resulting 'colour shock' can be exciting, almost dangerous (see pages 144-45).

LEFT Massed plantings of pink azaleas in a woodland garden in spring. Up to twenty plants of each colour have been used to create substantial drifts, which are in scale with the area covered.

BELOW Ribbons of the pink-edged tulip 'Meissner Porzellan', with the lilac-pink tulip 'Pandour' and the purple tulip 'Queen of Night' behind, echo the underplanting of lilac and pink pansies. This is only a small section of a vast border in which tens of thousands of bulbs are used as a public spectacle. But you could envisage the same idea of interlocking drifts of tulips on a much smaller scale; you could even achieve a pattern of different pinks in a large container. Bedding schemes are labour-intensive as they involve changing the plantings two or three times a year, but one advantage is that the colour schemes can be changed at the same time as the plants.

FAR LEFT Deep pink *Verbena* 'Sissinghurst' and *V.* 'Kemerton' are accompanied on a raised bed by pale pink *Diascia vigilis* and *Penstemon* 'Evelyn'. Below them are bright pink *Phlox paniculata* 'Cherry Pink' and the paler *P. p.* 'Sandringham'. The phlox have a short flowering season, but when they are over, their place will be taken by *Sedum* 'Herbstfreude', shown here still in bud.

CENTRE LEFT The young flowers of tender perennial *Argyranthemum* 'Vancouver' have mid-pink centres that become paler as they mature. Here they are planted with *Lavatera* 'Rosea'.

NEAR LEFT An inspired autumn planting brings together pale pink Japanese anemones (*Anemone* x *hybrida*), and a dendranthema of the same flower colour and size. Another, low-growing rusty pink dendranthema marks the edge of the border, with *Sedum* 'Ruby Glow' beyond.

Cool Pinks

Cool pinks – those which have some blue in them – run the gamut from very pale shell pink to magenta. Most associate well together, the paler colours making calmer, sweeter harmonies than the deeper ones. The most vivid pinks make assertive statements in the garden. If you are unsure of including them in a permanent planting, you can put them in containers that are easy to move.

Biased as they are towards blue, cool pinks are allied to violets and lilacs. Some pinks turn violet as they fade, creating lovely transitional colours on the way.

ABOVE Two perennial peas (*Lathyrus latifolius*), one deep pink, one pale, grow together through chicken wire against a wall. The flowers fade to lilac and grey as they age, so there seem to be at least four colours here.

LEFT Deep pink pansies and drumstick primulas (*Primula denticulata*) are a close colour match in an underplanting for tulips in a spring bedding scheme. Normally the primulas prefer damp, boggy ground, whereas the pansies like it to be merely moist. In a short-lived planting like this you can get away with partnering plants that favour slightly different conditions. In permanent plantings, though, it is important that partners should thrive in the same situation.

LEFT The recently introduced Japanese Surfinia trailing petunias accompany burgundy petunias and the perennial pink *Verbena* 'Sissinghurst' in a collection of terracotta pots. All the flower colours here are in the family of cool pinks, but the lighter petunias are noticeably more blue, and so cooler, than the verbenas.

BELOW Feathery-leaved annual *Cosmos* 'Imperial Pink' has flowers of the same colour as those of perennial *Salvia involucrata* 'Bethellii', but of contrasting shape. To make such a close colour match, you need to see the flowers together, so grow the cosmos to flowering size in pots before planting them.

BOTTOM Spikes of *Gladiolus communis* subsp. *byzantinus* grow through *Geranium psilostemon* in a summer border, giving matching colours in a variety of shapes.

Warm Pinks

BELOW The rambling rose 'Albertine' is the perfect partner for the honeysuckle (*Lonicera periclymenum* 'Belgica'), whose young flowers are pink and become yellow with age, thus tying in with the yellow undertones of the pink rose.

Warm pinks contain a touch of yellow, and the more yellow they contain, the closer they come to apricot or pale orange. This yellow content makes them the only pinks to harmonize with pale yellows. Many flowers such as some echinaceas and rock roses appear warm pink because of their orange or yellow centres. Others, such as honeysuckles, are bicoloured, with yellow and pink appearing on separate flowers within a flowerhead. An interesting feature of this elusive colour is that many flowers change as they mature, and are often dark in bud, and lighten as they open. Several roses, including 'Albertine', have orange-red buds that give flowers of pink with a hint of copper. Because of the fugitive nature of warm pinks, relatively few flowers hold onto this colour for long, making it difficult to create a large-scale planting in this range alone.

ABOVE The black-leaved elder (*Sambucus nigra* 'Guincho Purple') has flat heads of small flowers that are pink in bud and cream in flower, making a good colour match for warm, pale pink foxgloves (*Digitalis purpurea* 'Sutton's Apricot'.) These cultivated foxgloves have flowers arranged all round the stem, making a substantial flower spike, whereas the wild deep pink ones have flowers on only one side, giving a lighter, more open effect.

RIGHT ABOVE The copper-pink *Verbascum* 'Helen Johnson' warms up its much cooler pink neighbours, *Nicotiana* x *sanderae* 'Domino Salmon Pink' and *Monarda* 'Beauty of Cobham'. The monarda's purple bracts provide a strong supporting colour for the pale pink flowers, and help them to hold their own in the company of the powerful colour of the verbascum.

RIGHT BELOW The rich orange centres of *Echinacea purpurea* 'Leuchstern', and the yellow throats of *Hemerocallis* 'Catherine Woodbery' have a warming effect on the pink colours.

Magenta and Deep Pinks

SPRING

Malus x *moerlandsii* 'Profusion' CRAB APPLE A good, vigorous crab apple tree, with wine-red flowers in great profusion, young leaves tinged red, and small ox-blood red fruits in autumn. Requires full sun. H 7.6m (25ft) S 6m (20ft) Z5

Rhododendron 'Praecox' A compact shrub with slightly aromatic, small dark green leaves, and bunches of rosy-purple flowers in very early spring. Best in neutral to acid conditions, with some protection from late frosts. H 1.2m (4ft) S 1.5m (5ft) Z6

SUMMER

Bougainvillea glabra PAPER FLOWER Vigorous woody-stemmed climber with glossy oval leaves. Rich magenta floral bracts in quantity in the summer. Requires full sun. H and S 4.6m (15ft) Z9

Clematis The following climbing varieties can be cut hard back in early spring to flower from midsummer onwards: 'Jackmanii Rubra' with single velvety magenta flowers with cream stamens; 'Niobe' with rich purple-red flowers with light greenish stamens [ill.p.66]; and 'Rouge Cardinal' with large magenta flowers. All H and S 4m (13ft) Z6

Geranium Invaluable border perennials. *G. psilostemon* has deep magenta flowers with black centres, and forms a large clump of elegantly cut broad leaves that colour brilliantly in autumn. H and S 1.2m (4ft) Z4 [ill.pp.55, 181,182,184]. *G. sanguineum* BLOODY CRANESBILL has flowers of deep or paler pink over a long period, and makes slowly increasing clumps of deeply divided dark green leaves. H 25cm (10in) S 30cm (12in) Z4 [ill.pp.116,183]

Gladiolus communis subsp. *byzantinus* Corm producing prettily shaped purple and magenta flowers. Can seed itself about quite energetically in light soils. Requires sun. H 75cm (30in) S 15cm (6in) Z7 [ill.pp.55,180]

Lychnis coronaria ROSE CAMPION Biennial or short-lived perennial has much-branched stems carrying a succession of single deep magenta flowers, and downy grey foliage. Requires sun. H 50cm (20in) S 30cm (12in) Z4

Malva sylvestris var. *mauritiana* TREE MALLOW A perennial that will produce rich purple flowers in its first year from seed. H 90cm (3ft) S 30cm (1ft) Z6

Petunia Surfinia cultivars Tender perennials grown as annuals that will flower all summer in shades of pink, purple or white. Can be used as groundcover or to cascade out of pots. Overwinter with cuttings. H 20cm (8in) S 60cm (24in) Z9 [ill.pp.55,146]

Rosa ROSE Good shrub roses in this colour range include 'Cerise Bouquet' which has a strong, graceful, arching habit, clusters of double blooms of an intense pink, and lots of prickles, H and S 6ft (1.8m) Z6; 'Charles de Mills' which has the typical strong scent of a Gallica rose and purplish magenta flowers, H 1.2m (4ft) S 90cm (3ft) Z5 [ill.p.157]; 'Chianti' which is a free-blooming Shrub rose with clusters of rich purple-maroon flowers, H and S 1.5m (5ft) Z6 [ill.p.162]; and 'William Lobb' which has mossy buds that open purple and fade slightly to lavender grey, (peg down the long new growths to get the most flowers), H and S 2m (6ft6in) Z5 [ill.pp.7,119]

Verbena A number of perennial hybrid verbenas are grown for their continual flowering. The following are good for containers, for groundcover or for the border: 'Cleopatra' with purple and white blooms Z9 [ill.p.144]; 'Homestead Purple' with rich purple crimson flowers Z9; 'Sissinghurst' with deep pink flowers Z7 [ill.pp.53,55,121, 182]. All H 30cm (12in) S 45cm (18in)

Mid-Pinks

SPRING

Anemone coronaria St Brigid Group POPPY ANEMONE Corm producing lacy leaves and large double or semi-double flowers in a range of colours. Tolerates sun or partial shade. H 30cm (12in) S 15cm (6in) Z8 [ill.p.116]

Bellis perennis Pomponette Perennial. This cultivated daisy has fully double flowers in shades of red, pink or white. Requires sun. H and S 15cm (6in) Z4 [ill.p.144]

Cornus florida f. *rubra* FLOWERING DOGWOOD Large shrub or small tree with an open, spreading habit, rosy foliage in spring with pink bracts and reddish new growth. Best in light shade in deep, lime-free soil. H 6m (20ft) S 7.6m (25ft) Z7

Cyclamen Large tubers of *C. coum* produce rounded, prettily marked leaves and delicate flowers in a range of pinks and white. Will spread if happy, for instance in light woodland. H 10cm (4in) S 15cm (6in) Z5 [ill.pp.27,113]. *C. repandum* has variously marbled and toothed leaves, and flowers with slightly twisted petals. Prefers deep shade. H 10cm (4in) S 15cm (6in) Z8

Daphne mezereum MEZEREON Shrub wreathed in sweetly scented rose-pink flowers in late winter, before the leaves appear. Tolerates sun and partial shade in moist, alkaline soil. H and S 1.2m (4ft) Z5

Erythronium Tuberous perennnial that requires partial shade and moist soil. *E. dens-canis* DOG'S TOOTH VIOLET has green leaves spotted purple-brown, and pink or lilac flowers with reflexed petals. H and S 15cm (6in) Z3. *E. revolutum* TROUT LILY has gently mottled leaves and delicate pink flowers on taller stems. H 30cm (12in) S 15cm (6in) Z5

Primula denticulata DRUMSTICK PRIMULA Perennial with round flowerheads in white, lavender-blue, as well as pinks, on a stout stem that elongates as it develops. Tolerates sun or partial shade in moist soil. H 30cm (12in) S 20cm (8in) Z6 [ill.p.54]

Tulipa TULIP Bulb needing a sunny position. Good late spring-flowering tulips for this colour range include Lily-flowered 'China Pink' H 55cm (22in) S 23cm (9in) Z4; and Triumph tulip 'Peerless Pink' H 40cm (15in) S 23cm (9in) Z4 [ill.p.112]

Bougainvillea glabra

Lychnis coronaria

Rosa 'Charles de Mills'

Cyclamen repandum

Erythronium dens-canis

SUMMER

Allium ORNAMENTAL ONION
Perennial bulb needing sun.
A. carinatum subsp. *pulchellum*
KEELED GARLIC has graceful
miniature fountains of pinky
flowers. H 45cm (18in) S 10cm
(4in) Z6. *A. cernuum* LADY'S LEEK
is unusual in its nodding flower
heads, varying from pale pink to
deep rose-purple. Lacks the
oniony smell. H 45cm (18in)
S 12cm (5in) Z3

Armeria maritima THRIFT\SEA PINK
Evergreen perennial. Forming
tussocks of threadlike foliage,
with fragrant pink flowers.
Requires sun. H 20cm (8in)
S 30cm (12in) Z4 [ill.p.176]

Astrantia maxima
Clump-forming perennial with
bold three-lobed foliage, and
long-lasting pink flowers. Best in
sun. H 60cm (24in) S 30cm
(12in) Z4 [ill.p.178]

Cistus 'Silver Pink' ROCK ROSE
Evergreen shrub with pleasing
clear pink flowers and greyish
foliage. Requires sun. H and S
1m (3ft3in) Z8

Clematis
The following climbing varieties
tolerate sun or partial shade in
moist, alkaline soil: **'Comtesse de
Bouchard'** with abundant
flowers, and should be cut back
hard in late winter, H and S 3m
(10ft) Z6; *C. montana* **var.**
rubens with purplish foliage, and
vanilla-scented rosy flowers in
spring, it does not need pruning,
H 12m (40ft) S 3m (10ft) Z6; **C.
m.'Tetrarose'** has slightly larger
and richer foliage and flowers,
although is less vigorous, H 7.5m
(25ft) S 3m (10ft) Z6

Cleome hassleriana (syn. *C. spinosa*)
SPIDER FLOWER Annual with
pretty, spidery flowers in shades
of rose, purple and white.
Aromatic foliage and spiny
stems. Requires sun. H 1.2m (4ft)
S 30cm (12in)

Cosmos bipinnatus
Annual with feathery foliage and
stout stems flowering in various
pinks and whites. Requires sun
and moist soil. **'Imperial Pink'** is a
strong pink. H 1.2m (4ft) S 75cm
(30in) Z8 [ill.pp.11,55,114]

Dianthus CARNATION/PINK
Evergreen perennial,best in a
sunny open position over chalk
[ill.p.7]. **'Pike's Pink'** makes an
extensive, weed-smothering
mat of foliage, and has scented
pale pink double flowers.
H 15cm (6in) S 30cm (12in) Z4.
Modern pinks, such as **'Gran's
Favourite'** which has pink-laced
white flowers, have blue-grey
foliage. H 25cm (10in) S 40cm
(15in) Z4

Diascia **'Ruby Field'**
Half-hardy perennial that makes
neat mats of small green leaves
with generous sprays of copper-
pink flowers from midsummer.
Requires sun and soil that is not
too dry. H 25cm (10in) S 30cm
(12in) Z8 [ill.p.112]

Dicentra BLEEDING HEART
D. spectabilis Perennial with
heart-shaped rosy flowers that
dangle from arching stems with
prettily divided foliage. H 75cm
(30in) S 50cm (20in) [ill.p.112].
D. 'Stuart Boothman' is smaller
with grey-green leaves. H 45cm
(18in) S 30cm (12in) [ill.p.111].
Best in partial shade and humus-
rich soil. Z3

Dierama pulcherrimum ANGEL'S
FISHING ROD Evergreen perennial
with grassy foliage and deep
pink bell-like blossoms that
shower from tall, wiry stems in
late summer. Needs a sheltered,
sunny site and moist soil. H 1.5m
(5ft) S 90cm (3ft) Z7 [ill.p.116]

Digitalis FOXGLOVE
D. purpurea is biennial with tall
spikes of pink, purple or white
flowers, spotted on the inside.
H 1.5m (5ft) S 45cm (18in) Z3
[ill.pp.113,175]. **D. x
mertonensis** is perennial if
divided after flowering, and has
much shorter flower spikes of a
buff rose colour. H 60cm (2ft) S
30cm (1ft) Z4 [ill.p.131]. Both
do best in partial shade and
moist soil.

Echinacea purpurea CONEFLOWER
Perennial for late summer with
robust daisy-flowers, each with a
distinctive, prominent central
boss. Requires sun and a humus-
rich soil. **E. p. 'Leuchtstern'** (syn.
E.p.'Bright Star') is a good
cultivar. H 1.2m (4ft) S 45cm
(18in) Z4 [ill.p.57]

Geranium CRANESBILL
Invaluable border perennials. **G.
cinereum** 'Ballerina' makes neat
mounds of rounded, grey-green
foliage, and has relatively large
lilac-pink flowers with darker
veining. Likes well-drained soil.
H 20cm (8in) S 30cm (12in) Z4.
G. x oxonianum 'Claridge Druce'
makes weed-proof clumps and
flowers over a long season in a
rich rose-pink; it is quite a
vigorous spreader. H and S 90cm
(3ft) Z3 [ill.p.163]. **G. x
riversleaianum** 'Mavis Simpson'
throws out long trailing stems
with silvery pink flowers; lobed
leaves are a soft, silky green H
23cm (9in) S 60cm (2ft) Z7.
G. x r. **'Russell Prichard'** has
similar foliage but is shorter, and
has magenta flowers over a long
period in summer. H 23cm (9in)
S 60cm (2ft) Z6 [ill.p.119]

Helianthemum **'Rhodanthe
Carneum'** (syn. *H.* 'Wisley Pink')
ROCK ROSE Evergreen shrub that
makes a spreading mound of
silver-grey foliage and produces
myriads of short-lived pink
flowers in early summer. Needs
sun. H 45cm (18in) S 60cm
(24in) Z6 [ill.p.180]

Lathyrus PEA
Perennial **L. grandiflorus**
EVERLASTING PEA has largish
flowers of deep magenta with
lighter pink. Suckers and can be
invasive. H 1.5m (5ft) Z6
[ill.p.163]. **L. latifolius** PERENNIAL
SWEET PEA has robust, almost
lush, flowers over a long period,
sadly lacking scent. Strong
magenta, pink and pale pink,
and white forms are available
H and S 1.8m (6ft) Z 5 [ill.p.54].
Annual **L. odoratus** SWEET PEA has
a unique and indispensable
scent. Many different colour
forms available as seed. H and S
1.8m (6ft) All need sun and
humus-rich soil.

Lavatera MALLOW
Annuals and shrubs requiring full
sun. **L. trimestris** 'Silver Cup' is a
bushy annual smothered in large
glowing pink trumpets. H and S
60cm (24in). **'Rosea'** TREE
MALLOW is a quick-growing
shrubby plant with downy leaves
of a soft sage-green, and soft
pink flowers in quantity through
summer and autumn. H and S
3m (10ft) Z8 [ill.pp.53,184]

Lilium LILY
Bulb. **L. martagon** TURKSCAP LILY
has nodding flowers with
reflexed petals in shades ranging
from white through dull pink to
wine-red and buff, variously
spotted. Will self-seed if happy,
in humus-rich soil. H 1.2m (4ft)
Z4. **L. speciosum** var. *rubrum* has
larger flowers, carmine pink and
white spotted. H 1.5m (5ft) Z5.
Good hybrids include **'Journey's
End'** also carmine pink and
white. H 1.5m (4ft) Z5; and the
Pink Perfection Group which has
pink trumpets with deep
carmine reverse. H 1.2m (4ft) Z5
[ill.p.184]

Allium carinatum subsp. *pulchellum*

Clematis montana 'Tetrarose'

Digitalis x *mertonensis*

Geranium x *riversleaianum* 'Russell
Prichard'

Lilium speciosum var. *rubrum*

Lupinus 'The Chatelaine' LUPIN
Perennial with pretty palmate foliage and stout flower spikes in two-tone pink and white. Best in sandy, well-drained soil in sun. H 1.2m (4ft) S 45cm (18in) Z3 [ill.pp.3,184]

Nicotiana x sanderae (syn. N. alata) TOBACCO PLANT These sweetly scented annuals produce five-pointed flowers profusely all summer. Best in sun. H 75cm (30in) S 30cm (12in) [ill.p.163]

Osteospermum 'Pink Whirls'
A half-hardy perennial making tufts of narrow, aromatic leaves, with soft old rose pink daisy flowers from early summer until the frosts. Requires sun. H and S 60cm (2ft) Z9 [ill.p.109]

Paeonia lactiflora PEONY
In the wild this perennial has large single white flowers with silky petals and lots of yellow stamens, but in cultivation a broad colour range of blooms, single and double, has arisen. Good pink cultivars include single **'Bowl of Beauty'** and double, paler pink **'Ballerina'** [ill.p.113]. Prefers sun. H and S 60cm (2ft) Z5

Penstemon 'Evelyn'
Bushy semi-evergreen perennial covered in tubular pink flowers from midsummer. Requires sun. H and S 45cm (18in) Z7 [ill.pp.53,157,181]

Phlox paniculata 'Bright Eyes'
Perennial forming clumps of tall stout stems topped with large

pink sweetly scented flower heads. Best in moist soil. Tolerates sun and partial shade. H 1.2m (4ft) S 60cm (2ft) Z4

Rehmannia elata CHINESE FOXGLOVE
Perennial that makes a clump of soft, prettily lobed leaves, and has surprisingly large foxglove-like flowers of a rich pink with orangey markings. H 90cm (3ft) S 45cm (18in) Z9 [ill.p.112]

Rosa ROSE
Good climbing varieties include: **'Mme Grégoire Staechelin'**, vigorous with good foliage and large pale pink flowers, deeper on the reverse, H 6m (20ft) S 3.7m (12ft) Z6 [ill.p.65]; and **'Zéphirine Drouhin'**, thornless, with fragrant pink flowers that repeat well, H 2.4m (8ft) S 1.8m (6ft) Z6. Good shrub roses include: **'Complicata'** which can be trained as a climber, and makes long arching growths with flat, single pink flowers all along their length, in midsummer, H 2.1m (7ft) S 2.4m (8ft) Z5; **'Comte de Chambord'** with fragrant pinkish lilac flowers, and an erect habit, H 1.2m (4ft) S 90cm (3ft) Z5 [ill.pp.176, 178]; **'De Rescht'** with small brilliant flowers that verge on magenta, H 1.2m (4ft) S 90cm (3ft) Z6 [ill.p.162]; **R. gallica var. officinalis** APOTHECARY'S ROSE with soft light green foliage and deep pink flowers, generously borne although not repeated, H and S 90cm (3ft) Z5 [ill.p.116]; and

R. g. 'Versicolor' ROSA MUNDI similar, but the flowers are splashed pink and white, H 75cm (2ft6in) S 90cm (3ft) Z5 [ill.p.162]

Salvia involucrata 'Bethellii'
Perennial with rich green, aromatic leaves and large spikes of bright cerise flowers with pink bracts: lovely in bud. Requires sun. H 1.5m (5ft) S 90cm (3ft) Z9 [ill.p.55]

Sidalcea malviflora MALLOW
Perennial with silky flowers on stately branching spires. Good varieties include **S. m. 'William Smith'** Requires sun. H 90cm (3ft) S 40cm (15in) Z5

Silene dioica RED CAMPION
Perennial with clear pink flowers over dark hairy leaves; the double **S. d. 'Flore Pleno'** has a blowsy charm. H 60cm (2ft) S 30cm (1ft) Z5

AUTUMN

Colchicum speciosum MEADOW SAFFRON Also known as Naked Ladies, as this bulb flowers without its leaves. The large, shiny leaves appear in spring, then die down. Requires an open, sunny situation. H and S 15cm (6in) Z5 [ill.p.146]

Cyclamen hederifolium (syn. C. neapolitanum) Tuberous perennial with delicate pink or white flowers with reflexed petals followed by pretty heart-shaped leaves, variously marked

and marbled with silver. Tolerates sun and shade and requires humus-rich soil. H 10cm (4in) S 15cm (6in) Z5 [ill.p.147]

Nerine bowdenii
Bulb that throws up a cluster of bright pink flowers on a tallish stem in autumn; the colour is a wonderful shock so late in the year. Tolerates full sun and requires a light sandy soil. H 60cm (24in) S 15cm (6in) Z8

Schizostylis coccinea 'Mrs Hegarty' KAFFIR LILY Spreading rhizomes produce tufts of narrow leaves followed by strong stems of flowers of pretty pale pink. Requires sun and moist soil. H 60cm (24in) S 15cm (6in) Z6

Sedum STONECROP
Perennial requiring sun. **'Herbstfreude'** (syn. S. 'Autumn Joy') has stout clumps of grey-green fleshy leaves and large flowerheads that turn rich pink and, gradually, coppery red. H and S 60cm (2ft) Z4 [ill.pp.146,171]. **'Ruby Glow'** is a sprawler, with deep ruby-pink flowers. H to 23cm (to 9in) S 45cm (18in) Z4 [ill.p.53]

Pale Pinks

SPRING

Daphne x burkwoodii 'Somerset'
Semi-evergreen shrub. Small, narrow leaves and gloriously scented flowers in late spring.

Requires full sun but not dry soil. H and S 1.2m (4ft) Z5

Magnolia
Shrub requiring neutral to acid soil, but tolerant of pollution. **M. x loebneri 'Leonard Messel'** has elegant, slender-petalled flowers that appear before the leaves. H 8m (25ft) S 6m (20ft) Z5. **M. x soulangeana** is a wide-spreading shrub or small tree with large tulip-shaped flowers, white flushed purple, on bare branches. H and S 6m (20ft) Z5

Malus floribunda JAPANESE CRAB
A gracefully spreading tree, early to flower. Deep pink buds open to pale pink, and are followed by small red and yellow fruits. Prefers full sun. H and S 10m (30ft) Z4

Tulipa TULIP
Bulb that appreciates summer baking. **'Angélique'** is Peony-flowered, delicately scented and late to flower. H 40cm (16in) S 23cm (9in) [ill.p.111]. **'Elegant Lady'** is Lily-flowered, cream edged with mauve-pink, and flowers in mid spring. H 45cm (18in) S 23cm (9in). **'Meissner Porzellan'** is ivory flushed apple blossom pink, and flowers in mid spring. H 40cm (15in) S 23cm (9in) [ill.p.53]. **'Pandour'** is a Greigii tulip, and although pale yellow flamed red, it appears pink, mottled foliage, and flowers in mid spring. H 30cm (12in) S 20cm (8in) [ill.p.53]. All Z4

Paeonia 'Bowl of Beauty'

Rosa 'Zéphirine Drouhin'

Sidalcea malviflora 'William Smith'

Sedum 'Herbstfreude'

Magnolia x loebneri 'Leonard Messel'

SUMMER

Clematis
Climber that prefers partial shade with a cool root run include 'Duchess of Albany' with small tulip-shaped flowers; 'Hagley Hybrid' with large rosy-mauve flowers with purplish anthers, produced in quantity for three months at midsummer. Both H 2.4m (8ft) S 90cm (3ft) Z5

Dianthus 'Doris' PINK
Evergreen perennial producing a succession of well-scented flowers, salmon-pink with a ring of deeper pink. Prefers an open, sunny situation in slightly alkaline soil. H 30cm (12in) S 40cm (15in) Z4

Diascia
Perennial requiring sun. *D. fetcaniensis* has creeping stems clothed in small rounded leaves and loose spikes of flowers. H 40cm (15in) S 45cm (18in) Z8. *D. rigescens* has a denser habit with stiffer flower stems crowded with silvery-pink flowers. H 40cm (15in) S 30cm (12in) Z8 [ill.p.131]

Erigeron karvinskianus (syn. *E. mucronatus*) Charming but untidy perennial producing dainty daisies throughout the summer. Likes to seed itself around warm, sunny walls and steps. H 20cm (8in) S 30cm (12in) Z8

Geranium CRANESBILL
Invaluable border perennials. *G.* x *oxonianum* 'Wargrave Pink' has small flowers over attractive, lobed, semi-evergreen foliage. H 45cm (18in) S 60cm (24in) Z4 [ill.p.180]. *G. macrorrhizum* 'Ingwersen's Variety' makes good groundcovering clumps of aromatic foliage. H 38cm (15in) S 60cm (24in) Z4. *G. traversii* var. *elegans* has distinctly silvery leaves, and clear pink flowers. H 10cm (4in) S 25cm (10in) Z8 [ill.p.178]

Hemerocallis 'Catherine Woodbery' DAYLILY Semi-evergreen perennial with flowers that are palest peach flushed crimson, and very fragrant. Requires full sun and moist soil. H 70cm (28in) S 75cm (30in) Z4 [ill.p.57]

Kolkwitzia amabilis BEAUTY BUSH
A graceful shrub with an arching habit, softly draped with masses of bell-shaped flowers in early summer. Requires full sun. H and S 3m (10ft) Z5

Lavatera 'Barnsley' TREE MALLOW
Shrub with soft grey-green foliage and an abundance of pale pink flowers with a red eye. Requires sun. H and S 1.8m (6ft6in) Z8 [ill.p.176]

Lonicera periclymenum 'Belgica' HONEYSUCKLE\WOODBINE Climber with tubular flowers that are creamy inside, deep pink outside, and very fragrant in the evening. Tolerates sun and shade. H and S 3m (10ft) Z5 [ill.p.56]

Monarda 'Beauty of Cobham' BERGAMOT This perennial herb has aromatic, purplish foliage, and pale pink tufts of flowers. H 90cm (3ft) S 45cm (18in) Z4 [ill.p.57]

Papaver orientale ORIENTAL POPPY
Perennials that die back by midsummer, so careful siting is required. Petals emerge like folded crepe paper from furry buds. H and S 90cm (3ft) Z4. Good varieties include: *P. o.* 'Cedric Morris' with large, pale buff pink flowers which have black blotches; and salmon pink *P. o.* 'Mrs Perry' [ill.p.180]

Penstemon 'Apple Blossom'
Bushy semi-evergreen perennial producing pale pink tubular flowers all summer. Best in full sun. H and S 45cm (18in) Z9 [ill.p.176]

Rosa ROSE
Good climbing varieties include 'Albertine' with copper-pink buds that open to pale salmon-pink, and a fruity scent. H 5m (15ft) S 3m (10ft) Z6 [ill.p.56]; 'Blairii Number Two', which is shell-pink and susceptible to mildew, H 3.5m (12ft) S 1.8m (6ft) Z6 [ill.p.114]; 'Francis E. Lester' with clusters of very pale pink, strongly scented, single flowers, tolerant of shade, and suitable for growing up tree, H 4.5m (15ft) S 3m (10ft) Z7[ill.p.183]; 'New Dawn' with pale pink, well-formed flowers, tolerant of shade, H and S 5m (15ft) Z6 [ill.pp.1,176,178]; and 'Paul's Himalayan Musk' which makes a curtain of small, double sweet-scented flowers, H and S 10m (30ft) Z5. Good shrub roses include 'Céleste' (syn. *R.* 'Celestial') with flat, shell-pink flowers, which is good for hedging, H 1.5m (5ft) S 1.2m (4ft) Z4; 'Fantin-Latour' a blowsy, sweet-scented old rose with petals arranged in a whorl, H 1.5m (5ft) S 1.2m (4ft) Z5; and 'Königin von Dänemark' with beautifully formed flowers, H 1.5m (5ft) S 1.2m (4ft) Z4

Verbena 'Silver Anne'
This tender perennial is a vigorous trailer, with small heads of fragrant flowers. Requires sun. H 20cm (8in) S 45cm (18in) Z9 [ill.p.121]

AUTUMN

Amaryllis belladonna
Bulb with sweetly fragrant pink flowers that darken as they age, and broad strap-shaped leaves that appear later. Requires a sunny, sheltered situation. In cool areas, grow against a sunny wall. H 50cm (20in) S 30cm (12in) Z8 [ill.p.121]

Anemone x *hybrida* (syn *A. japonica*) JAPANESE ANEMONE
Perennial making hearty clumps of lobed, dark green leaves that throw up branching stems of rounded rose-pink flowers; a long-lasting feature of late autumn. Tolerates partial shade and requires humus-rich soil. H 1.5m (5ft) S 60cm (2ft) Z5 [ill.pp.53,107]

Dendranthema (formerly *Chrysanthemum*) Perennial with daisy-like flowers that last from late summer through the autumn. A vast number of varieties are available, in colours ranging from wine-red, through pinks to rust, yellow and white, with different ones suitable for gardens or greenhouse. H from 30cm (1ft) to 1.5m (5ft) Z5-9 [ill.p.53]

BERRIES

Sorbus vilmorinii
Tree with elegant, ferny foliage that colours well in the autumn. Hanging clusters of rosy fruits gradually fade to pinky-white. Tolerates sun and partial shade in moist soil. H and S 6m (20ft) Z5

WINTER

Prunus x *subhirtella* 'Autumnalis Rosea' Tree that produces semi-double blush pink flowers intermittently throughout the winter. H 9m (30ft) S 6m (20ft) Z5

Viburnum x *bodnantense* 'Dawn'
Erect, arching shrub, with clusters of very fragrant rose pink flowers over a long period from early winter. Tolerates sun and partial shade in soil that is not too dry. H 3m (10ft) S 1.8m (6ft) Z7 [ill.p.171]

Erigeron karvinskianus

Hemerocallis 'Catherine Woodbery'

Rosa 'Paul's Himalayan Musk'

Rosa 'Königin von Dänemark'

Viburnum x *bodnantense* 'Dawn'

Violets

Violet is one of the richest and most opulent of colours. In some cultures, violet and purple are used as symbols of rank, prestige and wealth. They are also associated with mourning. Dark violet can help to to create a meditative mood in the garden. It even has a melancholy quality that can be used to offset the exuberance of brighter flower colours. True violet can be regarded as the colour on the edge of the rainbow; it actually extends over the edge, merging with ultra-violet that the human eye cannot detect. Bees and other insects can perceive it, though, and this explains why they are most attracted to violet and related colours that reflect ultra-violet.

Violet is a cool colour, almost as cool as blue, and so in the garden it may tend to recede and take a background role. Like the wayside flower with which it shares its name, violet can be discreet and retiring. It is also a fugitive colour, in the sense that the slightest addition of another hue will tip the colour away from violet. Add red to violet and it becomes purple. Add a touch of blue and the colour appears more blue than violet. And as if to emphasize the transient nature of these colours, violet and blue flowers sometimes appear far pinker in photographs than they do to the eye.

Because it is so recessive, violet can be eclipsed by stronger colours in a mixed group. It needs to be isolated somewhat, and used in massed plantings for maximum effect. For depth of colour you can hardly improve upon dark geraniums and delphiniums underplanted with the darkest violas and pansies. Violet clematis can be useful, too, either as a vertical feature on an obelisk, or as a dark curtain at the back of a border.

For subdued harmonious associations, partner violet and lilac flowers with blue and blue-pink ones. *Viola cornuta,* for instance, looks marvellous as an underplanting for old-fashioned pink roses. The cottage garden annual clary, *Salvia viridis,* comes in seed mixtures of violet, pink, and cream, which harmonize well together and look equally good mixed with blue larkspurs and cornflowers. For a much richer colour incident, deep violet flowers can make an exotic combination with strong reds and oranges. Try planting violet pansies with fierce red tulips such as *Tulipa praestans.*

Violet is the darkest colour in the colour wheel and therefore the nearest to black. Its complementary is yellow, the lightest of the rainbow colours. But when you exploit this relationship and place a dark violet heliotrope, say, with pale yellow daisies, the light-dark contrast makes a stronger statement than the colour contrast. For a more balanced relationship between the colours, use unsaturated versions of each: pale violet *Campanula lactiflora,* for instance, makes a good partner for powder-yellow *Thalictrum flavum* subsp. *glaucum.*

ABOVE Two clematis – 'Etoile Violette' with small flowers, on the purple side of violet, and the larger-flowered 'Perle d'Azur' whose colour verges towards the blue of the accompanying sweet pea (*Lathyrus odoratus* 'Noel Sutton') – cover an ornamental wooden obelisk that has been stained dark green so that it merges with the foliage.

ABOVE LEFT To the eye, the dwarf bearded irises appear the same violet as the *Aubrieta* 'Doctor Mules' that accompanies it, but on film the relationship is distorted, and the aubrieta appears purple.

ABOVE RIGHT Violets and violas, together with two distinct varieties of *Lathyrus vernus*, make up this tightly-knit spring grouping at the front of a border. Violet is the base colour of this pea and of most violas, but they can both be highly variable.

RIGHT Lying flat across the top of a wall, *Clematis* 'Jackmanii Superba' makes a colour link with *Delphinium* Black Knight Group, and with clumps of *Verbena bonariensis* in the border beyond. Clematis is usually grown vertically up walls and fences, but it can also be encouraged to grow horizontally through a border, supported by other shrubs, where its colour can relate more closely with that of the other plants.

Soft Violets

BELOW LEFT An ancient wall supports *Wisteria sinensis* and shelters the somewhat tender but fast-growing *Abutilon vitifolium* with similar-coloured lilac flowers.

BELOW RIGHT *Clematis* 'Lasurstern' needs support, which it receives here from the potato vine (*Solanum crispum* 'Glasnevin'). This, in turn, is supported by wires attached to the wall.

The paler, unsaturated forms of violet are lilac and lavender, and an unsaturated version of purple is mauve. Colours in this range can vary with the age of a flower; violet flowers often fade to mauve and then to lilac as they pass their prime. Light conditions also have an effect. In the cool light after sundown, or in deep shade, lilac can seem quite blue; in warm sunshine, as at dawn and dusk, it appears pink.

Violet is a recessive colour, and the shy charms of its paler, softer versions are even more easily overlooked. So plant it with closely-related colours with which it does not need to compete for attention, and plant it abundantly for effect. You can make the most of it in a herb garden with chives, hyssop, thyme, sage and lavender.

It is a good colour to use to soften the lines of hard landscaping. A wall hung with wisteria becomes light and insubstantial when the climber is in flower; the straight edge of a terrace will dissolve beneath the pale violet haze of a lavender hedge.

ABOVE A herb garden occupies the narrow space between a tunnel of apple trees and a stone wall, that supports the climbing rose 'Mme Grégoire Staechelin'. It has been planned so that several lilac-flowered herbs bloom simultaneously in summer. Chives (*Allium schoenoprasum*) have been partnered with their taller relatives, *Allium aflatunense*, and colour-matched with a narrow-leaved sage (*Salvia lavandulifolia*) and the flower-covered wands of *BuddleJa alternifolia*.

Deep Purple-Violet

The slightest hint of red tips the colour violet toward purple and magenta. You can exploit violet's range by putting together flowers that are close but not identical in hue, so that the colours shimmer together like a rich shade of shot silk. Large-flowered clematis are ideal candidates for this treatment because they offer such a wide selection of hybrids with similar flowers but subtly different hues. Irises offer similar opportunities for close colour matching. You can put close-hued bearded irises together, exploiting the rich variation of colour within each flower, or else partner an iris with other plants of contrasting form such as the globe-shaped flowerheads of violet alliums.

To introduce a colour that will make an attractive contrast to deep purple-violet, try muted yellows such as the lime-yellow of euphorbias, or the palest lemons of evening primrose or of *Verbascum* 'Gainsborough'.

RIGHT ABOVE Violet *Clematis* 'The President' makes a voluptuous combination with magenta-flowered *C.* 'Niobe'. You need only slight variations between deep, rich colours to create a vibrant effect that is more charged than either colour on its own. To grow clematis together like this, plant them about a metre apart so that their roots do not compete for nourishment.

RIGHT BELOW Violet bearded irises combine with *Allium aflatunense* 'Purple Sensation' to make a resonant mixture of deep colour with interesting differences in flower shape. The allium bulbs can be planted in the gaps between the iris rhizomes, and both benefit from baking in the sun after flowering.

Deep and Mid Violets

SPRING

Aquilegia vulgaris GRANNY'S BONNET
Perennial with intriguing crown-shaped flowers with long spurs. The colours are very variable, coming in violet, blue, pink and cream which cross and mix promiscuously. Needs sun or partial shade. H 90cm (3ft) S 50cm (20in) Z5 [ill.pp.73,183].

Aubrieta 'Doctor Mules'
Evergreen perennial that makes a plumped-up cushion in crevices between stones. Useful to soften the outlines of walls and steps. Best in full sun. H 15cm (6in) S 45cm (18in) Z5 [ill.p.63]

Crocus tommasinianus 'Whitewell Purple' The flowers of this corm open in full sun, revealing bright orange stamens. It will naturalize in undisturbed ground. H 10cm (4in) S 8cm (3in) Z5

Lathyrus vernus SPRING VETCH
Non-climbing perennial pea that makes a compact mound. Very variable with pale pink and creamy forms as well as violet. Needs humus-rich soil and full sun. Difficult to transplant. H and S 30cm (12in) Z5 [ill.p.63]

Tulipa 'Negrita' TULIP
Bulb that produces a good tall, sturdy, late-flowering tulip. H 50cm (20in) S 23cm (9in) Z5 [ill.p.112]

Viola VIOLET
The best violets are the wild ones. Good cultivated evergreen perennial violets include **V. riviniana** Purpurea Group PURPLE DOG VIOLET with dark purple foliage, H 10cm (4in) S 20cm (8in) Z2; and **V. odorata** SWEET VIOLET H 7cm (3in) S 25cm (10in) Z8 [ill.p.136]. All tolerate both sun and shade.

SUMMER

Allium ORNAMENTAL ONION
The eye-catching spherical flowerheads of these bulbous perennials, which like an open, sunny position, are each a mass of single flowers. Good varieties include **A. aflatunense** [ill.pp.65, 139] and deeper violet **A. a.** 'Purple Sensation' [ill.pp.11,66, 108]. Both H 75cm (30in) S 20cm (8in) Z4

Brachyscome iberidifolia SWAN RIVER DAISY Prolifically flowering annual, useful in containers. Needs a sunny, sheltered position. H and S 45cm (18in)

Buddleja davidii BUTTERFLY BUSH
Late-summer flowers in pointed racemes are irresistible to butterflies. Regular dead-heading needed to make the shrub look tidy. Requires full sun. H and S 5m (15ft) Z6

Campanula BELLFLOWER
Good perennial varieties include **C. lactiflora**, which makes dense clumps that are covered with a mass of open bell-shaped flowers, H 1.2m (4ft) S 60cm (2ft) Z4; and **C. persicifolia**, which has tall spires of flowers that self-seed freely, H 90cm (3ft) S 30cm (12in) Z4 [ill.p.174]. All tolerate both sun and shade, and benefit from regular division.

Clematis
Most summer-flowering climbing varieties like sun but a shaded root run. 'Etoile Violette' is covered with small velvet-textured flowers in late summer. H and S 4m (12ft) Z6 [ill.pp.62, 183]. 'Jackmanii Superba' has large flowers with sepals lightly striped purple. S 3m (10ft) Z5 [ill.p.63]. 'The President' has large flowers with pointed sepals. H and S 3m (10ft) Z5 [ill.p.66]. 'Venosa Violacea' H and S 3m (10ft) Z6. Late-flowering **C. viticella** produces a mass of small, bell-shaped flowers. H and S 3m (10ft) Z6 [ill.p.150]

Delphinium
Some varieties of this perennial, which carries its flowers on tall spires, diverge from the familiar blue and have violet and lilac flowers, among them **King Arthur Group**, 'Honey Bee' and 'Purple Triumph'. Requires an open, sunny position. H 1.8m (6ft) S 60cm (2ft) Z3

Erigeron 'Dunkelste Aller'
A perennial producing a mass of daisy flowers with yellow eyes.

Requires sun and moist soil, but resents winter damp. H 80cm (32in) S 60cm (24in) Z3

Erysimum 'Bowles' Mauve'
Makes a mound of blue-green foliage, covered prolifically with flower-spikes through the season. A somewhat short-lived perennial that needs to be propagated by cuttings and replaced every three or four years. Requires sun. H 75cm (30in) S 1.2m (4ft) Z8 [ill.pp.109,116,132]

Galega orientalis GOAT'S RUE
Perennial member of the pea family, with pea-like flowerheads surmounting mounds of dense foliage which may need staking with peasticks. After flowering cut to the ground to encourage fresh foliage. Requires an open, sunny position. H 1.2m (4ft) S 60cm (24in) Z5 [ill.p.181]

Geranium CRANESBILL
Indispensable perennial for the border, easy to grow, resistant to disease, and producing densely-covered domes of flowers. **G. x magnificum** needs sun, and tolerates any but water-logged soil. H 60cm (2ft) S 90cm (3ft) Z4 [ill.pp.11,184]. **G. clarkei** 'Kashmir Purple' has rich purple flowers with reddish veins and deeply cut leaves. H and S 60cm (24in) Z4. **G. pratense** 'Plenum Violaceum' MEADOW CRANESBILL has clusters of double flowers. H 75cm (30in) S 60cm (2ft) Z4 [ill.p.183].

G. sylvaticum 'Mayflower' has bright flowers with white centres, and prefers shade. H and S 60cm (2ft) Z4

Hebe 'Autumn Glory'
Evergreen shrub that provides a reliable, if not particularly glamorous touch of violet for late summer. Grows well in coastal areas and likes full sun. H 60cm (24in) S 75cm (30in) Z8

Heliotropium arborescens
Evergreen shrub, propagated by cuttings, or may be used as an annual, grown from seed. Sweet-scented and tender, suited to planting out in pots or bedding schemes, or growing in a conservatory where it can be trained as a standard. Likes full sun. A good variety is **H.** 'Princess Marina' H and S 60cm (2ft) Z10 [ill.p.182]

Iris
Several tall bearded varieties of this rhizomatous perennial are such deep violet as to be near black, including 'Dusky Challenger', whose rhizomes need to bake in sun, and although the flowers are short-lived, fans of blue-green sword-shaped foliage are an asset. H 90cm (3ft) S 45cm (18in) Z4 [ill.p.136]. The following irises prefer partial shade and water or bog garden conditions: **I. ensata** 'Royal Purple' JAPANESE WATER IRIS H 90cm (3ft) S 50cm (20in) Z5; and **I. laevigata** H 90cm (3ft) S 50cm (20in) Z5

Crocus tommasinianus 'Whitewell Purple'

Brachyscome iberidifolia

Clematis 'Jackmanii Superba'

Geranium pratense 'Plenum Violaceum'

Iris ensata 'Royal Purple'

Lathyrus odoratus SWEET PEA
An abundance of violet, purple and mauve varieties of this annual climber are available from different seed merchants. Effective to grow plants of a single colour supported on pea sticks in a container, which can be moved around a border to augment a colour scheme. Requires full sun and rich soil. H and S 3m (10ft) [ill.pp.62,175]

Lavandula LAVENDER
Grow this grey-leaved aromatic shrub with other Mediterranean herbs to give a pot-pourri of summer scents. More tender varieties can be grown in pots, to overwinter indoors. All require full sun and thrive on poor soil. Good varieties include *L. stoechas* subsp. *pedunculata* whose flowers form little 'topknots'. H and S 45cm (18in) Z8 [ill.pp.108,109]. *L. angustifolia* 'Hidcote' has dense spikes of very aromatic violet-blue flowers. H and S 60cm (2ft) Z6

Linaria purpurea TOADFLAX
Slender violet flower spikes provide useful vertical incidents. Perennial, but self-seeds freely in light soil. Tolerates full sun or light shade. H 90cm (3ft) S 60cm (2ft) Z5

Lunaria annua (syn. *L. biennis*) HONESTY Biennial, double performer, with violet-mauve flowers in summer followed by dainty wafer-thin seed-pods, surviving on the plant well into

winter. Prefers light shade. H 75cm (30in) S 30cm (12in) [ill.p.167]

Papaver somniferum OPIUM POPPY
Varying in colour from near-black purple through mauve to knicker pink, and available in single and double forms, this annual poppy also produces a wonderful 'pepperpot' seedpod. Tolerates sun or partial shade in moist soil. H 75cm (30in) S 30cm (1ft)

Penstemon
Reliable producers of spires of foxglove-like flowers. Most need full sun. Good evergreen perennial varieties include *P. fruticosus* 'Purple Haze', which is suitable for rock gardens, H and S 30cm (12in) Z4; and deep purple-violet 'Blackbird', 'Midnight' and 'Raven' H 60cm (24in) S 40cm (15in) Z9

Rosa ROSE
Good climbing roses include 'Veilchenblau', which is especially suitable for arches and combines well with violet or blue. H 3.7m (12ft) S 2.1m (7ft) Z6. Good shrub roses include 'Reine des Violettes' H 1.8m (6ft) S 1.5m (5ft) Z6

Salvia SAGE
Good perennial varieties include: *S. lavandulifolia* H and S 60cm (2ft) Z8 [ill.p.65]; *S. nemorosa* 'Ostfriesland', which is best grown in clumps, H 75cm (30in) S 45cm (18in) Z5 [ill.p.119]; *S. pratensis* Haematodes Group

MEADOW CLARY H 90cm (3ft) S 45cm (18in) Z6 [ill.p.175, 183]; and *S. x superba* H 90cm (3ft) S 45cm (18in) Z5 [ill.p.183]. *S. officinalis* Purpurascens Group PURPLE SAGE is an evergreen shrubby herb grown for its velvety purple foliage. H 60cm (2ft) S 90cm (3ft) Z6 [ill.pp.147, 149,182]. Most prefer sun.

Solanum crispum 'Glasnevin'
Semi-evergreen climber whose yellow-'eyed' flowers look like those of a potato. Requires full sun. H 6m (20ft) S 3m (10ft) Z8 [ill.p.64]

Verbascum phoeniceum PURPLE MULLEIN Annual or short-lived perennial that produces spires of small flowers of variable colour; the best are reddish purple. Tolerates shade but prefers an open sunny site. H 90cm (3ft) S 45cm (18in) Z5

Verbena
Good varieties of this perennial, which prefers sun, include *V. bonariensis*, a 'see-through' plant, with small bobbles of violet flowers that wave in the wind, atop impossibly narrow stems. It will seed itself in sun-baked paths and terraces. H 1.5m (5ft) S 50cm (20in) Z9 [ill.p.146]. *V. rigida*, often grown as an annual, has flowers that are slightly pinker and on shorter stems but is otherwise similar to *V. bonariensis*. H 60cm (24in) S 30cm (12in) Z8 [ill.pp.19, 63,139]

Viola VIOLET\PANSY
Good evergreen perennial varieties include 'Huntercombe Purple', 'Maggie Mott' [ill.p.133] and 'Vita' H 25cm (10in) S 40cm (15in) Z4; 'Prince Henry' is deepest violet, verging on black and smaller H 15cm (6in) S 25cm (10in) Z4. Good annual varieties include 'Universal Purple' PANSY which will flower through the winter in mild conditions H and S 25cm (10in) Z4. All tolerate sun or shade and prefer cool conditions.

AUTUMN

Callicarpa bodinieri var. *giraldii* 'Profusion' Shrub producing a mass of small violet berries that stand out well against yellow autumn foliage. Likes full sun. H 1.8m (6ft) S 1.6m (5ft) Z6

Liriope muscari LILYTURF
Evergreen, rhizomatous perennial whose small, round flowers, clustered in spikes among the grassy foliage, resemble berries. Useful as an edging plant. Requires sun. H and S 45cm (18in) Z6

Soft Violets

SPRING

Anemone blanda WINDFLOWER
Tuberous perennial that will naturalize to make a soft violet

carpet on the edge of woodland. Likes a humus-rich soil and will tolerate both full light and partial shade. H 10cm (4in) S 15cm (6in) Z5 [ill.p.136]

Clematis
Good spring-flowering climbers include *C. alpina* with single, nodding lantern-shaped flowers with white centres. H 3m (10ft) S 1.5m (5ft) Z5; *C. macropetala* has similar, but semi-double flowers, H 3m (10ft) S 90cm (3ft) Z5. They prefer partial shade and do not need pruning.

Crocus tommasinianus
The first crocus of spring, it may poke up through snow. Bright orange stigmas light up the wispy flowers when they open in sun. The corms need a sunny site to naturalize well. H 10cm (4in) S 8cm (3in) Z5 [ill.pp.27,113]

Hepatica nobilis
Semi-evergreen perennial, with three-lobed leaves. Cut away old foliage to expose the shy clumps of elegant, many-petalled cup-shaped flowers of variable colour. Requires partial shade and deep, humus-rich soil. H 15cm (6in) S 25cm (10in) Z5

Tulipa TULIP
The bulbs need a sunny, open position and appreciate a good summer baking. Good cultivars include 'Blue Parrot', which is lilac, despite its name, H 60cm (2ft) S 23cm (9in) Z3; and 'Lilac Perfection' H 45cm (18in) S 23cm (9in) Z3.

Lavandula angustifolia 'Hidcote'

Salvia pratensis Haematodes Group

Verbena bonariensis

Liriope muscari

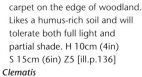
Hepatica nobilis

SUMMER

Abutilon vitifolium
Try growing this stately, fast-growing shrub against a sheltered wall on which you have trained a harmonizing wisteria. Tolerates sun and partial shade. H 4m (12ft) S 2.4m (8ft) Z9 [ill.p.64]

Allium ORNAMENTAL ONION
Bulbous perennials with globe-shaped flowerheads like starbursts. They like an open, sunny position. **A. christophii** STAR OF PERSIA has flowerheads like bubbles of soft lilac. H 40cm (15in) S 20cm (8in) Z4 [ill.pp.175,182].
A. rosenbachianum has longer stems and looser flowerheads. H 90cm (3ft) S 30cm (12in) Z4 [ill.p.10]. **A. schoenoprasum** CHIVES makes a good edging plant, not just confined to the herb garden. H 25cm (10in) S 10cm (4in) Z3 [ill.p.65].
A. schubertii needs a sheltered spot to produce its enormous umbels of up to 45cm (18in) wide. H 60cm (24in) S 30cm (12in) Z4

Buddleja BUTTERFLY BUSH
Good varieties of this shrub include the early-summer flowering **B. alternifolia** that is usually trained as a standard, and produces long, arching wands of violet flowers. H and S 4m (12ft) Z6 [ill.p.65]. **B. davidii** var. **nanhoensis** has flowers of a subtle pale violet-blue. H and S 3m (10ft) Z6. The more tender **B. davidii** 'Glasnevin' has felty grey-green foliage. H and S 1.8m (6ft) Z6 [ill.p.139]. All require full sun and cutting back hard in spring.

Campanula lactiflora 'Loddon Anna' Perennial producing clouds of milky lilac-pink flowers. Tolerates both sun and shade. H 1.2m (4ft) S 60cm (2ft) Z4 [ill.p.181]

Erigeron alpinus ALPINE FLEABANE
Perennial that looks good colonizing a wall or raised bed, where it can bake in the sun. Resents winter damp, but does not like to dry out in the summer. H 25cm (10in) S 20cm (8in) Z5

Galega officinalis GOAT'S RUE
Very variable perennial, with lilac flowers usually bicoloured with white. Requires an open, sunny site. H 1.5m (5ft) S 60cm (2ft) Z4

Hesperis matronalis SWEET ROCKET
Perennial that self-seeds through the border, producing frothy sweet-scented flowerheads. It may need thinning out to prevent it swamping less vigorous companions. Will tolerate poor soil but does best in full sun. H 75cm (30in) S 60cm (2ft) Z4 [ill.p.109]

Hydrangea aspera Villosa Group
Shrub with so-called 'lacecap' flowerheads that have pinkish central flowers and pale lilac outer ones. Likes moist soil in either sun or partial shade. H 3m (10ft) S 2.7m (9ft) Z8

Lantana montevidensis SHRUB VERBENA The flowers of this evergreen perennial have a sparkling yellow 'eye'. A conservatory plant in most climates, it needs full light. H 1m (3ft 3in) S 1.5m (5ft) Z10

Limonium latifolium SEA LAVENDER
Perennial producing a diaphanous cloud of tiny lilac flowers. Likes full sun. H 30cm (12in) S 45cm (18in) Z4 [ill.pp.134,151]

Penstemon
Valuable for their long flowering season, which can be extended if you cut back finished flower-spikes. Good evergreen perennial varieties include 'Alice Hindley' which has lilac flowers with white throats, H 1m (3ft 3in) S 60cm (2ft) Z9; and deeper violet 'Stapleford Gem' H 50cm (20in) S 30cm (12in) Z8 [ill.pp.119,175,181]; 'Sour Grapes' H 40cm (15in) S 30cm (12in) Z8; and P. virens H 40cm (15in) S 30cm (12in) Z4. All do best in sun.

Prostanthera ovalifolia
Evergreen shrub that will flower over a long period in a conservatory. Will grow in full sun or partial shade. H 1.8m (6ft) S 2.1m (7ft) Z9

Salvia SAGE
S. sclarea var. **turkestanica** CLARY, a biennial grown as an annual, produces many spikes of hooded lilac and white flowers, making a soft cloud of colour. It thrives in dry soil and needs sun. H 75cm (30in) S 30cm (12in) Z5 [ill.p.181]. **S. leucantha** MEXICAN BUSH SAGE, an evergreen shrub, has white flowers hung on purplish sepals to give a lilac haze. Needs sun. H and S 60cm (2ft) Z10

Syringa LILAC
Good varieties that make small trees or large shrubs include **S. vulgaris** COMMON LILAC that has countless cultivars incuding 'Katherine Havemeyer' and 'Pocahontas' H 3.5m (12ft) S 3m (10ft) Z4; **S. x persica** PERSIAN LILAC has more delicate sprays of flowers, still with characteristic lilac scent H and S 1.8m (6ft) Z3. All require sun and soil that is prejudiced towards alkaline.

Thalictrum MEADOW RUE
Perennials with sprays of tiny flowers, suspended on strong, but slender stems, that create a haze of thin colour, and finely divided leaves. All require sun or light shade. Good varieties include **T. aquilegiifolium** H 1.2m (4ft) S 45cm (18in) Z5; **T. delavayi** H 1.8m (6ft) S 60cm (2ft) Z5; and **T. rochebruneanum** H 2.1m (7ft) S 75cm (30in) Z5

Tulbaghia violacia SOCIETY GARLIC
Bulb producing rounded flowerheads of funnel-shaped flowers. May be eclipsed by more ostentatious plants in the border, but looks well grown in a pot.
Requires full sun. H 60cm (24in) S 30cm (12in) Z7

Verbena tenuisecta
Good perennial performer in a raised bed or a container planting, where it can be allowed to hang down over the edge. Prefers sun. H 40cm (15in) S 75cm (40in) Z9 [ill.p.109,181]

Viola cornuta HORNED VIOLET
Prolifically flowering perennial that makes good under-planting for roses. Cut back to the ground when it begins to look shaggy and it will reward you with new growth and a further flush of flowers. Tolerates sun or partial shade. H 40cm (15in) S 60cm (24in) Z4 [ill.pp.114, 176,184]

Wisteria
Slow-growing at first, this climber is unlikely to flower in the first ten years. Needs sun. Both **W. floribunda** H and S 9m (30ft) Z5 and **W. sinensis** H and S 30m (100ft) Z5 [ill.p.64] have fragrant lilac- to violet-blue flowers on racemes followed by velvety pods in late summer.

WINTER

Iris unguicularis (syn. *I. stylosa*) ALGERIAN IRIS An evergreen rhizomatous perenial, this iris is better planted in clumps rather than singly. Requires a sunny, sheltered position and will tolerate lime and poor soil. H 40cm (15in) S 75cm (30in) Z8

Allium schoenoprasum

Hesperis matronalis

Penstemon 'Sour Grapes'

Syringa 'Pocahontas'

Iris unguicularis (syn. *I. stylosa*)

Blues

Blue is the ultimate cool colour. It only takes the sight of sparkling blue water to offer relief from the heat of summer. Blue also suggests space and distance, like the sky that stretches to infinity and distant hills that seem all the more blue the further back they are. In the garden, blue carries similar connotations, suggesting coolness, space, and distance. Blue flowers act like frames in the garden picture, giving their neighbours a visual nudge forward while appearing to recede themselves. Put a bank of blue delphiniums at the back of a border, and you can imagine space stretching back far beyond them.

Along with green, blue is the most agreeable of colours in the garden. It associates well with all other colours; it makes gentle harmonies with closely related cool colours such as violets and blue-greens, and it remains the calm, passive partner in contrasting associations, even with orange, its complementary, and bright yellow, both of which seem even brighter in its company.

Unlike red, blue retains its character when diluted with white. A pale blue flower is still blue, and it remains cool too. Blue with a touch of red is slightly warmer; the more pronounced the red, the more it tips the colour toward violet and blue-pink; yet it remains essentially a cool colour.

Blues can be found in foliage too, though here the 'blue' is actually blue-green and much more muted than the blue found in flowers. To enhance the blueness of foliage, combine it with yellow-green leaves or creamy flowers. Blue-green hostas, for instance, look all the more blue when partnered with yellow-leaved ones.

Blues appear coolest and most blue in shade. You can take advantage of this and create the illusion of a blue pool under trees by allowing blue-flowered bulbs and perennials to naturalize there. Bluebells do this in the wild, and you can emulate them in the garden in spring with violet-blue *Anemone blanda*, scillas and *Corydalis flexuosa* under trees. You can repeat the effect in summer with shade-tolerant *Campanula latiloba*. Sunlight, on the other hand, makes blue flowers seem warmer and slightly pinker. To exploit this, partner blue with pink flowers in sunny situations to give a warmer version of a cool harmony.

At dusk blue flowers have a special value. Together with whites, they remain visible longer than any other colour. This is because the eye is more sensitive to blue than other colours in dim conditions, and also because the light after sunset has a blue cast and so it is reflected back by blue objects. You can take advantage of this effect by concentrating blue and white flowers around the area where you like to sit on summer evenings.

ABOVE A spring carpet of blue and light blue flowers is composed of low-growing bulbs. The palest are *Puschkinia scilloides* var. *libanotica*, each of which has a blue stripe along its near-white petals. The upward-facing star-shaped flowers are *Chionodoxa luciliae*, and the clump of darker flowers is grape hyacinth (*Muscari armeniacum*). These, and other blue bulbs such as *Scilla siberica,* are good for underplanting deciduous shrubs. In early spring the bare branches allow light to reach the bulbs' foliage, while in summer the dormant bulbs enjoy being shaded by the foliage above them, and being kept dry by the surrounding roots competing for moisture.

TOP *Camassia cusickii* is a bulb that shoots up spikes of star-shaped flowers. The perennial *Amsonia tabernaemontana* has slightly paler blue flowers of similar shape but in more compact flowerheads. Planted together, they create a pale blue haze in early summer.

ABOVE A blue viola makes a successful marriage with a bugle (*Ajuga reptans*). Both thrive in partial shade. The two will compete for the same ground, the bugle spreading by runners and the viola by seed, but you can easily adjust the balance by removing plants of the dominant partner.

ABOVE A late spring partnership of blue flowers and blue-green foliage. The perennial *Omphalodes cappadocica* 'Cherry Ingram' weaves between three clumps of *Hosta* 'Halcyon' with blue fescue grass (*Festuca glauca*) and a silvery santolina at bottom right of the picture. Scattered creamy flower spikes of *Tellima grandiflora* add a nuance of colour contrast that underlines the blueness of the hosta leaves. Although this planting looks attractive, it is flawed because not all the plants are suited to the same conditions. The hostas, omphalodes and tellima like moist soil and shade, whereas the fescue and santolina would prefer drier conditions and more sun.

All-Blue Plantings

A sea of wild bluebells, stretching through woodland, is an inspiring sight. Although its sheer bounty cannot be imitated in the garden, you can plant quantities of bulbs of a single kind – chionodoxas or scillas, for instance – and allow them to spread through otherwise undisturbed ground.

More formal blue plantings may be more difficult to achieve, and a whole border, rigidly restricted to blue flowers and foliage, may seem a touch too sombre. Blue is a distant, ethereal colour, and almost seems hard to grasp. On a small scale, groupings of blue flowers, such as veronicas with blue violas, backed by delphiniums and aconitums, can look very effective, especially in an area designated to feel cool in summer. However, on a large scale the eye might yearn for some relief, provided either by the refreshing contrasts of a few yellows and creams, or by the pleasing harmonies of some pinks and violets.

A good approach is to regard blue as a base for plantings that change colour through the year, perhaps being blue for only one season. You could create the framework with blue-flowered shrubs and climbers, beginning with ceanothus and clematis in late spring, with buddleja, hydrangea and caryopteris to follow in late summer. Between the shrubs you could plant blue perennials, lightly infiltrated with plants in other colours, such as yellow narcissi for spring contrast, and pink and magenta geraniums and white and soft violet sweet rocket to make cool harmonies for high summer.

LEFT *Centaurea montana* and Jacob's ladder (*Polemonium caeruleum*) fill the foreground section of a box-edged parterre; beyond is a good stand of the Himalayan blue poppy (*Meconopsis betonicifolia*).

RIGHT The framework for this informal planting includes a Californian lilac with rich blue flowers (*Ceanothus* 'Puget Blue') to the left of the path, and an unusual blue lilac (*Syringa vulgaris* 'Firmament') with a white-flowered viburnum (*V. opulus* 'Xanthocarpum') to the right. In the foreground is *Polemonium caeruleum*, which comes true to colour when it seeds itself, and columbine (*Aquilegia vulgaris*), which spreads equally prolifically but varies between blue, pink, and purple. Further back, beyond the foliage of ferns, daylilies and hellebores, is the black-flowered *Geranium phaeum* growing with *Tellima grandiflora*.

BELOW This section towards the front of a predominantly blue border has passed through a blue and yellow phase, as revealed by the foliage of narcissi which have gone over. A pale blue viola is coming into flower just as the forget-me-nots are finishing. *Centaurea montana* will go on flowering all summer provided it is regularly dead-headed.

Blues

SPRING

Ajuga reptans BUGLE
Semi-evergreen perennial that makes mats of shiny dark green foliage, with short spires of dusky blue flowers. Makes good groundcover for sun or shade. H 10cm (4in) S 40cm (15in) Z4 [ill.pp.71,151]. **A. r. 'Atropurpurea'** has dark purple foliage. H 15cm (6in) S 40cm (15in) Z4 [ill.p.133]

Brunnera macrophylla SIBERIAN BUGLOSS Perennial with flowers like those of forget-me-nots, and the added bonus of attractive heart-shaped leaves. Prefers light shade. H 45cm (18in) S 60cm (24in) Z4

Ceanothus CALIFORNIAN LILAC
The best of all blue-flowered shrubs. Evergreen **C. arboreus** makes a mound of almost uninterrupted blue if left to its own devices. Usually trained against a wall, for frost protection and to contain its size. Favours light soil and partial shade. H and S 4m (12ft) Z9. **C. 'Puget Blue'** H 6m (20ft) S 8m (25ft) Z8 [ill.p.73]. **C. 'Cascade'** is evergreen, with pale blue fflowers and narrow oval leaves. It has arching branches that are easily trained. H and S 6m (20ft) Z8 [ill.p.132]

Chionodoxa luciliae GLORY-OF-THE-SNOW An early-flowering bulb

whose upward-facing flowers, blue with white centres, open to the sun. Will seed itself and spread in undisturbed ground. H 10cm (4in) S 5cm (2in) Z4 [ill.pp.5,70]

Clematis alpina
Climbers that are small enough to be grown in containers and through wall-trained shrubs. Normally left unpruned, most alpina types tolerate partial shade. Good cultivars include **C. a. 'Frances Rivis'** which has flowers with long sepals, like a tensed claw; and **C. a.'Pamela Jackman'**with lantern-shaped flowers with white centres. Both H and S 2.5m (8ft) Z5

Gentiana verna subsp. **balcanica** SPRING GENTIAN Evergreen perennial with incomparable jewel-blue flowers. It prefers sun and needs humus-rich soil with sharp drainage. H and S 5cm (2in) Z5

Hyacinthoides hispanica SPANISH BLUEBELL If left undisturbed, the bulbs will spread into clumps, and will ultimately make sheets of blue. In borders it can become invasive. Prefers heavy soil and requires partial shade with plenty of moisture. H 40cm (15in) S 10cm (4in) Z4

Iris
Good varieties of these early-flowering bulbous perennials include **I. histrioides 'Major'** with dark blue flowers, H 10cm (4in) S 7cm (3in) Z5; and **I. 'Cantab'**

with paler, clear blue flowers, H 4in (10cm) S 6cm (2½in) Z5

Lithodora diffusa
Shrubby perennial that makes a low carpet of vivid blue flowers. Resents root disturbance and needs full sun and acid soil. Best varieties include **L. d. 'Heavenly Blue'** and the pale blue **L. d. 'Cambridge Blue'**. H 60cm (2ft) S 90cm (3ft) Z6

Muscari GRAPE HYACINTH
These small bulbs with dense flower spikes require a sunny situation. Good varieties include **M. armeniacum** with deep blue flowers, H 15cm (6in) S 8cm (3in) Z6 [ill.pp.5,70]; and **M. latifolium** with blue flowers and violet buds, H 15cm (6in) S 8cm (3in) Z6

Myosotis alpestris FORGET-ME-NOT
A self-seeding biennial, but over generations the flower colour becomes progressively more insipid. For the brightest blue, use bought seed. Prefers full sun but tolerates light shade. H 15cm (6in) S 30cm (12in) Z6 [ill.pp.10,73,141]

Omphalodes cappadocica
Perennial with exquisite blue flowers, that spreads by creeping stems. It is useful for giving colour in open shade. H 20cm (8in) S 25cm (10in) Z6 [ill.p.71]

Phlox stolonifera CREEPING PHLOX
Short-lived perennial, with pale blue flowers, pink at the centre. It makes attractive clumps, but does not spread. **P.s. 'Blue Ridge'**

spreads by creeping shoots making a pale blue carpet under deciduous trees. Needs moist, peaty, acid soil. H 15cm (6in) S 30cm (12in) Z4

Pulmonaria LUNGWORT
Early-flowering perennial that prefers shade and moist soil. Good varieties include **P. angustifolia** and its spp. **azurea**, as well as **P. a. 'Munstead Blue'**, all of which have intense blue flowers with unpatterned mid-green foliage. H 23cm (9in) S 30cm (12in) Z4. **P. longifolia 'Bertram Anderson'** has long dark green leaves spotted with white. H 30cm (12in) S45cm (18in) Z5. **P. saccharata 'Frühlingshimmel'** has pale blue flowers. H 30cm (12in) S 45cm (18in) Z4

Puschkinia scilloides var. **libanotica** (syn. **P. libanotica**) STRIPED SQUILL Early-flowering bulbs, needing sun. They are most effective planted en masse. Delicate-looking, the flower petals are near-white, with a blue midline that makes them appear pale blue overall. H 15cm (6in) S 5cm (2in) Z4 [ill.p.70]

Rosmarinus officinalis 'Benenden Blue' ROSEMARY Evergreen shrubs that require sun, rosemaries are usually grown for their aromatic foliage, but this one also has rich blue flowers. Can be shaped and even used as a hedge, if only new growth is clipped after flowering. H and S 1.5m (5ft) Z9

Scilla
Early-flowering bulbs that need an open site in sun or partial shade. **S. siberica** SIBERIAN SQUILL has down-turned mid-blue flowers. H 15cm (6in) S 5cm (2in) Z3. **S. mischtschenkoana** has the palest blue flowers. H 10cm (4in) S 5cm (2in) Z6

SUMMER

Aconitum napellus MONKSHOOD
Tuberous perennial with spikes of hooded, dusky blue flowers and deeply cut leaves. Prefers sun, but will tolerate partial shade. H 1.5m (5ft) S 30cm (1ft) Z5 [ill.p.181]

Agapanthus
Perennial, with globes of blue flowers atop long stems, and strap-like leaves. The plants like to bake in the sun, so a place in front of a border, or at the foot of a sunny wall or in a container is ideal. Good varieties include **A. campanulatus** with narrow leaves and good blue flowers, H 90cm (3ft) S 50cm (20in) Z8 [ill.p.116]; **Headbourne Hybrids** have slightly larger flowers of a more variable blue, H and S 90cm (3ft) Z7 [ill.p.181]

Amsonia tabernaemontana BLUE STAR Perennial with dainty flowerheads of pale sky-blue on a rounded plant. The flower colour is discreet, and dominated by the mass of lance-shaped leaves. Best if left

Brunnera macrophylla

Gentiana verna subsp. balcanica

Lithodora diffusa

Pulmonaria angustifolia

Aconitum napellus

undisturbed for years. Needs partial shade. H 60cm (24in) S 30cm (12in) Z4 [ill.p.71]

Anchusa azurea '**Loddon Royalist**' One of the most desirable of all blue flowers, giving generous spires of intense blue. Although perennial, it may be short-lived, and can be propagated by root cuttings. Requires sun and dislikes winter damp [ill.pp.116,184]. For a lighter, forget-me-not blue, try *A. a* '**Opal**' H 1.2m (4ft) S 60cm (2ft) Z4

Aquilegia '**Hensol Harebell**' COLUMBINE The best of the blue aquilegias. Prefers sun. H 75cm (30in) S 50cm (20in) Z4 [ill.p.183]

Aster x *frikartii* '**Mönch**' One of the best of the perennial late summer daisies, valuable for its good lavender-blue flowers (with yellow centres) and long flowering season. Prefers sun or partial shade. H 70cm (28in) S 40cm (15in) Z5

Baptisia australis FALSE INDIGO Perennial with blue flowers like small lupins, though less compact, and pretty lupin-like foliage. It needs staking, likes full sun and deep, neutral to acid soil, and is best left undisturbed. H 75cm (30in) S 60cm (2ft) Z3

Borago officinalis BORAGE This herbaceous annual, an ornamental and culinary asset to any herb or vegetable garden, has clear blue, star-shaped

flowers and attractive downy grey foliage. It self-seeds profusely, and so may become invasive. Prefers sun. H 90cm (3ft) S 30cm (1ft)

Buddleja '**Lochinch**' BUTTERFLY BUSH With only a suggestion of lilac in its pale flowers, this is the closest a buddleja comes to blue. The foliage is slightly hairy, giving the shrub a silvery look. It requires full sun, and should be cut back hard in spring. H and S 3m (10ft) Z7 [ill.p.181]

Camassia cusickii QUAMASH Spikes of starry mid-blue flowers grow from a fringe of strap-like foliage. The bulbs will multiply in the right conditions, and they may naturalize in damp meadows. Tolerates shade or partial shade in a clay soil. H 80cm (30in) S 30cm (12in) Z3 [ill.p.71]

Campanula BELLFLOWER Perennial varieties include *C. latiloba* which makes spreading groundcover under trees, where the shady light intensifies the blueness of the flowers, H 1.2m (4ft) S 60cm (2ft) Z3 [ill.p.180]; *C. portenschlagiana* which is mat-forming, H 15cm (6in) S 45cm (18in) Z4 [ill.p.116]; *C. poscharskyana* is similar, with slightly paler flowers, shaped like deeper bells, and it has a tendency to creep up low walls, H 15cm (6in) S 45cm (18in) Z3 [ill.p.133]. All tolerate sun and partial shade.

Catananche caerulea CUPID'S DART Flowers of this perennial are cornflower-like, with papery white bracts around their bases. The plants need staking with discreet peasticks, and do best in sun and light soil. H 90cm (30in) S 45cm (18in) Z4

Centaurea CORNFLOWER Good varieties include annual *C. cyanus* which has intense blue flowers, though there are varieties available in white, pink or deepest purple. Keep them dead-headed to ensure repeat-flowering. H 90cm (3ft) S 30cm (1ft) [ill.p.164]. *C. montana* PERENNIAL CORNFLOWER is a spreading and potentially invasive plant, but rewarding for its intense blue flowers, larger than the annual, and for its grey-green foliage. H 50cm (20in) S 60cm (2ft) Z3 [ill.p.184]. All are best in full sun.

Clematis Good climbing varieties that tolerate both sun and shade so long as they have a shaded root run, include '**Lasurstern**' with large flowers in midsummer, H 3m (10ft) S 90cm (3ft) Z5 [ill.pp.64,114];.'**Perle d'Azur**' is vigorous with large pale blue flowers, H 4.6m (15ft) S 90cm (3ft) Z5 [ill.pp.11,62,164]; '**Prince Charles**' is smaller-flowered and less vigorous, H 2.4m (8ft) S 90cm (3ft) Z5 [ill.p.151]. Good semi-herbaceous varieties include *C.*

heracleifolia var. *davidana* H 90cm (3ft) S 75cm (30in) Z3; and *C.* x *durandii* H 1.8m (6ft) S90cm (3ft) Z4. Both can be trained into other shrubs.

Consolida ambigua (syn. *C. ajacis*) LARKSPUR Very similar to their perennial cousins, the delphiniums, only these are annuals, growing to full size in a season. Effective when the seed is scattered in open ground between perennial. They require sun. H 60cm (2ft) S 30cm (1ft)

Convolvulus *C. sabatius* (syn.*C. mauritanicus*) is an evergreen perennial, good for a container. It is not a climber, but will trail elegantly over the side and produce a profusion of small, funnel-shaped blue-violet flowers. H 20cm (8in) S 30cm (1ft) Z9. *C. tricolor* (syn. *C. minor*) is an annual with intense blue, saucer-shaped flowers with bright yellow throats. H 30cm (12in) S 20cm (8in). Both need full sun.

Corydalis flexuosa A perennial with delicate flowerheads of sky blue combined with intricately cut foliage. Ideal for naturalizing under deciduous trees, where a massed planting looks like a blue pool. Requires a loose, leafy soil in shade or partial shade. H 30cm (12in) S 40cm (15in) Z5

Cynoglossum amabile CHINESE FORGET-ME-NOT A sun-loving biennial with intense turquoise-

blue flowers among downy grey-green foliage. H 60cm (2ft) S 40cm (15in) Z7

Delphinium Star performers of the blue galaxy, these perennials can provide the backbone to a blue border in summer, and are available in all tints and shades of blue, as well as white, cream and violet [ill.pp.8,180,182]. Good blue ones include **Black Knight Group** H 1.8m (6ft) S 40cm (15in) Z3 [ill.pp.63,143]; '**Chelsea Star**' H 1.8m (6ft) S 75cm (30in) Z3; *D. grandiflorum* '**Blue Butterfly**', which is usually grown as an annual, H 45cm (18in) S30cm (12in) Z3; **Pacific Hybrids** H 1.8m (6ft) S 40cm (15in) Z3 [ill.pp.176,183]; and **Summer Skies Group** H 1.8m (6ft) S 40cm (15in) Z3. All require sun.

Echinops ritro GLOBE THISTLE A reliable perennial with spiky and compact globes of tiny blue flowers surmounting tall clumps of hairy jagged-edged foliage. Best in sun and in poor soil. H 1.2m (4ft) S 40cm (15in) Z3 [ill.p.11]

Echium '**Blue Bedder**' VIPER'S BUGLOSS Annual that produces mounds of mid-blue flowers that ultimately become untidy, and because they are shy of re-flowering if cut right back, it is best to remove them altogether after flowering. Requires sun. H 30cm (1ft) S 20cm (8in)

Baptisia australis

Campanula poscharskyana

Catananche caerulea

Corydalis flexuosa

Echinops ritro

Eryngium SEA HOLLY
Good perennial varieties include *E. alpinum* which has a flowerhead like a pin-cushion surrounded by a prickly fringe of dusky blue bracts, H 1m (3ft3in) S 60cm (2ft) Z5 [ill.pp.25,157]; *E. x oliverianum* has less elaborate bracts, H 90cm (36in) S 60cm (24in) Z5; *E. x tripartitum* has much smaller flowers but more of them, arranged in clusters, with all flower-parts suffused with blue, H 1.2m (4ft) S 50cm (20in) Z5 [ill.p.108]. All require sun.

Felicia amelloides 'Santa Anita'
Since this evergreen shrub with daisy-like flowers is tender, it is best for containers or for a summer bedding scheme. Requires full sun. H and S 1ft (30cm) Z10

Geranium CRANESBILL
Invaluable, reliable perennials that tolerate sun and partial shade. **'Johnson's Blue'** makes a lovely mound of rounded blue flowers above cut foliage. H 30cm (1ft) S 60cm (2ft) Z4 [ill.pp.11,151]. *G. pratense* '**Mrs Kendall Clark**' has palest blue-grey flowers with pink stamens. H and S 60cm (2ft) Z4 [ill.p.7]. *G. pratense* 'Plenum Caeruleum' has double mid-blue flowers. H and S 75cm (30in) Z4 [ill.p.175]

Hibiscus syriacus 'Oiseau Bleu'
(syn. *H.s.* 'Blue Bird') The blue flowers of this shrub have magenta throats and close up in damp weather. May be planted in a row and clipped to make a hedge. Requires sun. H 3m (10ft) S 2m (6ft6in) Z6

Hydrangea macrophylla 'Mariesii Perfection' (syn. *H. m.* 'Blue Wave') This shrub is best in partial shade and moist soil, and it needs acid soil if the elegant 'lacecap' flowerheads are to be bright blue. In neutral to alkaline soils they become quite pink. H 2m (6ft6in) S 2.4m (8ft) Z6

Ipomea tricolor 'Heavenly Blue' (syn. *I. rubrocaerulea* 'Heavenly Blue') MORNING GLORY Fast-growing, this annual climber produces intense blue funnel-shaped flowers, made all the more scintillating by their ephemerality. They are barely open at breakfast, and over by lunch. Requires full sun. H and S 3m (10ft)

Iris
The following rhizomatous perennial irises need a sunny position in moist soil: *I. cristata* is a miniature that spreads to form a blue mat in gravel or on the rock garden, H 10cm (4in) S 30cm (12in) Z3; *I. ensata* 'Favourite' (syn. *I. kaempferi* 'F.') thrives in a water or bog gardens, H 1m (3ft3in) S 40cm (15in) Z5; and *I. pallida* is evergreen with bluish sword-shaped leaves, H 1.2m (4ft) S 45cm (18in) Z4. *I. missouriensis* (syn *I. tolmieana*) needs sun or partial shade, and resents being moved. H 75cm (30in) S 40cm (15in) Z3. *I. sibirica* forms clumps of grass-like foliage, with tall flowering stems carrying relatively small rich blue flowers. H 1.2m (4ft) S 45cm (18in) Z4 [ill.p.11]

Linum perenne PERENNIAL FLAX
Perennial that makes a clump of narrow, grass-like leaves, surmounted by small, open saucer-shaped flowers of exquisite blue, which appear in succession through the summer. Requires sun. H 60cm (24in) S 15cm (6in) Z4

Lobelia erinus TRAILING LOBELIA
An annual stalwart for the edges of bedding schemes, and for containers, especially window boxes and hanging baskets, where the tiny blue flowers can be used to best effect. Requires moist soil in either sun or partial shade. Good varieties include trailing *L. e.* '**Blue Cascade**' H 20cm (8in) S 15cm (6in); and *L. e.* '**Cambridge Blue**' which is more compact.

Meconopsis
These most desirable of perennial plants are very choosy about their living conditions. The privileged minority of gardeners will be rewarded with enviable drifts of blue poppies in broken shade and moist, acid soil. *M. betonicifolia* HIMALYAN BLUE POPPY H 1.2m (4ft) S 45cm (18in) Z5 [ill.p.72]; *M. grandis* H 1.5m (5ft) S 30cm (1ft) Z5

Nemophila menziesii BABY BLUE EYES The little scalloped blue flowers of this annual have white centres, which give them a welcome touch of lightness for the blue border. Tolerates both sun and partial shade. H 20cm (8in) S 15cm (6in)

Nepeta CATMINT
The aromatic foliage of this perennial is irresistible to cats and the genus is indispensable to gardeners wanting to create a diaphanous haze of lavender-blue. Useful varieties include **N. x faassenii** H and S 45cm (18in) Z4 [ill.pp.119,175]; **N. nervosa** H 60cm (2ft) S 40cm (15in) Z5 [ill.p.21]; **N. sibirica** H and S 90cm (3ft) Z4; and, the most desirable of all, **N. sibirica** '**Souvenir d'André Chaudron**', with shorter habit but larger flowers [ill.p.183]. '**Six Hills Giant**' is one of the most vigorous varieties, floppy in habit and well suited for use as an edging to a path. As soon as the flowers go over, cut the plant right back and it will regenerate surpris-ingly quickly. H 75cm (30in) S 1.2m (4ft) Z4 [ill.pp. 106,141]. All do best in sun and moist soil.

Nigella damascena LOVE-IN-A-MIST
The semi-double flowers of this annual are intriguingly shaped and framed by spindly bracts. The inflated seedpods are shapely too, and can be used for dried flower arrangements - but leave some *in situ* so that seed is scattered to colonize your garden. Best in sun. H. 60cm (24in) S 20cm (8in). Good cultivars include **N. d.** '**Miss Jekyll**' H 45cm (18in) S 20cm (8in) [ill.p.143]

Parahebe perfoliata DIGGER'S SPEEDWELL The stems of the branching sprays of small blue flowers are clasped by evergreen oval blue-green leaves. A sub-shrub that requires sun, and peaty and sandy soil, the plant tends to flop and needs the discreet support of peasticks. H 45-60cm (18-24in) S 45cm (18in) Z8

Penstemon heterophyllus
This perennial and its varieties *P. h.* '**Blue Gem**' and *P. h.* '**Heavenly Blue**' are the best of the blue penstemons, giving a succession of spikes of tubular flowers, provided the flowering stems are cut back as soon as they go over. All do best in sun. H 40cm (15in) S 30cm (12in) Z8 [ill.pp.11,114]

Perovskia 'Blue Spire' RUSSIAN SAGE
The spires of small blue flowers, combined with the small, silvery, toothed leaves, create a haze of colour for late season. This aromatic sub-shrub needs full sun and very well-drained soil. H 90cm (3ft) S 80cm (2ft8in) Z6

Phacelia campanularia CALIFORNIA BLUEBELL Deep blue bell-shaped flowers on reddish stems combine with oval serrated foliage on this annual that needs sun. H 20cm (8in) S 15cm (6in)

Geranium pratense 'Mrs Kendall Clark'

Ipomea tricolor 'Heavenly Blue'

Iris sibirica

Nemophila menzeisii

Phacelia campanularia

Phlox

P. divaricata subsp. *laphamii* '**Chattahoochee**' is a short-lived perennial that makes clumps of bright lavender-blue flowers with crimson throats. Best in sun. H 40cm (15in) S 30cm (12in) Z3; *P. drummondii* '**Blue Beauty**' is an annual with rounded flowerheads of open, clear lavender-blue flowers. Best in sun. H 15cm (6in) S 10cm (4in)

Platycodon grandiflorus BALLOON FLOWER This perennial member of the campanula family has striking balloon-shaped buds, which open into shallow bell-shaped flowers with fused petals. Likes sun and a light, sandy soil. H and S 45cm (18in) Z4

Polemonium caeruleum JACOB'S LADDER Forms a clump, with finely divided foliage and clusters of clear blue flowers with contrasting yellow stamens. Although it is a perennial, it spreads by self-seeding. Requires sun. H and S 60cm (2ft) Z4 [ill.p.73]

Plumbago auriculata (syn. *P. capensis*) CAPE LEADWORT This evergreen climber is confined to conservatories and summer containers in cooler climates. Produces clouds of exquisite pale blue flowers over a long period in summer. Requires sun. H and S 6m (20ft) Z9

Salvia SAGE The salvias with the best blue flowers are mostly perennials or annuals. *S. farinacea* '**Victoria**' MEALY SAGE has spikes of small dark blue flowers, reminiscent of lavender. It is a perennial that can be grown as an annual, and prefers sun. H 45cm (18in) S 30cm (12in) Z9. *S. guaranitica* is a perennial, that becomes quite shrubby in appearance, with dark green leaves and claw-shaped flowers of an intense blue. H 1.5m (5ft) S 60cm (2ft) Z9. *S. viridis* '**Blue Beard**' (syn. *S. horminum* 'B.B.') is an annual whose colour interest comes from the terminal bracts, which are blue-violet and long-lasting; the flowers themselves are modest. Does best in sun. H 45cm (18in) S 20cm (8in) [ill.p.132]. *S. patens* is a perennial with bright blue flowers. Requires sun. H and S 45cm (18in) Z9. A variety with pale blue flowers is *S. p.* '**Cambridge Blue**'. H 45cm (18in) S 60cm (24in) Z9

Scabiosa caucasica '**Clive Greaves**' SCABIOUS Perennial whose round flowers with fluffed petals and creamy centres, wave in the wind on long stems. Requires sun and prefers alkaline soil. H and S 45cm (18in) Z4

Stokesia laevis '**Blue Danube**' STOKE'S ASTER This evergreen perennial, which tolerates sun and partial shade bears its cornflower-like flowers on short stems above narrow mid-green leaves. H and S 45cm (18in) Z5

Syringa vulgaris '**Firmament**' LILAC The bluest of the lilacs, with good scent, this tree requires sun or partial shade. Amenable to pruning to keep it within bounds. H and S 7m (24ft) Z4 [ill.p.73]

Teucrium fruticans TREE GERMANDER The lipped pale blue flowers look well against the shrub's own evergreen, grey-green leaves, which are aromatic. There is a desirable variety with dark blue flowers called *T. f.* '**Azureum**'. Both require full sun. H 2m (6ft6in) S 4m (12ft) Z9

Veronica SPEEDWELL Among the best varieties of this perennial is *V. austriaca* '**Crater Lake Blue**', an ideal plant for the front of the border, making a mound of spikes of small flowers of an intense blue, lightened by tiny white eyes, H and S 50cm (20in) Z5 [ill.p.133]; *V. gentianoides* puts out spikes of palest blue flowers, H and S 45cm (18in) Z5 [ill.p.141]; *V. peduncularis* '**Georgia Blue**' is a recent introduction with intense blue flowers on a compact plant, H 25cm (9in) S 45cm (18in) Z6. All require sun.

Viola VIOLET\PANSY Good varieties that tolerate both sun and shade include the perennial '**Boughton Blue**' that flowers throughout the summer. Cut back to base when it begins to look tired, and will sprout and flower again if new growth is kept fed and watered. H 40cm (15in) S 60cm (24in) Z5

AUTUMN

Aconitum carmichaelii MONKSHOOD The hooded dark blue flowers of this perennial are an unexpected feature of the autumn garden and so more prized than they would be in competition with summer flowers. Prefers sun, but tolerates some shade. H 1.5m (5ft) S 90cm (3ft) Z3

Caryopteris x clandonensis BLUEBEARD Attractive throughout the summer, this small shrub has blue-green lance-shaped leaves, and pointed racemes of clear blue flowers in late season. Good named varieties are *C. c.* '**Heavenly Blue**' with the deepest blue flowers; and *C. c.* '**Kew Blue**' with paler flowers. All require full sun. H and S 90cm (3ft) Z7

Ceratostigma The rich blue flowers make a marvellous combination with the shrub's own orange and red autumn foliage. Requires full sun and benefits from the shelter of a wall. Good varieties include *C. plumbaginoides* a low, spreading plant, good for groundcover, H 45cm (18in) S 75cm (30in) Z5; and *C. willmottianum* a more substantial shrub, H and S 1m (3ft3in) Z5

Crocus speciosus The blue-violet flowers, with bright orange stigmas, appear in advance of the leaves. The best blue variety of this sun-loving corm is *C. s.* '**Oxonian**'. H 10cm (4in) S 8cm (3in) Z4

Gentiana sino-ornata A creeping evergreen perennial, with large, intense blue trumpet-shaped flowers, that thrives in an alpine trough, or on the edge of woodland, provided it has lime-free soil, a cool root-run and is never allowed to dry out. H 5cm (2in) S 30cm (12in) Z6

Geranium wallichianum '**Buxton's Variety**' CRANESBILL A creeping perennial with blue flowers that have pink veining and brilliant white centres. Tolerant of sun, shade and any except water-logged soil. H 30cm (12in) S 90cm (3ft) Z7

Salvia uliginosa BOG SAGE A lovely 'see-through' perennial for late autumn, its flower-heads of the most intense pale blue are suspended on insubstantial stems that wave prettily in the wind. Requires sun. H 2m (6ft6in) S 45cm (18in) Z9

WINTER

Viola '**Universal Blue**' PANSY Annual that produces flowers in mild winter spells. Tolerant of sun or shade, it is always worth growing a few in pots or on the edge of borders to bring a little winter cheer. H and S 20cm (8in) Z4

Plumbago auriculata

Salvia patens

Veronica peduncularis 'Georgia Blue'

Caryopteris x *clandonensis* 'Kew Blue

Crocus speciosus

Greens

ABOVE A planting of aromatic herbs and grasses in terracotta containers make a rich tapestry of greens. Bowles' golden grass (*Milium effusum* 'Aureum') is planted with young fennel in front of yellow-leaved *Lonicera nitida* 'Baggesen's Gold'. Miniature standard box globes are underplanted with golden thyme (*Thymus* x *citriodorus* 'Aureus') and, on the opposite side, with germander (*Teucrium* x *lucidrys*). The variegated holly (*Ilex aquifolium* 'Silver Queen') has silver-leaved *Tanacetum densum* subsp. *amani* at its foot.

Green is the backdrop to all other colours in the garden. But it is not an entirely neutral background, as a mid-grey screen would be. It plays an active part in colour associations and has an effect on its neighbours, contrasting most strongly with its complementary – red – and harmonizing most closely with its adjacent hues on the colour wheel – yellow and blue. Green also has a calming influence on other colours because of its associations with peace and nature. In fact, green can be so calming that sufferers from migraine have reported that their symptoms can sometimes be relieved by staring at green grass and foliage.

We sometimes apologise that there is not much colour in the garden, forgetting perhaps that green is a wonderful colour in itself. It is all that we need to create a mood of tranquillity and peace. Foliage has a purely practical advantage over flowers too, in that it is longer- lived and generally easier to maintain, often needing only an occasional weed and trim. If you use evergreen plants, you can create foliage efffects that last throughout the year.

Mid-greens are neutral in terms of colour temperature and tone. They lie on the borderline between hot and cold colours, and near the middle of the scale of dark and light tones. That is why green foliage works so well as a transition between other colours, softening contrasts that would appear too intense if colours were placed side by side without its intervening influence. Some foliage greens are fairly dark on the tonal scale, and so help to show up light-coloured flowers, while dark-coloured flowers, such as violets, purples and deep blues, merge with the similar tones of their green background.

Greens offer the gardener greater diversity than any other colour family. They range from the fresh lime-green of emerging leaf-buds in spring to the near-black evergreen foliage of yew, from the bright yellow-green leaves of golden privet, to the blue-green foliage of *Hosta* 'Halcyon'. There is also an extraordinary range of shapes, sizes, and textures from which to choose. Foliage forms vary from the wispy filaments of grasses such as *Miscanthus sinensis* 'Gracillimus' to the stolid, ear-flap leaves of *Bergenia cordifolia*, and the elaborate filigree of ferns. Textures range from the felty softness of verbascums to the shiny, prickle-edged hardness of hollies.

Patterned foliage adds yet another dimension to the greens. The possibilities include grasses and irises with white striped leaves, spotted pulmonarias, white-splashed dogwoods, marbled arums and white- or yellow-edged hostas. Variegation like this gives the effect of broken colour and fragmented shape and form. When you see a green-and white-striped leaf, it looks as though several leaves are shimmering together, rather than a single one. Pale spots and smudges on leaves can look like sunbeams filtering through the foliage. You can capitalize on this and bring the illusion of dappled light to a shady area by using variegated plants, such as hostas.

Variegated foliage also presents opportunities for subtle colour associations. You could plant the white-edged *Hosta* 'Albomarginata' with green and white striped *Tulipa* 'Spring Green'. Or grow a yellow-variegated ivy, like *Hedera helix* 'Oro di Bogliasco', on a trellis screen with *Clematis tangutica*, whose yellow dangling heart-shaped flowers echo the yellow variegations in the ivy leaves.

One important point to remember when growing variegated plants is that they are not usually as vigorous as their unvariegated relations. And since some variegations are caused by viruses, patterned foliage can look sickly. Use them with restraint. Remember too that variegated plants may need more sunlight than plain varieties do. This is because they contain less of the green pigment, chlorophyll, which is needed in photosynthesis, the process by which plants harness sunlight to make energy.

With such a range of greens available in foliage, it is easy to forget that there are some choice plants with green flowers. These are an acquired taste and novice gardeners tend not to notice them. But as the gardening passion takes hold, green flowers reveal their special charms. Like green foliage, they are useful in any plant association; they look good with any other flower colour and they provide a buffer between stronger and brighter flowers.

Green-flowered hellebores are among the first flowers to appear in early spring. They sometimes accompany snowdrops, whose flowers have echoing touches of green. Green catkins of evergreen *Garrya elliptica* are followed by lime-green euphorbias. A few months on, the foamy green-flowered lady's mantle (*Alchemilla mollis*) provides the perfect foil for all the other colours of the summer garden. Among the annuals, bells of Ireland (*Moluccella laevis*) and the flowering tobacco plants, *Nicotiana langsdorffii* and *N.* x *sanderae* 'Lime Green', have flowers that are only slightly lighter green than their own leaves, but make a matching partnership with the lime-green foliage of tender perennial *Helichrysum petiolare* 'Limelight'.

ABOVE The common ivy (*Hedera helix*) is immensely variable. Here two varieties, the yellow-leaved *H.h.* 'Buttercup' and the grey-variegated *H.h.* 'Glacier', create a patterned green drape over a low wall. In a situation like this, ivy needs regular trimming to prevent it spreading out into the adjacent borders and choking the plants. It thrives in most conditions, including poor soil and full shade, although the variegated and yellow-leaved varieties, which have reduced chloropyll, are less tolerant of shade.

ABOVE In early summer, a clever combination of perennials – many of them evergreens – shows the broad range of greens that can be used. The lime-yellow of the long-flowering *Euphorbia polychroma* and of the Bowles' golden grass (*Milium effusum* 'Aureum') dominate, and enhance the silver of the foliage of the artemisia. Most of these plants thrive in semi-shade, making solid mounds of colour, and some are good groundcover. (Full planting details of this scheme are given on page 173.)

Foliage Associations

You do not need flowers to create colour interest in the garden. A variety of green foliage can be enough, certainly on a small scale. To exploit the limitless repertory of greens, try puting yellow-greens with blue-greens, rusty greens with silvers, and spotty variegated patterns beside stripes. For interesting differences in shapes and textural effects, put together plants with strong outlines – jagged against smooth, spear shapes against fuzzy ones, shiny surfaces against felty ones. The advantage of foliage plantings is that they are longer-lived than floral associations, and their colour effects ebb and flow with the changing seasons.

FAR LEFT ABOVE Purple fronds of *Cordyline australis* 'Purpurea' and stems of purple-leaved *Lobelia* 'Queen Victoria' grow through a cluster of glossy green *Darmera peltata* and the smaller felty leaves of *Ballota pseudodictamnus. Heuchera micrantha* var. *diversifolia* 'Palace Purple' picks up the purple theme in the foreground.

FAR LEFT BELOW Leaves of *Atriplex hortensis* var. *rubra* and frothy love-in-a-mist (*Nigella damascena*) grow through stems of golden-leaved hop (*Humulus lupulus* 'Aureus') and brightly variegated *Euonymus fortunei* 'Silver Queen'.

LEFT ABOVE A variegated iris (*I. pallida* 'Argentea Variegata') grows through the feathery young foliage of *Nigella damascena*.

LEFT BELOW The creamy veins of an ornamental cabbage are echoed by the pale flowers of a tobacco plant (*Nicotiana* x *sanderae* 'Domino Lime'), the plumes of squirrel tail grass (*Hordeum jubatum*) and leaves of yellow-green variegated sage (*Salvia officinalis* 'Icterina'). Foliage of the mallow (*Lavatera trimestris* 'Mont Blanc') and of the plume poppy (*Macleaya microcarpa* 'Kelway's Coral Plume') contribute darker tones.

TOP The shiny seven-fingered variegated leaves of *Fatsia japonica* 'Variegata' contrast with the blue-green foliage of the *Macleaya microcarpa* 'Kelway's Coral Plume' and the velvet foliage of *Hydrangea aspera* subsp. *sargentiana*. The fatsia keeps its variegation best in sun.

ABOVE Ornamental rhubarb (*Rheum palmatum* 'Atrosanguineum'), *Angelica archangelica*, golden feverfew (*Tanacetum parthenium* 'Aureum'), *Macleaya microcarpa* 'Kelway's Coral Plume', *Ligularia przewalskii* and gardener's garters (*Phalaris arundinacea* var. *picta* 'Picta') make a tapestry of greens. Take care with these plants: the rhubarb needs space, gardener's garters can be invasive, and angelica will die if its seedheads are left on.

TOP In early summer, green fennel (*Foeniculum vulgare*) softens the link between the blue hostas (*H.* 'Blue Diamond', *H.* 'Halcyon' and *H.* 'Krossa Regal') and the cream-margined *Hosta fortunei* var. *aureomarginata*. The cream motif is repeated in the flower spikes of *Tellima grandiflora*.

ABOVE In a moist shady site in early summer, the yellowish autumn fern (*Dryopteris erythrosora*) links the felty young foliage of a rhododendron (*R. yakushimanum*), the pointed leaves of *Persicaria campanulata* and the green and purple ones of *Cimicifuga racemosa* and *C. simplex* Atropurpurea Group, with a couple of decorative leaves of *Hosta tokudama* f. *flavocircinalis* appearing at the bottom.

81

All-Green Gardens

BELOW Its strict geometry softened by the silvery boughs of a weeping pear tree, this formal garden retains its structure through the year with little maintenance. The box domes, hedges and obelisks need trimming twice during the growing season, as does the ivy on the arbour to keep it from filling the spaces in the trellis.

No colour is as peaceful as green, and by restricting your palette to green plants, you can create a garden – or corner of a garden – of absolute tranquillity, whether it is formal and highly structured, or informal and natural-looking.

The formality of the garden *below*, relies on its permanent geometric structure. Its sense of ordered calm depends upon its symmetry. A low maze has been created from clipped box. Topiary and ivy-covered treillage add vertical emphasis, and a seat has been placed for silent contemplation. A very limited range of colour has been used

here, but it could be extended by infilling the parterre with other evergreens such as variegated ivy or pachysandra, or grey-leaved santolina, and by using dark bottle green yew for the obelisks instead of lightly variegated box. If you wish to add more colour, introduce pots of pale flowers that can be changed as soon as they go over.

Ferns, hostas and other shade-tolerant plants have been used to imitate nature in the informal garden *below*. There are no blue-greens, and the yellow-greens are largely the result of the sun filtering through the young foliage. Although it looks entirely natural, a lot of skill and effort are needed to maintain the lushness, while keeping the less vigorous plants from being swamped by their more rampant neighbours.

BELOW Later in the summer, the leaves of the giant rhubarb (*Gunnera manicata)* in the foreground will swell to meet the overhanging branches of the Japanese maple (*Acer palmatum*) and Indian horse chestnut (*Aesculus indica*). The extra shade will make the groundcover foliage more attenuated, as the hostas, ferns, and dinner-plate leaves of *Astilboides tabularis* compete for the remaining light.

Dark Greens

EVERGREEN

Camellia japonica
Handsome shrub with glossy leaves and flower colour ranging from pure white through all the pinks to deep mauve and red. Requires neutral to acid soil and a cool root-run. H 4.6m (15ft) S 3.7m (12ft) Z8

Ilex aquifolium 'J. C. van Tol' HOLLY
Hardy shrub with glossy, almost spineless leaves, and a reliable crop of red berries. Can be clipped to make a solid hedge. Tolerates sun or shade. H 3.7m (12ft) S 3m (10ft) Z6

Laurus nobilis SWEET BAY
Culinary herb with aromatic foliage. Fierce winters can cut it to the ground but it will come again. Clipped specimens need winter protection. *L. n. f. angustifolia*, the narrow-leaved form, is slightly hardier and more elegant. Tolerates sun and partial shade. H 6m (20ft) S 4.6m (15ft) Z8

Mahonia japonica
An imposing shrub with deep green, pinnate, spiny leaves and long lax racemes of fragrant lemon-yellow flowers over a long period from late autumn to spring. Tolerates sun and partial shade. H and S 2.4m (8ft) Z8

Osmanthus x burkwoodii
Shrub with neat, shiny dark foliage that will make a substantial hedge. Flowers freely in a sunny position. *O. delavayi* has flowers with an even sweeter scent. Both H and S 3m (10ft) Z7

Phillyrea latifolia MOCK PRIVET
Will make a very elegant small tree with glossy masses of foliage. *P. angustifolia* has longer, narrower leaves, and can be clipped to make a good compact hedge or topiary forms. Requires full sun. H and S 8m (25ft) Z8

Prunus lusitanica PORTUGAL LAUREL
A beautiful tree, given room, with glossy leaves, paler when new. Can be shaped. Tolerates sun or shade in any except water-logged soil. H and S 6m (20ft) Z8

Taxus baccata YEW
Essential hedging material, dark and dense; the backbone of so many fine gardens. Can be cut back very hard. Tolerates sun or shade and any type of soil. H and S to 9m (30ft) Z7 [ill.pp.178,184]

Teucrium x lucidrys GERMANDER
Sub-shrub densely clothed with small, dark toothed leaves, small deep pink flowers appearing in quantity in late summer. Can be clipped to make a dwarf hedge. Requires sun. H 30cm (1ft) S 60cm (2ft) Z6 [ill.p.78]

Viburnum davidii
Shrub that generally makes a wide-spreading mound of glossy, dark green foliage. Plant at least one male in a group of female plants to ensure a good crop of the bright blue berries in winter. Requires sun or partial shade. H 1.2m (4ft) S 1.5m (5ft) Z8

SPRING AND SUMMER

Cotoneaster horizontalis WALL SPRAY
The fan-like growth of this shrub will send its 'herringbone' branches climbing high if planted against a wall. The small leaves colour richly in autumn and last well, as do the red berries. In summer it is a buzz of bees (and wasps). Tolerates sun or partial shade. H 50cm (20in) S 1.5m (5ft) Z5

Hydrangea aspera subsp. *sargentiana* The huge, velvety leaves of this shrub are a fine setting for the wide heads of white flowers in mid summer. Tolerates sun and partial shade. H 2.4m (8ft) S 2m (6ft6in) Z8 [ill.p.81]

Mid-greens

EVERGREEN

Asplenium scolopendrium HART'S TONGUE FERN Perennial fern with strap-like leaves that unfurl from spirals in spring. Requires moist soil and partial shade. H 60cm (2ft) S 45cm (18in) Z5

Bergenia cordifolia
Perennial with clumps of rounded leaves, tinted red in winter. Useful groundcover in shade. Panicles of pink flowers in spring. Tolerates sun and shade and poor soil. H 45cm (18in) S 60cm (2ft) Z3 [ill.pp.96,170]

Buxus sempervirens COMMON BOX
Slow-growing shrub or small tree with small shiny leaves. Amenable to training and clipping. The perfect plant for compact hedging. Requires sun or partial shade, and any but water-logged soil. H and S 5m (15ft) Z6 [ill.pp.39,82,176, 183]

Choisya ternata MEXICAN ORANGE BLOSSOM Shrub with shiny three-lobed leaves, aromatic when cut or crushed, with scented white flowers in late spring. Requires sun or partial shade. H and S 3m (10ft) Z8

Epimedium pinnatum subsp. *colchicum* Perennial with heart-shaped leaves colouring in autumn and winter. Cut the foliage down in late winter to reveal the delicate yellow flowers. Requires partial shade and humus-rich soil. H and S 30cm (12in) Z5

Fatsia japonica
Shrub with elegant, large shiny divided leaves. Produces sprays of white flowers in autumn, followed by black fruits. Ideal for sheltered town gardens away from cold winds. Tolerates sun or shade. H and S 3m (10ft) Z8 [ill.p.81]

Griselinia littoralis
Wind-resistant shrub with luxuriant apple-green foliage. Requires sun. H 6m (20ft) S 4.6m (15ft) Z9

Hedera helix ENGLISH IVY
Excellent climber for covering sound walls or the ground, with a wide variety of leaf forms, colour, and vigour. Tolerant of shade and poor soil. *H. h.* 'Sagittifolia' H 3m (10ft) Z5; *H. h.* 'Gracilis' H 5m (15ft) Z5

Ligustrum ovalifolium OVAL-LEAVED PRIVET Justly popular shrub for hedging, the privet will also make a lovely soft mass of greenery whether in shade or sun and whatever the soil, although it will flower more freely in the sun. H 3.7m (12ft) S 3m (10ft) Z6

Lonicera pileata PRIVET HONEYSUCKLE
Spreading shrub with small, narrow leaves. Useful for groundcover and as a substitute for box for low hedging. Tolerates sun or shade. H 1.2m (4ft) S 90cm (3ft) Z6

Prunus laurocerasus CHERRY LAUREL
Large-leaved shrub or small tree, useful for screens and hedges. May also be shaped into cones and domes, but not fine topiary. White flower spikes in spring. Tolerates sun and shade. H 6m (20ft) S 9m (30ft) Z7

Tellima grandiflora FRINGECUPS
Semi-evergreen perennial forming spreading clumps of hairy, lobed leaves that make

Mahonia japonica

Phillyrea latifolia

Asplenium scolopendrium

Epimedium pinnatum subsp. colchicum

Hedera helix

pretty groundcover. The long stems of pale cream flowers smell of honey. Seeds itself about generously but not invasively. Requires a cool position in partial shade. H and S 60cm (2ft) Z4 [ill.pp.81,139]

Vinca major GREATER PERIWINKLE
A rampant spreader in any position, with glossy green leaves and bright blue flowers through spring and early summer. Tolerates sun and shade in all except dry soils. H 45cm (18in) S 90cm (3ft) Z7

SPRING AND SUMMER

Acanthus spinosus BEAR'S BREECHES
Perennial producing clumps of arching broadly-cut leaves, and tall, silky, purple and white flowers in summer. Best in full sun, but tolerates light shade. H 1.2m (4ft) S 1.5m (5ft) Z6

Angelica archangelica ANGELICA
Tall statuesque biennial producing in its second year a stout stem ending in rounded pale green umbels. Cut off the seedheads to prevent it seeding itself everywhere. Tolerates sun and shade. H 2.1m (7ft) S 90cm (3ft) Z4 [ill.p.157]

Astilboides tabularis (syn. *Rodgersia tabularis*) Perennial with creamy-white plumes of flowers held high above the bold, circular leaves, which can be 90cm (3ft) wide. Requires either sun or partial shade in

moist soil. H 1.5m (5ft) S 1.8m (6ft) Z5 [ill.p.83]

Carpinus betulus COMMON HORNBEAM Can either be grown as a specimen tree, or for hedging, where it resembles beech, but with more fine, ribbed, ovate leaves. Tolerates sun and partial shade. H 25m (80ft) S 20m (70ft) Z5

Darmera peltata (syn. *Peltiphyllum peltatum*) INDIAN RHUBARB Bog-loving and waterside perennial with umbrella-like leaves. Pink flowers appear in spring before foliage. Tolerates sun or shade. H 1m (3ft3in) S 60cm (2ft) Z5 [ill.p.180]

Dryopteris
Perennial fern that requires shade and moist soil. Good varieties include the deciduous *D. erythrosora* AUTUMN FERN H 45cm (18in) S 30cm (12in) Z8 [ill.pp.81,178]; and semi-evergreen *D. filix-mas* MALE FERN H 1.2m (4ft) S 90cm (3ft) Z2 [ill.p.178]

Epimedium x *versicolor*
Perennial with heart-shaped leaves; spring growth tinted red. Useful groundcover in shade or partial shade. Grows best in moist soil. H and S 30cm (12in) Z5

Ferula communis GIANT FENNEL
This unscented fennel makes a huge mound of perennial, finely cut dark foliage. The umbels of yellow flowers in late summer can be as tall as 3.7m (12ft)

Requires sun. H 2m (6ft6in) S 1.2m (4ft) Z7

Foeniculum vulgare FENNEL
Perennial herb with sprays of wire-like aromatic foliage. Requires an open, sunny position. H 2m (6ft6in) S 45cm (18in) Z5 [ill.pp.81,172]

Gunnera manicata GIANT RHUBARB
Waterside and bog-loving perennial with immense leaves and curious green flower spikes. Requires a sunny position in moist soil. Needs shelter from high winds and the crowns need extra protection during the colder months. H 2m (6ft6in) S 2.4m (8ft) Z8 [ill.p.83]

Hosta PLANTAIN LILY
Perennials. Most grow best in shade in rich, moist soil. Slug and snail control is essential. [ill.p.83]. *H. lancifolia* makes good groundcovering clumps of shining, dark green pointed leaves, with lilac flowers freely produced in late summer. H 45cm (18in) S 75cm (30in) Z3. *H. plantaginea* is, untypically, a sun-loving hosta with glossy pale green leaves and fragrant white flowers in late summer. H 60cm (2ft) S 1.2m (4ft) Z3. *H. ventricosa* has broad heart-shaped ribbed leaves of dark glossy green and rich violet flowers held well above the mound of foliage. H 70cm (2ft4in) S 90cm (3ft) Z3

Kirengeshoma palmata
A beautiful perennial for light

shade with clear green vine-like leaves on purple stems. Cool yellow, waxy flowers appear in autumn. Prefers moist, lime-free soil. H 90cm (3ft) S 60cm (2ft) Z5

Matteuccia struthiopteris OSTRICH FEATHER FERN Has arching, feathery fronds fanning out from the base like a shuttlecock. Brown fertile lacy fronds grow from the centre like ostrich plumes. Best with some protection and in moist, even wet, conditions. H 60cm (2ft) S 45cm (18in) Z2 [ill.p.9]

Miscanthus sinensis
Perennial grass that slowly forms a clump of narrow leaves with paler midriffs. Sends up tall, soft inflorescences in autumn that last well into winter. H 1.2m (4ft) S 45cm (18in) Z5

Myrrhis odorata SWEET CICELY
Perennial with leaves smelling of aniseed when crushed. Fragrant creamy white flowers appear in early summer. Tolerates sun or shade. H 90cm (3ft) S 60cm (2ft) Z4

Osmunda regalis ROYAL FERN
Tall, graceful perennial that tolerates sun but prefers shade. Needs wet conditions and lime-free soil. H 1.8m (6ft) S 90cm (3ft) Z3 [ill.pp.32,172]

Polypodium vulgare POLYPODY FERN
Perennial with mid-green deeply cut leaves that makes effective groundcover. Needs partial shade and fibrous, well-drained soil. H and S 30cm (12in) Z3

Polystichum setiferum SOFT SHIELD FERN Unusually tolerant evergreen fern, fresh and luxuriant even in relatively dry conditions. H and S 90cm (3ft) Z5

Rheum palmatum RHUBARB
Perennial with large, decorative deeply-cut leaves. Tall plumes of muted red flowers appear in summer. Requires sun or partial shade in deep, rich soil. H and S 2m (6ft6in) Z6 [ill.pp.81,177]

Rodgersia pinnata
Perennial with heavily ribbed, divided leaves with bronze sheen. Panicles of cream or pink flowers appear in summer. Tolerates sun, or partial shade if placed in a sheltered position, and needs moist soil. H 1.2m (4ft) S 75cm (30in) Z6 [ill.p.38]

Selinum tenuifolium
A tall, elegant perennial sending up many stems with lacy foliage and flat white flower umbels in summer. Prefers sun and will tolerate any well-drained soil. H 1.5m (5ft) S 60cm (2ft) Z6

Vitis GRAPEVINE
A number of varieties of grapevine have been selected for their ornamental value: '**Brant**' colours particularly well in autumn; *V. vinifera* 'Ciotat' has attractively divided leaves; *V. v.* 'Purpurea' has claret-coloured foliage in autumn[ill.p.20]. They require fertile chalky soil in sun or partial shade. H and S 7m (23ft) Z6

Angelica archangelica

Darmera peltata

Gunnera manicata

Miscanthus sinensis

Vitis vinifera

Yellow-Greens

EVERGREEN

Carex elata 'Aurea' BOWLES' GOLDEN SEDGE Perennial that forms clumps of bright foliage in spring, greener in late summer. Likes sun and moist soil. H 1m (3ft3in) S 1.2m (4ft) Z5 [ill.p.172]

Choisya ternata 'Sundance' MEXICAN ORANGE BLOSSOM The foliage is bright yellow in good light but will scorch in hot sun. Best in partial shade. H and S 1.8m (6ft) Z8

Hedera helix 'Buttercup' IVY Climber with variable heart-shaped leaves, yellow in sun but green in shade. Good for cutting. Like all ivies, prune back to avoid maturation to arborescent form. Tolerates sun or shade and prefers alkaline soil. H 2m (6ft6in) S 2.4m (8ft) Z5 [ill.pp.79,184]

Ligustrum ovalifolium 'Aureum' GOLDEN PRIVET Amenable shrub, tolerant of shade, it gives best colour in full sun. H 3.7m (12ft) S 3m (10ft) Z6 [ill.pp.18,147]

Lonicera nitida 'Baggesen's Gold' BOXLEAF HONEYSUCKLE Small-leaved shrub, amenable to clipping into low hedges, or simple shapes. Leaves are yellow in summer, greener in winter. Requires sun or partial shade. H and S 1.5m (5ft) Z7 [ill.pp.32, 78,167,172]

Phormium cookianum 'Cream Delight' MOUNTAIN FLAX Perennial with long, lax, shiny leaves and a tall spike of yellowish brown flowers that provides a good contrast to more rounded shapes. Requires sun. H 1.8m (6ft) S 30cm (1ft) Z9 [ill.p.143]

Rhododendron yakushimanum A compact shrub with leathery leaves, dark above and rusty beneath, carrying a truss of bell-shaped pale pink flowers in early summer. Requires partial shade and tolerates neutral to acid soil. H 90cm (3ft) S 1.5m (5ft) Z5 [ill.p.81]

Taxus baccata 'Aurea' GOLDEN YEW Slow-growing conifer with needle-like leaves. Amenable to hard pruning. Tolerates shade H and S 4.6m (15ft) Z5 [ill.pp.139,181]

SPRING AND SUMMER

Acer shirasawanum 'Aureum' (syn. A. japonicum) JAPANESE MAPLE Slow-growing shrub or small tree with fan-like leaves of light greenish gold. Best in partial shade. H and S 6m (20ft) Z5 [ill.p.143]

Berberis thunbergii 'Aurea' Compact shrub with vivid yellow leaves in spring, greener in late summer. Pale yellow flowers in early summer. Tolerates sun or partial shade in any but water-logged soil. H and S 1.5m (5ft) Z5

Cornus alba 'Aurea' DOGWOOD Shrub with pointed yellow leaves and reddish bark on young stems. Prune back to base in spring to encourage new growth with larger leaves and bright stems. Tolerates sun and partial shade. H and S 3m (10ft) Z3 [ill.pp.122,184]

Gleditsia triacanthos 'Sunburst' HONEY LOCUST Tree with elegant foliage, bright yellow when young. Likes sun. H 13m (44ft) S 7.5m (25ft) Z4 [ill.p.178]

Helichrysum petiolare 'Limelight' LIQUORICE PLANT Tender sub-shrub with white woolly stems and yellowy green woolly leaves held on long, wide-spreading branches. Can be trained up a support to give a more vertical effect. Requires sun. H and S 1.5m (5ft) Z9

Hosta 'Gold Standard' GOLDEN PLANTAIN LILY Perennial with deeply veined leaves, thinly edged with green, becoming a deeper yellow as they mature. Requires partial shade and moist, neutral soil. H and S 75cm (30in) Z3

Humulus lupulus 'Aureus' GOLDEN HOP Climber with soft divided leaves. Ideal for covering unsightly buildings, but may be invasive. Tolerates sun and partial shade. H 6m (20ft) Z5 [ill.pp.80,143,184]

Milium effusum 'Aureum' BOWLES' GOLDEN GRASS Perennial grass with dainty foliage and slender yellow flowerheads in summer. H and S 3m (10ft) Z5 [ill.pp.11,78,79,167,173]

Origanum vulgare 'Aureum' GOLDEN MARJORAM Perennial herb, forming low clumps of aromatic pointed leaves and inconspicuous flowers in summer. Useful for long-term summer colour. Prefers sun and alkaline soil. H 25cm (10in) S 60cm (2ft) Z4 [ill.p.147]

Philadelphus coronarius 'Aureus' GOLDEN MOCK ORANGE A substantial shrub with lovely fresh yellow foliage in spring and creamy, fragrant flowers in early summer. Needs protection from full sun. H 2.4m (8ft) S 1.5m (5ft) Z5 [ill.pp.10,184]

Physocarpus opulifolius 'Dart's Gold' One of the best yellow-green shrubs, with lobed leaves, coloured best when young in spring. Clusters of greeny-white flowers in early summer. Requires sun and prefers acid soil. H 4m (13ft) S 3m (10ft) Z3

Robinia pseudoacacia 'Frisia' FALSE ACACIA One of the best yellow-leaved trees, not fading to green later in the season. Elegant pinnate foliage. Requires sun and tolerates poor, dry soil. H 11m (35ft) S 6m (20ft) Z3 [ill.pp.11,169,184]

Sambucus racemosa 'Plumosa Aurea' RED BERRIED ELDER Shrub with deeply divided golden leaves with serrated leaflets; the richest effect is achieved by cutting older growths nearly to the ground in early spring, and then feeding. Likes sun. H and S 3m (10ft) Z4

Spiraea japonica 'Goldflame' Shrub with spectacular rich golden orange foliage in spring, and somewhat unfortunate deep pink flower heads in late summer. Needs sun and prefers moist soil. H and S 90cm (3ft) Z5 [ill.p.10]

Tanacetum parthenium 'Aureum' GOLDEN FEVERFEW Semi-evergreen perennial with lime-yellow, finely divided, aromatic foliage and sprays of little white daisies through the summer. Self-seeds. Requires sun. H and S 30cm (12in) Z5 [ill.pp.81,172,179]

Valeriana phu 'Aurea' Perennial with rosettes of bright yellow-green foliage in spring, turning green in summer. Requires sun. H 40cm (15in) S 30cm (12in) Z6

Blue-Greens

EVERGREEN

Arctostaphylos patula GREEN MANZANITA This medium-sized shrub has neat foliage and pinky white flowers in spring. Requires full sun and acid soil. H and S 1.8m (6ft) Z6

Eucalyptus gunnii CIDER GUM Although this gum will make a large tree with pretty sage-green

Hedera helix 'Buttercup'

Berberis thunbergii 'Aurea'

Milium effusum 'Aureum'

Physocarpus opulifolius 'Dart's Gold'

Valeriana phu 'Aurea'

leaves if left to its own devices, it can be stooled and thus kept to shrub size, with round, silver-blue juvenile foliage, lovely for cutting. H 25m (80ft) S 8m (23ft) , or H and S 2.1m (7ft) Z8

Euphorbia characias SPURGE
The stiff stems are crowded with narrow blue-grey leaves, and from late winter the drooping heads begin to look up and open their heads of lime-green flowers, which last in beauty until early summer. Cut the flowered stems close to the ground to encourage next year's flowering shoots. Tolerates sun or partial shade. H 1.2m (4ft) S 90cm (3ft) Z8

Festuca glauca BLUE FESCUE
Perennial tufts of steely blue-green grass, good for edging. H and S 20cm (8in) Z4 [ill.pp.71,90,91]

Picea pungens 'Koster' BLUE SPRUCE
A conical tree with stout leaves of an intense silvery blue. Tolerates sun or shade in any soil except overlying chalk or limestone. H 6m (20ft) S 3m (10ft) Z3

Ruta graveolens 'Jackman's Blue' RUE Shrub with divided leaves of a good blue-green and bright yellow flowers in summer. Cut hard back in late spring to keep the mound compact and reduce flowering (but wear gloves to avoid allergy). Requires sun. H 50cm (20in) S 75cm (30in) Z5 [ill.p.181]

SPRING AND SUMMER

Acaena 'Blue Haze'
This makes a nearly evergreen mat of finely cut bluish leaves on bronze stems. The flowers are little brown spiny burrs, in summer. Tolerates sun and partial shade. H 20cm (8in) S 75cm (30in) Z6

Hosta PLANTAIN LILY
Perennials that do best in partial shade and rich, moist soil. Good 'blue' leaved varieties include *H.* **'Halcyon'** with heart-shaped glaucous leaves, and lilac-grey flower spikes in summer, H 20cm (8in) S 30cm (12in) Z3 [ill.pp.71,81]; *H. sieboldiana* var. *elegans* with deeply puckered leaves and near white flowers in summer, H 90cm (3ft) S 1.5m (5ft) Z3 [ill.pp.94,139]

Macleaya microcarpa 'Kelway's Coral Plume' PLUME POPPY An impressive perennial with a running rootstock. Beautiful lobed leaves, grey-green above and nearly white beneath, and fluffy plumes of coral flowers in summer. Requires sun. H 2.5m (8ft) S 1.2m (4ft) Z4 [ill.pp.80,81]

Melianthus major HONEYBUSH
Perennial with sumptuous frilled and incised blue-green foliage. Can be cut to the ground in colder winters but will generally sprout again from the base. Requires sun. H and S 1.2m (4ft) Z9 [ill.p.182]

Mertensia simplicissima (syn. *M. mertensia* subsp. *asiatica*) Perennial with very blue leaves that are pretty with the bunches of drooping pale blue flowers in early summer. Tolerates sun and shade in deep soil. H and S 30cm (12in) Z6 [ill.p.175]

Green Flowers

Alchemilla mollis LADY'S MANTLE
Perennial with round, furry leaves, and sprays of lime-green flowers in summer. Useful for edging paths and borders. Cut back after flowering to encourage fresh new foliage. Tolerant of sun or shade in any but boggy soil. H and S 50cm (20in) Z4 [ill.pp.167,172]

Astrantia major MASTERWORT
Perennial forming clumps of divided leaves that throw up many branched stems of pinchusion-shaped flowerheads, of a pleasing greenish-white with a hint of pink. Tolerates sun and partial shade. H 60cm (24in) S 45cm (18in) Z4

Bupleurum fruticosum SHRUBBY HARE'S EAR Evergreen shrub with dark green glossy foliage that is a good foil for the umbels of yellow-green flowers that last all summer. Requires full sun. H 1.8m (6ft) S 2.5m (8ft) Z7

Eucomis bicolor PINEAPPLE FLOWER
In late summer this bulbous plant produces substantial spikes of starry pale green flowers edged with dark red, making a strong contrast to the broad dark green leaves. Requires full sun. H and S 45cm (18in) Z8

Euphorbia SPURGE
Euphorbias with green flowers include *E. amygdaloides* var. *robbiae* WOOD SPURGE, rampant but useful for shade, even on poor soil, with dark green rosettes, H 45cm (18in) S 60cm (24in) Z7; *E. characias* subsp. *wulfenii* has large flowerheads and good blue-green evergreen leaves, H and S 3ft (90cm) Z7 [ill.pp.142,172,184]; *E. palustris*, which needs deeper soil, but rewards with brilliant yellow-green flowerheads in summer, and good foliage colouring in autumn, H and S 90cm (3ft) Z5; *E. polychroma*, which makes tidy mounds of bright yellow-green in early spring, lasting well, H and S 50cm (20in) Z4 [ill.pp.79,184]; and *E. schillingii*, which is a strong plant that produces its impressive yellowy flower heads later in the summer, H and S 90cm (3ft) Z7

Garrya elliptica SILK TASSEL BUSH
A well-furnished shrub with leathery evergreen leaves and long catkins of greyish green flowers in late winter. The good male form *G. e.* 'James Roof' has the longest catkins, purple-tinted. Will be happy on a shady wall, and tolerates poor soil. H 5m (16ft) S 3m (10ft) Z8

Helleborus HELLEBORE
Evergreen perennials. *H. argutifolius* (syn. *H. corsicus*) forms a clump of stout stems with handsome three-fingered leaves of a cool green, producing its large clusters of apple-green cups from late winter. H 90cm (3ft) S 50cm (20in) Z7. *H. foetidus* STINKING HELLEBORE has much-divided, darkest green leaves, with clusters of flowers like pale green bells, edged with purple. *H. f.* **Wester Fisk Group** has reddish stems and larger flowers. H and S 45cm (18in) Z6. All require partial shade and moist soil.

Itea ilicifolia
Evergreen shrub bearing mid-green holly-like leaves and long racemes of honey-scented flowers in profusion in late summer. Tolerates sun or partial shade. H and S 3m (10ft) Z8

Kniphofia 'Green Jade'
Evergreen perennial that forms a clump of long, thin, lax leaves and sends up tall 'pokers' of cool jade green with a hint of cream in late summer. Requires full sun and moist soil. H 1.2m (4ft) S 75cm (30in) Z5

Moluccella laevis BELLS OF IRELAND
Annual that sends up long spires of cool emerald green bells that are good for cutting. Requires sun and rich soil. H 60cm (24in) S 20cm (8in)

Ruta graveolens 'Jackman's Blue'

Melianthus major

Eucomis bicolor

Garrya elliptica

Heleborus argutifolius

Nicotiana FLOWERING TOBACCO
Perennials grown as annuals that require sun and rich soil. **N. x sanderae** 'Lime Green' has bright yellow green flowers in profusion over a long period. H 60cm (24in) S 20cm (8in) [ill.pp.44,180,182]. **N. langsdorffii** is a tall, open plant, with panicles of drooping green flowers; it self-seeds willingly but not oppressively. H 1m (3ft3in) S 30cm (12in)

Veratrum viride INDIAN POKE
Perennial with gloriously pleated fresh green leaves followed by tall spikes densely packed with starry green flowers. Requires partial shade and fertile soil. H 1.2m (4ft) S 60cm (2ft) Z3

Green Variegated with White or Cream

EVERGREEN

Euonymus fortunei
These plants are normally semi-prostrate, but will climb if given support. They do best in sun. **E. f.** 'Emerald Gaiety' has rounded leaves and the whitest variegation H 90cm (3ft) S 1.5m (5ft) Z5. **E. f.** 'Silver Queen' makes an elegant, compact shrub when not climbing, with

yellow variegation becoming creamy white later. H 2.4m (8ft) S 5ft (1.5m) Z5 [ill.pp.80,143]

Hedera helix 'Glacier' IVY
Evergreen climber that makes a good background with clear markings in grey and white. H and S 3m (10ft) Z6 [ill.p.79]

Lamium galeobdolon 'Florentinum' DEADNETTLE
Perennial that roots as it spreads, with dark green leaves, marbled with white. Has yellow 'deadnettle' flowers. May be invasive, but not difficult to keep within bounds. Requires sun. H 25cm (10in) S 45cm (18in) Z5

SPRING AND SUMMER

Arum italicum subsp. **italicum** 'Marmoratum' ITALIAN ARUM
Tuberous bulb that produces glossy dark green spear-shaped leaves, veined with white, that are very effective in winter. Stalks of orange-red berries appear in late summer. Requires sun. H 25cm (10in) S 30cm (12in) Z6 [ill.p.146]

Brunnera macrophylla 'Dawson's White' Perennial that makes good groundcover, its large heart-shaped leaves boldly variegated with creamy white. Long sprays of forget-me-not blue flowers in spring. Requires partial shade and moist soil. H 45cm (18in) S 60cm (24in) Z4

Cornus alba 'Elegantissima' DOGWOOD Shrub with pale

green leaves edged with creamy white. Cut back half the shoots to the ground in early spring to get red stems for winter. Needs sun. H and S 3m (10ft) Z2

Glyceria maxima var. **variegata** (syn. **G. aquatica** 'Variegata') VARIEGATED MANNA GRASS This spreading grass prefers pond margins or boggy soil, and has broad spiky leaves striped with white and cream. Best in sun but tolerates partial shade. H 80cm (2ft8in) S 60cm (2ft) Z5 [ill.p.32]

Holcus mollis 'Albovariegatus' VARIEGATED CREEPING SOFT GRASS
Grass whose fresh growth in spring and autumn gives the effect of a white carpet, the soft leaves having only an narrow central green stripe. The creeping rhizomes are easily uprooted. Requires partial shade. H 25cm (10in) S 45cm (18in) Z5 [ill.p.149]

Hosta PLANTAIN LILY
Perennials that do best in shade. **H. crispula** has undulating leaf margins, boldly edged with white H 30in (75cm) S 3ft (90cm) Z3 [ill.p.18]. **H. f.** 'Marginata Alba' has rich sage-green leaves broadly edged with white. H and S 60cm (2ft) Z3. **H. undulata** var. **albomarginata** (syn. **H.** 'Thomas Hogg') is a robust plant with smooth fresh leaves, edged with cream, and tall lilac flowers in summer. H 75cm (30in) S 90cm (3ft) Z3

Iris pallida 'Argentea Variegata' DALMATIAN IRIS Rhizomatous perennial with superb sword-shaped leaves, boldly striped blue-green and white. Tall blue flowering stems in summer. Requires sun. H 60cm (2ft) S 30cm (1ft) Z5 [ill.p.80]

Lunaria annua 'Alba Variegata' VARIEGATED HONESTY Biennial that produces loose spires of white flowers in spring, and leaves irregularly marked creamy white. Comes true from seed. Requires partial shade. H 90cm (3ft) S 30cm (1ft) Z6 [ill.pp.111, 183,184]

Miscanthus sinensis 'Variegatus' Perennial that form clumps of ribbon-like leaves, prettily striped green and white. H 1.5m (5ft) S 90cm (3ft) Z6 [ill.p.176]

Phalaris arundinacea var. **picta** 'Picta' GARDENER'S GARTERS Dense, running grass with white-striped leaves. Can be cut to the ground in summer to make fresh growth for the autumn. Needs partial shade and moist soil. H and S 90cm (3ft) Z4 [ill.pp.32, 81, 172,181]

Phlox paniculata 'Norah Leigh' Perennial with tall, willowy stems which have cream-variegated leaves, and pale lilac flowers in late summer. Requires sun and moist soil. H 1m (3ft3in) S 60cm (24in) Z4

Pulmonaria LUNGWORT
Spring-flowering perennials. **P. longifolia** has narrow, dark

green leaves with white spots, and deep blue flowers. **P. officinalis** has heart-shaped spotted leaves and pink flowers that turn pale blue [ill.p.111]. **P. o.** 'Sissinghurst White' has white flowers. All make good groundcover in moisture-retentive soil All H 30cm (12in) S 45cm (18in) Z4

Scrophularia auriculata 'Variegata' (syn. **S. aquatica**) VARIEGATED WATER FIGWORT
Perennial making evergreen clumps with particularly good cream variegation. Cut off the flower spikes to prevent seeding. Requires partial shade and moist soil. H 75cm (30in) S 30cm (12in) Z5 [ill.p.131]

Silybum marianum OUR LADY'S THISTLE Biennial with very prickly thistle leaves that are dark greensplashed with white. Reliable self-seeder. Requires sun. H 1.2m (4ft) S 60cm (2ft) Z7

Green Variegated with Yellow

EVERGREEN

Agave americana 'Variegata' CENTURY PLANT Perennial succulent. Makes a huge rosette of sharply pointed striped grey-

Nicotiana langsdorffii

Cornus alba 'Elegantissima'

H. undulata var. albomarginata

Pulmonaria longifolia

Silybum marianum

green and yellow leaves. Only hardy in our warmest gardens. Requires sun. H and S 2m (6ft6in) Z9

Carex hachijoensis 'Evergold' (syn. *C. oshimensis* 'E.') JAPANESE SEDGE Perennial that forms dense tufts of grass-like foliage, bright yellow with narrow green margins. Requires sun. H and S 30cm (12in) Z7

Cortaderia selloana 'Aureolineata' (syn. *C. s.*'Gold Band') PAMPAS GRASS Perennial with large, luxuriant clumps of yellow-striped leaves, and creamy, erect plumes from late summer. Requires sun. H 1.8m (6ft) S 1.2m (4ft) Z8

Elaeagnus pungens 'Maculata' Shrub at its cheerful best in winter sunlight. The new growth is brownish in colour, maturing to dark green, leathery leaves with bright yellow centres. Requires sun. H 3m (10ft) S 3.7m (12ft) Z7

Euonymus fortunei 'Emerald 'n' Gold' A good groundcovering shrub, densely covered with small leaves with bright variegation. It will also climb with good support. Requires sun. H 60cm (2ft) S 90cm (3ft) Z5 [ill.p.178]

Hedera IVY Climbers that do well in sun or shade, good or poor soil. They will grow horizontally, for groundcover, as well as vertically. *H. colchica* 'Dentata

Variegata' COLCHIS IVY has large elliptic leaves, shaded green and margined creamy-yellow Z6. *H. c.* 'Sulphur Heart' (syn. *H. c.* 'Paddy's Pride') has dark green margins and deep yellow and paler green centres Z6 [ill.p.170]. *H. helix* 'Oro di Bogliasco' (syn. *H. h.*'Goldheart') has neat, very dark green leaves with a splash of yellow in the centre [ill.p.150]. All H and S 3m (10ft) Z5

Ilex aquifolium'Aurea Marginata' HOLLY A very solid shrub, or small tree, with spiny leaves broadly edged with creamy yellow. Red berries. Amenable to shaping. Tolerates both sun and partial shade. H 6m (20ft) S 5m (16ft) Z6 [ill.p.181]

Pleioblastus auricomus (syn. *P. viridistriatus*) Bamboo whose leaves are bright yellow with irregular green striping. A runner but controllable. Requires sun. H 1.2m (4ft) S indefinite Z7

Salvia officinalis 'Icterina' SAGE This shrub's soft, rounded leaves are light green variegated with yellow, and strongly aromatic. Requires sun. H 60cm (2ft) S 90cm (3ft) Z7 [ill.p.80]

Vinca major 'Variegata' GREATER PERIWINKLE A carpeting shrub that roots as it spreads, with glossy dark green leaves splashed with cream. Lavender-blue flowers in spring. Requires partial shade and moist soil. H 40cm (15in) S 1.5m (5ft) Z7

SPRING AND SUMMER

Cornus alba 'Spaethii' DOGWOOD Shrub with brilliant yellow variegation in the leaves and deep red stems in winter. Requires sun. H 2.3m (7ft6in) S 1.8m (6ft) Z3

Hakonechloa macra 'Alboaurea' HAKONE GRASS Perennial grass that makes slowly increasing clumps of arching leaves variegated cream and yellow, colouring rusty-yellow in autumn. H and S 45cm (18in) Z5

Hosta PLANTAIN LILY Perennial that tolerates sun and partial shade in moist soil. *H. fortunei* var. *aureomarginata* (syn. *H.* 'Yellow Edge') has sage-green pointed leaves edged with yellow and spires of lavender flowers in midsummer. H 30cm (12in) S 45cm (18in) Z3 [ill.p.81]. *H. sieboldiana* 'Frances Williams' has puckered glaucous leaves with a bold yellow margin, and pale mauve spikes in summer. H 60cm (2ft) S 90cm (3ft) Z3

Iris Rhizomatous perennials. *I. pallida* 'Variegata' VARIEGATED DALMATIAN IRIS, which needs a sunny position, has sword-shaped leaves striped blue-green and yellow, and tall blue flowers in early summer. H 60cm (2ft) S 30cm (1ft) Z4 [ill.pp.136,157]. *I. pseudacorus* 'Variegata' is

best in a moist position. The dramatic foliage has bold yellow stripes in spring, turning green later, and yellow flowers in early summer. H 1.2m (4ft) S 30cm (1ft) Z5 [ill.p.32]

Mentha suaveolens 'Variegata' APPLEMINT Like all mints, this can be invasive, but is a very fresh groundcover with creamy white variegation. Requires sun. H 45cm (18in) S 60cm (24in) Z5

Symphoricarpos orbiculatus 'Foliis Variegatis' CORAL BERRY A graceful shrub with small leaves irregularly edged with yellow, colouring best in full sun. H 90cm (3ft) S 1.5m (5ft) Z3 [ill.p.167]

Green Variegated with Reds and Pinks

EVERGREEN

Berberis thunbergii 'Rose Glow' Generally the leaves of this shrub open purple and become more and more variegated with pink as the season progresses. Good autumn colour. Tolerates both sun and partial shade. H and S 1.2m (4ft) Z5 [ill.p.130]

Brassica oleracea Acephala Group 'Red Peacock' ORNAMENTAL KALE

These annual kales are grown for their autumn value: they need low night temperatures before they colour up well, but a severe frost will finish them off. Requires sun and fertile, lime-rich soil. H and S 45cm (18in) Z7 [ill.p.109]

Trifolium repens 'Purpurascens' WHITE CLOVER Semi-evergreen perennial that makes effective groundcover with good foliage that is dark green mottled with chocolate brown. Requires sun. H 12cm (5in) S 30cm (12in) Z4 [ill.p.131]

SPRING AND SUMMER

Acer negundo 'Flamingo' ASH-LEAVED MAPLE The large, trifoliate leaves of this fast-growing tree are pinkish green, turning white. Requires sun. H 15m (50ft) S 8m (26ft) Z2

Actinidia kolomikta Twining climber with large leaves that are variously splashed in shades of pink, white and green as they develop, but revert to green as the summer progresses. Needs full sun. H and S 5m (16ft) Z5

Houttuynia cordata 'Chameleon' Perennial with pungent heart-shaped leaves in shades of dark green, red, yellow and bronze, bearing single white flowers in summer. The roots are invasive in moist ground. H and S 30cm (12in) Z5

Carex hachijoensis 'Evergold'

Pleioblastus auricomus

Hosta fortunei var. *aureomarginata*

Mentha suaveolens 'Variegata'

Actinidia kolomikta

Silver-Greys

Silver is often used as a setting for brilliant jewels, because it flatters its surroundings by reflecting them back. The colour of silver is elusive, since its character derives from its brilliance. Without that sheen, silver would be grey. It is a near-neutral colour, almost as inert as white, though not so bright and assertive.

In the garden, silver foliage can be used like silver in jewellery as a background against which other colours are set. The leaves of many silver and grey plants, such as some artemisias and santolinas, are fine-cut like filigree and seem to shimmer with light. Other, paler grey plants are soft, even dusty-seeming, like the felty leaves of some verbascums. Being lighter in tone than most green foliage, and more neutral, silver-grey reacts less with other colours. Because of this, silver-leaved plants make good 'peace-keepers'. Like white flowers, but more long-lasting, they can be used to keep warring colours such as pink and yellow apart in a border, and can be even more effective than green foliage as a buffer between colours. Repeating incidents of silver in a border will hold together a diverse range of colours with a unifying strand of neutrality.

Silver is a particularly good foil for magenta flowers, such as *Geranium psilostemon* or *Lychnis coronaria*, two plants which many gardeners are nervous to use because their colour is so intense. For a longer-lasting planting with striking tonal contrasts, use silver-leaved plants with the darkest available foliage plants, such as the plum-coloured and muted-red varieties of beech, plum, berberis, hazel and cotinus.

Silver-leaved plants are good components for pale harmonious plantings involving cream, blues and pinks, because they will make the pastel colours seem brighter. Like white variegation, silver foli-

LEFT A coat of silver-grey paint has been given to an obelisk to forge a link with the foliage of the silver spear astelia (*A. chathamica*) in a black-painted terracotta pot. Bright green box, clipped into spirals, contributes to the geometric formality of the scene.

RIGHT The giant, many-fingered leaves of the cardoon (*Cynara cardunculus*) loom over blue fescue (*Festuca glauca*) and silver lamb's ears (*Stachys byzantina*), with the silver-leaved shrub, *Elaeagnus* 'Quicksilver', glimmering behind. The clump of phlox on the right is going to have white flowers. All the silver-leaved plants here do best in full sun, and so you would need to place the cardoon where it will not shade the smaller plants, or else keep cutting back the lower leaves.

age can also be valuable in an all-white planting. Being light in tone, it enhances the overall impression of lightness made by the white flowers. Actually it is intermediate in tone between white and green, and so it helps to reduce what might otherwise be harsh tonal contrasts between white flowers and their own green leaves.

An exclusively silver planting can be effective on a relatively small scale, but will rely for interest on strong contrasts of shape and texture, because the colour itself is so inert and the range of colour so narrow. The majestic cardoon, with its deeply cut leaves, could be used as an emphatic centrepiece for a combination that might include the fluttering leaves of a silver eleagnus and the woolly leaves of *Stachys byzantina*.

A silver garden would benefit, though, from a less purist approach. If you introduce a few blue or purple flowers or some blue-green foliage such as rue, or blue-green hostas, these will enhance the silver to give a cool, harmonious planting with far greater colour interest. You could use a fountain-like clump of blue fescue grass to reinforce the silver-grey of an accompanying curry plant. White, or clear mid-green partners, will lighten and sharpen a grey planting without adding strong colour. White tulips growing through artemisias, for instance, make bright highlights like pearls in a silver necklace.

When using silver-leaved plants it is important to bear in mind that most of them originate in arid climates, and so need dry and sunny conditions. Their silver sheen comes from masses of tiny white hairs on the surface of the leaves, which have evolved to protect the plants from overheating in the sun. But remember that this sheen is at its best in summer sunshine. Plants such as artemisias and lamb's ears that gleam like silver in the sun, seem transmuted into base metal in other lights. They can look leaden grey in damp or shade, and they do not thrive in these conditions either. They can also look insipid when lit by thin winter light.

LEFT *Hebe rakaiensis* makes a white-flowered mound surrounded by two kinds of artemisia, the filigree-leaved *A.* 'Powis Castle' and *A. ludoviciana* with lance-shaped leaves. The felty leaves and purple flower spikes of *Stachys byzantina* add textural and colour interest.

RIGHT The blue fescue (*Festuca glauca*) mingles with the curry plant (*Helichrysum italicum*) against the loose stone edging of a border – an ideal position since both plants favour dry, well-drained conditions.

Silvers and Greys

EVERGREENS

Anthemis punctata subsp. *cupaniana* DOG FENNEL A quick-growing perennial forming a low mound of finely-cut silvery foliage. The white daisies should be cut back after flowering is over. Requires sun. H 30cm (12in) S 60cm (24in) Z7 [ill.p.80]

Artemisia
Perennials and sub-shrubs that generally do best in open, sunny sites. *A. absinthium* 'Lambrook Silver' WORMWOOD has boldly divided silky grey leaves and tall sprays of tiny dirty yellow flowers in summer. H and S 75cm (30in) Z4. *A. arborescens* has beautiful silver filigree foliage. Given a warm wall and a dry position it will climb 1.8m (6ft), normally H 90cm (3ft) S 60cm (2ft) Z9 [ill.p.176]. 'Powis Castle' has elegant silvery foliage and does not usually flower. H 75cm (30in) S 90cm (3ft) Z6 [ill.pp.91,114,176]. *A. stelleriana* 'Mori' DUSTY MILLER is a prostrate carpeter, with broadly cut leaves of silvery grey felt. H 30cm (1ft) S 90cm (3ft) Z5

Ballota pseudodictamnus
Sub-shrub that, from a woody base, throws up many long stems clothed in woolly grey green leaves, with bobbly flowers opening along the stem in midsummer. Requires full sun and very well drained soil. H 60cm (2ft) S 90cm (3ft) Z8 [ill.p.80]

Brachyglottis 'Sunshine' (syn. *Senecio* 'Sunshine') Sprawling shrub with good grey foliage which can be pruned quite hard; either in spring to prevent its brassy yellow flowers, or in midsummer to remove the spent flower heads. Requires full sun. H 90cm (3ft) S 1.5m (5ft) Z8 [ill.p.172]

Convolvulus cneorum
A neat shrub well-clothed with narrow, silky leaves. It produces its white trumpets over a long period in summer. Requires sun. H and S 75cm (30in) Z9

Cortaderia selloana 'Pumila' PAMPAS GRASS Perennial that makes a clump of lax, sharp-edged leaves, with tall, silvery plumes in early autumn. Requires sun. H and S 1.5m (5ft) Z5 [ill.p.130]

Dianthus PINK
The pinks make evergreen mats of grey leaves, with very sweetly scented flowers in shades of white, pink, red and purple. Named varieties include 'Bridal Veil' with double white flowers, 'Brympton Red' with deep crimson flowers flecked with pink, 'Green Eye' with fresh white flowers with light green centres, 'Mrs Sinkins' with double white flowers, richly scented, 'Old Pink Clove' with double dark pink flowers, and 'Sops in Wine' with dusky pink flowers marked with white. All do best in full sun. H and S 30cm (12in) Z4.

Echeveria
These succulents are not hardy, but will make large clumps of neat rosettes in a range of greys and greens; shiny, matt or furry. Spikes of drooping orange or red flowers appear in summer. Require sun. H 15cm (6in) S 30cm (12in) Z10

Hebe pinguifolia 'Pagei'
A densely creeping shrub with very small leaves of a leaden grey, and small heads of white flowers in early summer. Requires sun. H 15cm (6in) S 60cm (2ft) Z8

Helichrysum
Annuals, perennials and shrubs that are best in sun. *H. italicum* CURRY PLANT is a pungent sub-shrub that is best clipped in spring to prevent the lanky stems of yellow flowers from forming. H 60cm (2ft) S 90cm (3ft) Z8 [ill.pp.91,176].
H. petiolare LIQUORICE PLANT is a shrub, usually grown as an annual with rounded grey leaves and a spreading habit. The vigorous growth can be trained vertically. H 45cm (18in) S 1.5m (5ft) Z9 [ill.pp.121,175]

Helictotrichon sempervirens (syn. *Avena candida*) BLUE OAT GRASS Perennial making dense clumps of narrow blue-grey leaves, with waving flower plumes of grey in summer. Requires sun. H 90cm (3ft) S 60cm (2ft) Z4 [ill.p.178]

Lavandula LAVENDER
Shrub with fine grey foliage and strongly aromatic flower spikes in summer. It grows best in sun and well-drained soil [ill.pp.95, 173]. A good pink variety is *L. angustifolia* 'Loddon Pink'; good blue and violet varieties include *L. a.* 'Hidcote' and *L. a.* 'Munstead' H and S 75cm (30in) Z6. *L. stoechas* FRENCH LAVENDER has heads of small violet flowers with prominent bracts like topknots; *L.s.* f. *leucantha* has white flowers, H and S 75cm (30in) Z4

Phlomis fruticosa JERUSALEM SAGE
A Mediterranean shrub of a woolly, grey-green appearance; the deep yellow flowers have long-lasting seedheads. Requires sun. H and S 1.2m (4ft) Z8 [ill.pp.162,169]

Santolina chaemaecyparissus COTTON LAVENDER This shrub is best clipped tight in early spring, to make a mound of neat grey foliage which has a pleasant scent. Its yellow flowers are usually removed. Requires sun. H 75cm (30in) S 90cm (3ft) Z7 [ill.pp.71,151]

Sedum spathulifolium STONECROP
Evergreen perennial that makes a close mat of grey-green rosettes, often flushed red. Sprays of yellow stars appear through late summer. Tolerates shade. H 10cm (4in) S 30cm (12in) Z5

Senecio viravira DUSTY MILLER
Sub-shrub, often grown as an annual. Exquisite woolly grey foliage, but not reliably hardy. Requires full sun. H and S 90cm (3ft) Z9

Stachys byzantina (syn. *S. lanata*) LAMBS EARS Woody perennial making mats of velvety leaves that cover the ground well. Spikes of deep pink flowers are almost swamped in grey fluff. Best in poor soil. H 30cm (12in) S 60cm (24in) Z5 [ill.pp.90,91, 98,178,183]. *S. b.* 'Silver Carpet' is similar but does not flower.

Tanacetum argenteum (syn. *Achillea argentea*) Perennial that forms mats of silvery filigree foliage with small pure white daisies. Requires sun. H 23cm (9in) S 20cm (8in) Z5

Teucrium fruticans GERMANDER
Quick-growing, open shrub with a softly grey-white overall appearance. Pale blue flowers are produced over a long period in summer. Requires full sun. H 1.8m (6ft) S 4m (12ft) Z9

Thymus x *citriodorus* 'Argenteus' LEMON THYME Evergreen, spreading shrub with tiny silvery, lemon-scented leaves. Requires sun. H 20cm (8in) S 40cm (15in) Z6

Artemisia 'Powis Castle'

Dianthus 'Mrs Sinkins'

Echeveria

Lavandula stoechas f. *leucantha*

Tanacetum argenteum

SPRING AND SUMMER

Argyranthemum MARGUERITE
Perennials with finely-cut grey-green leaves and a long season of flowering. H and S 75cm (30in) Z9 [ill.pp.172,182,183]

Artemisia
Perennials and shrubs that are not evergreen include *A. alba* 'Canescens' which has extremely lacy, finely curving, leaflets, giving it a rather spiky overall look, H 45cm (18in) S 30cm (12in) Z6 [ill.p.178];
A. ludoviciana 'Silver Queen' WESTERN MUGWORT which has lanceolate silver-grey leaves on running stems, H 75cm (30in) S 90cm (3ft) Z6 [ill.pp.91,130]; and *A. schmidtiana* which has creeping shoots forming low cushions of soft greenish grey, hair-like leaves and nodding white flowerheads in early autumn, H 15cm (6in) S 45cm (18in) Z6 [ill.p.182]

Astelia chathamica SILVER SPEAR
Perennial producing open tussocks of arching silver-grey sword-shaped leaves, with reddish, scented flowers on short spikes in summer. Tolerates both sun and partial shade, requiring fertile soil that does not dry out. H 1.2m (4ft) S 90cm (3ft) Z9 [ill.p.90]

Athyrium niponicum var. *pictum* PAINTED LADY FERN Deciduous, glaucous fronds with purple flushed stalks and midrib.

Requires shade and humus-rich, moist soil. H 60cm (2ft) S 45cm (18in) Z7

Centaurea cineraria
Quite a chunky plant, this perennial has loose rosettes of very beautiful, lacy, grey leaves. Best to remove the mauve thistle flower. Requires sun and will tolerate poor soil. H 75cm (30in) S 90cm (3ft) Z7

Cerastium tomentosum SNOW IN SUMMER Semi-evergreen perennial forming mats of grey foliage smothered in white flowers in late spring. Invasive. Requires sun. H 8cm (3in) S 45cm (18in) Z4 [ill.p.109]

Cynara cardunculus CARDOON
A magnificent perennial with pointed, deeply divided leaves that can be 1.2m (4ft) long. In the summer stout stems carry prickly purple thistles. Requires sun. H 2m (6ft6in) S 90cm (3ft) Z7 [ill.pp.90,149,174,181]

Eryngium giganteum MISS WILLMOTT'S GHOST Biennial producing rosettes of lightly-veined green leaves that throw up spiny silver flower spikes in their second year. Easy from seed, as Miss Willmott proved. Requires sun. H 90cm (3ft) S 30cm (1ft) Z6 [ill.p.172]

Elaeagnus angustifolia OLEASTER
Large shrub that can easily be pruned to make a small standard, with downy greyish green leaves and startling spines. The variety 'Quicksilver' is particularly silvery

[ill.p.90] Requires full sun and fertile soil. H and S 6m (20ft) Z4

Hippophaë rhamnoïdes SEA BUCKTHORN A silvery shrub with an open habit, this needs to be planted in a group with at least one male plant, and the females will then develop masses of translucent orange berries. Needs sun and tolerates poor soil. H and S 6m (20ft) Z4

Iris pallida DALMATIAN IRIS
Rhizomatous perennial. The strong fans of sword-shaped leaves remain glaucous blue throughout the summer, and tall stems of blue flowers are freely produced in early summer. Requires full sun and rich, preferably alkaline soil. H 1.2m (4ft) S 45cm (18in) Z4

Lamium maculatum 'Beacon Silver' DEADNETTLE Creeping and carpeting perennial with silver-patterned leaves and deep puce flowers. *L. m.* 'White Nancy' has white flowers. Tolerates shade and prefers moist soil. H 20cm (8in) S 90cm (3ft) Z3

Lotus hirsutus (syn. *Dorycnium hirsutum*) Sub-shrub with small silky leaves, at its best from late summer when the white pea-flowers mature into clusters of chocolate-brown seedpods. Prune in spring to keep it dense. Requires full sun and dry soil. H and S 60cm (2ft) Z8

Lychnis coronaria ROSE CAMPION
Biennial or short-lived perennial has a rosette of greyish leaves

and much-branched stems carrying a succession of sinple flowers, commonly deep magenta or white (Alba Group). Requires sun. H 50cm (20in) S 30cm (12in) Z4 [ill.pp.98,175]

Onopordum acanthium SCOTCH THISTLE Splendid biennial with large prickly leaves covered with silver white hairs, topped in its second year with a spire of mauve thistles. Tolerates both sun and partial shade and prefers rich soil. H 1.8m (6ft) S 90cm (3ft) Z6. *O. nervosum* will attain 2.4m (8ft) [ill.p.176]

Ornithogalum nutans DROOPING STAR OF BETHLEHEM Bulb producing spikes of satiny pale green and silvery white flowers in early spring. Tolerates both sun and partial shade. H and S 20cm (8in) Z6

Pyrus salicifolia 'Pendula' WEEPING WILLOW-LEAVED PEAR A graceful silvery-grey tree, although sometimes it needs a stake to help a leader make a good height. Requires full sun. H 5m (15ft) S 3.7m (12ft) Z5 [ill.pp.82,130]

Rosa glauca (syn. *R. rubrifolia*) ROSE A very useful rose with reddish stems and grey-green foliage. Simple pink flowers are followed by charming oval hips. Often self-seeds. Requires an open, sunny position. H 1.8m (6ft) S 1.5m (5ft) Z2 [ill.pp.120,176]

Salix alba var. *sericea* (syns. *S. a. argentea*, *S.a.* 'Splendens') SILVER

WILLOW Although this willow, which has leaves of an intense silvery hue, will make a tree, it takes kindly to coppicing and can thus be kept as small as 2.4m (8ft). Requires full sun and any but dry soil. H 15m (50ft) S 8m (25ft) Z2

Salvia argentea
Biennnial that produces large flat rosettes made up of silkily felted grey leaves in spring, followed by stems of white flowers. Requires sun. H 75cm (30in) S 45cm (18in) Z5

Tanacetum ptarmiciflorum (syn. *Pyrethrum p.*) This perennial has feathery pale grey foliage and is often grown as an annual for bedding, particularly in the variety 'Silver Feather'. Requires sun. H and S 50cm (20in) Z9

Verbascum MULLEIN
V. bombyciferum 'Polarsommer' (syn. *V.* 'Arctic Summer') has rosettes of large woolly leaves that are a good contrast to the more finely cut grey-leaved plants; though naturally biennial, it can be kept going for a few years if prevented from flowering. H 1.8m (6ft) S 60cm (2ft) Z6 [ill.p.142]. *V. olympicum* has large grey-felted leaves followed by statuesque flowering stems, branched like a candelabra, covered with bright yellow flowers for many weeks. H 1.8m (6ft) S 75cm (30in) Z6. Both tolerate shade but prefer an open, sunny site

Athyrium niponicum var. *pictum*

Eryngium giganteum

Lamium maculatum 'White Nancy'

Rosa glauca

Verbascum olympicum

Whites

White is the most mysterious of colours – is it a colour at all? It can seem empty of colour, yet white light is created when all the colours of the spectrum are combined, so it can be said to incorporate all colours. This is its greatest virtue for the gardener, since white will combine happily with any other colour. It also has sufficient impact to stand on its own. White can be regarded as an inert colour, since it does not react with other colours or change them in any way. Because of this, it is capable of acting as a buffer between two patches of colour in a border that might otherwise react uncomfortably together.

White also reflects all the light that strikes it. Its effect in gardens is to lighten them and make the mood more cheerful. You can capitalize on this by using white flowers that like shady conditions, such as foxgloves, and shrubs with white flowers, such as viburnums, to brighten up areas under trees.

The brilliance of white means that the shapes and patterns that white flowers make catch the eye and so are more intrusive than those of other colours in a mixed-colour planting. Because they are light-reflecting, flowers with a solid silhouette, such as lilies or phlox, tend to stand out most among other, darker colours. Plants that have sprays of tiny white flowers, on the other hand, like gypsophila or *Crambe cordifolia*, create a misty, diaphanous effect that is bright without being intrusive. Other colours, seen through this translucent haze, are fragmented and seem to shimmer.

Be sensitive to the subtle distinctions and degrees of whiteness – it is remarkable how few flowers are pure white. They range from

ABOVE Growing in the dappled shade of woodland, white foxgloves give the illusion that they are the flowers belonging to the blue-green foliage of the hostas (*H. sieboldiana* var. *elegans*). White flowers are useful for lightening up areas of shade. In shadow, the hosta leaves look most blue.

ABOVE Flowering together in open woodland in early summer, *Viburnum opulus* 'Roseum' and its relative *V. plicatum* 'Mariesii' introduce variety of shape as well as a subtle colour difference. For a similar effect later in the year, you could plant hydrangeas such as *H. arborescens* 'Grandiflora' with *H. quercifolia*. You could also extend the season by growing a late-flowering white clematis, such as *C.* 'Alba Luxurians' into shrubs such as these viburnums that flower earlier.

the ivory whites and creams of narcissi such as 'White Lion' to the 'blush-pink' whites of some roses and the bluish off-whites of white-flowered campanulas. Be aware too of the myriad ways that nature decorates whites. White lilies may be marked with crimson spots or blotches. The petals of white geraniums may have blue or purple veining. White daisies have an explosion of yellow florets at their centres. Match these details with plants of the appropriate colour. Blue or purple-veined geraniums will set up 'echoes' of colour with blue or purple flowers, while the daisies will enhance a yellow and orange planting.

Green leaves make a dark foil against which white flowers show up well. But silver-grey foliage is an even better partner for them. Silver and white are both neutral, non-reactive colours and so they make a close relationship. Silver-leaved anthemis and artemisia make elegant backdrops for the more solid shapes of white tulips and snapdragons. Similarly, white variegated foliage is useful with white flowers. Try the variegated grass *Holcus mollis* 'Albovariegatus', or the low-growing bamboo, *Pleioblastus variegatus,* with white-flowered mallows or roses, and grow white clematis into variegated shrubs like *Cornus alba* 'Elegantissima'.

White is always a popular choice of colour for garden furniture, but you should take care when using it. Its brightness can dazzle and it may eclipse other colours in nearby borders, so that it looks far too stark in comparison with them. It is usually best with white and silver plantings, but even here it is easy to overdo it. The cast-iron white bench with fine tracery *below* looks elegant with white flowers and silver foliage around it, but if the bench were more solid, it could easily overwhelm the delicate plants. In that case it would be better to paint it grey-green, to tone in with the foliage of the lavender and anthemis.

ABOVE An ornate cast-iron bench makes a fetching centrepiece for a white and silver late-spring planting that includes 'White Triumphator' tulips, white lavender, and clumps of the white daisy *Anthemis punctata* subsp. *cupaniana.* The anthemis has a long flowering season, and even when not in flower its feathery silvery-green foliage is attractive.

ABOVE In descending order of height, *Hydrangea paniculata* 'Kyushu', silver-leaved *Artemisia ludoviciana* and white snapdragons compose a section of a white border. The snapdragons are bedded out in late spring to take the place of white tulips.

All-White Plantings

BELOW Much of the success of this border is due to the contrasting shapes, sizes and textures of the plants. Whites range from the diaphanous sprays of crambe flowers, through denser clusters of valerian, to more solid-seeming heads of roses. Foliage is also varied: large leathery leaves of bergenia make an anchor for the border at the front, while piptanthus forms its backdrop – any of the piptanthus's yellow spring flowers that remain when the first white perennials appear in the border are clipped away. (Full planting details of this scheme are given on page 174.)

All-white schemes are among the classics of garden design. But because there is relatively little colour interest, the eye is drawn to the differing shapes, sizes and textures of the flowers. Think about combining the tightly-clustered flowers on delphinium spires with the loose sprays of crambe and gypsophila. Imagine softening the 'blobby' flowerheads of viburnums and azaleas with the more scattered flowers of dogwoods or *Magnolia stellata*. Foliage contrasts, particularly of shape, are equally important, especially in schemes for shade that are really studies in green with white highlights.

All-white plantings can be sustained through the seasons, and in the summer can be planned to reach a new peak every three or four weeks. The scheme's backbone would be plants that flower continuously, like white *Viola cornuta* or valerian, reinforced by those that are repeat-flowering, like some roses, and by annuals like snapdragons, most of which need regular deadheading. This is more important for whites than for other colours because any brown petals will muddy the purity of the whites.

BELOW White azaleas and the flowers of a dogwood tree (*Cornus florida*) lighten and brighten a shady foliage garden in the late spring. The scalloped leaves of the bloodroot (*Sanguinaria canadensis*) form a carpet at their feet. More foliage interest comes from the fountains of muscari foliage, and the box hedges that edge the lawn and snake away into the distance. The bloodroot's white flowers would have appeared in spring before the leaves, so setting in train the garden's white theme.

LEFT You can introduce white flowers early in the season by using bulbs that receive the light they need before the leaves appear on the trees above. Here snowdrops (*Galanthus elwesii*) grow with spring snowflakes (*Leucojum vernum*). Shade-tolerant white-variegated hostas, white foxgloves and white willow gentian (*Gentiana asclepiadea* var. *alba*) might carry the scheme through the summer.

A White Rose Garden

A small, scented rose garden, complete with an arbour in which to sit, makes an idyllic summer retreat. White is a particularly good choice of colour since there is a wide range of roses from which to choose, and the flowers will remain visible well after dusk. However, because many of the most beautiful, heavily-scented roses flower only once, the glory of such a garden can be short-lived. To make the rose garden into a bower of mixed scents, you might accompany the roses with white sweet rocket (*Hesperis matronalis* var. *albiflora*) and mock orange, and edge the beds with white lavender and white pinks such as *Dianthus* 'Mrs Sinkins'. Terracing of natural stone sets off white flowers. It also reflects and retains heat, so helping to bring out the garden's scents.

BELOW Behind a stone urn, an arbour is draped with the rambling rose 'Wickwar' and the path towards it is lined with mock orange (*Philadelphus* 'Belle Etoile'), with foxgloves and clematis (*C. recta*) underplanted with polyantha rose 'White Pet' and white lychnis. In the foreground are shrub roses 'Alba Maxima' and the dry soil around the urn harbours *Stachys byzantina* and feathery-leaved white anthemis.

Whites

SPRING

Amelanchier
Shrub that flowers in spring as the leaves, bronzey when young, develop; good colour in the autumn. Best on moist, acid to neutral soil. *A. canadensis* is a suckering shrub with an erect habit. H 5m (16ft) S 3m (10ft) Z5. *A. lamarckii* makes a spreading shrub or small tree . H 9m (30ft) S 6m (20ft) Z5

Anemone
Tuberous perennials. *A. blanda* 'White Splendour' WINDFLOWER has large glossy white flowers in early spring. H and S 20cm (8in) Z5. *A. nemorosa* has prettily divided foliage and smaller flowers, a little later. Both tolerates sun and partial shade in humus rich soil. H 10cm (4in) S 15cm (6in) Z4

Arabis caucasica
A mat-forming, evergreen perennial. Happiest in sunny, dry places, like the tops of walls. H 15cm (6in) S 25cm (10in) Z4

Camellia japonica 'Alba Simplex'
Evergreen shrub with leathery foliage and a mass of single flowers in spring. Needs shelter and partial shade. H 3m (10ft) S 1.5m (5ft) Z8

Clematis armandii
Evergreen climber with handsome foliage, coppery when young, and clusters of scented white flowers, sometimes tinged pink, in early spring. Deserves a warm, sheltered spot. H 5m (15ft) S 3m (10ft) Z9

Convallaria majalis LILY-OF-THE-VALLEY Spreading rhizomes make a thick carpet of pointed green leaves in moist, leafy, shady conditions. The bell-like flowers have a wonderful fragrance. H 15cm (6in) S indefinite Z4 [ill.p.151]

Cornus florida FLOWERING DOGWOOD Large shrub or small tree with white bracts surrounding the flowers in early summer. The leaves colour before they fall, revealing the glaucous young stem growth. Best in sun and deep, lime-free soil. H 6m (20ft) S 7.6m (25ft) Z6 [ill.pp.97,148]

Crocus chrysanthus 'Snow Bunting' Corm with white flowers delicately feathered purple. Requires an open, sunny position. H 10cm (4in) S 8cm (3in) Z4

Epimedium x youngianum 'Niveum' Rhizomatous perennial with pointed, heart-shaped leaves, often flushed purple when young, contrasting with the small white flowers, held well above the clump of foliage. Requires partial shade and humus rich, moist soil. Useful as groundcover. H 15cm (6in) S 30cm (12in) Z5

Erythronium californicum 'White Beauty' Perennial bulb with creamy-white flowers and mottled leaves. Requires partial shade and humus rich soil. H 30cm (12in) S 15cm (6in) Z5

Exochorda x macrantha 'The Bride' PEARLBUSH Somewhat lax, though graceful shrub; can be trained as a small tree. Chlorosis may be a problem on shallow, chalky soil. H 1.5m (5ft) S 2m (6ft) Z5

Halesia carolina
Shrub or small tree with clusters of charming bell-shaped flowers that hang from the bare branches before the leaves open. Oblong winged fruits follow in the autumn. Requires sun and neutral to acid soil. H 7.6m (25ft) S 10m (33ft) Z5

Hyacinthus 'L'Innocence'
Although hyacinth bulbs are often forced into early growth indoors, they will flourish outside in an open, sunny position, where the flowerheads will become less dense. H 20cm (8in) S 10cm (4in) Z4

Iberis sempervirens CANDYTUFT Evergreen sub shrub that makes a carpet of small dark green leaves, covered in pure white flowers in spring. Requires sun. H 30cm (12in) S 60cm (24in) Z3

Leucojum
Bulb that does best in partial shade. *L. aestivum* SUMMER SNOWFLAKE has nodding bells with green tips. H 60cm (24in) S 12cm (5in) Z4. *L. vernum* SPRING SNOWFLAKE appears a little earlier, and its scented flowers are much shorter. H 20cm (8in) S 10cm (4in) Z4 [ill.p.97]

Magnolia stellata STAR MAGNOLIA A very slow-growing, bushy shrub, covered in narrow-petalled white stars if late frosts do not catch the buds. H and S 1.8m (6ft) Z5

Malus hupehensis CRAB APPLE One of the best crab apple trees, with large flowers, followed by small orange red fruit in autumn. Prefers full sun. H and S 8m (26ft) Z4

Narcissus DAFFODIL
Bulb that tolerates sun and light shade. Good cultivars include 'Actaea' a Poeticus type, scented, with broad white petals and a yellowy eye, H 40cm (15in) Z4; 'Thalia' a multi-headed Triandrus type, with a cluster of snow-white, fragrant flowers, H 30cm (12in) Z4; and 'White Lion' which has double blooms, white mingled with cream, H 40cm (15in) Z3

Ornithogalum umbellatum STAR OF BETHLEHEM Bulb. Pretty, starry flowers, but can be invasive. Tolerates both sun and partial shade. H 30cm (12in) S 15cm (6in) Z5

Osmanthus delavayi
A substantial shrub with small, neat evergreen leaves and abundant strongly-scented small flowers. Tolerates sun and partial shade. H and S 3m (10ft) Z7

Prunus CHERRY
P. padus BIRD CHERRY bears almond-scented flowers that appear after the leaves. H 15m (50ft) S 7.5m (25ft) Z3. 'Shirotae' has a vigorously spreading habit; large flower clusters and soft green, serrated foliage. H 5.5m (18ft) S 7.6m (25ft) Z5.'Taihaku' GREAT WHITE CHERRY One of the largest of the flowering cherries, the young leaves emerge copper-coloured, as the flowers begin to fade. H 7.6m (25ft) S 10m (30ft) Z5. 'Ukon' has cream flowers, and its foliage colours well in the autumn. H 7m (22ft) S 10m (30ft) Z5

Pulmonaria officinalis 'Sissinghurst White' LUNGWORT Perennial with heart-shaped spotted leaves that makes good groundcover all year round. Requires shade. H 30cm (12in) S 45cm (18in) Z4

Sanguinaria canadensis BLOODROOT Rhizomatous perennial. The lobed leaves emerge vertically and gradually unfold, after the white flowers, to make an attractive, broad clump. Tolerates sun and partial shade, and requires humus-rich soil. H 15cm (6in) S 30cm (12in) Z3

Spiraea 'Arguta' BRIDAL WREATH Shrub with tiny flowers borne in great profusion all along its fine, arching branches. Requires sun. H and S 2.4m (8ft) Z5

Anemone blanda 'White Splendour'

Epimedium x *youngianum* 'Niveum'

Erythronium californicum 'White Beauty'

Magnolia stellata

Prunus 'Shirotae'

Tiarella wherryi FOAMFLOWER
Rhizomatous perennial with clumps of maple-like leaves that are often purplish in colour, and starry white flowers that are pink in the bud. Tolerates deep shade. H 20cm (8in) S 30cm (12in) Z3

Trillium grandiflorum WAKE ROBIN
Rhizomatous perennial with pointed, ovate leaves that grow in threes around the flowering stem, beneath the pure white flowers. Tolerates both full and partial shade. H 40cm (15in) S 30cm (12in) Z4

Tulipa TULIP
Bulb that appreciates summer baking. Good cultivars include 'Purissima' a Fosteriana hybrid, pure milky white, H 40cm (15in) S 23cm (9in) Z3; 'Spring Green' a Viridiflora tulip, with creamy flowers streaked green, H 40cm (15in) S 23cm (9in) Z3; and 'White Triumphator' a Lily-flowered type, with pointed petals, H 75cm (30in) S 25cm (10in) Z3 [ill.p.111]

SUMMER

Achillea
Perennial that tolerates most soil conditions in a sunny position. Good varieties include *A. chrysocoma* 'Grandiflora' with finely cut, lacy grey foliage, topped with flat heads of white daisy flowers in late summer, H 1.5m (5ft) S 90cm (3ft) Z6

[ill.p.172]; and *A. ptarmica* 'The Pearl' which has a tendency to be invasive, has stout, branching stems of neat button-flowers, H and S 75cm (30in) Z3 [ill.p.25]

Agapanthus campanulatus var. *albidus* AFRICAN LILY Perennial that forms clumps of fleshy, strap-shaped leaves in spring and in late summer throws up tall stems with round heads of white flowers. Requires full sun. H 90cm (3ft) S 50cm (20in) Z8

Allium ORNAMENTAL ONION
Bulbous perennials with spherical flowerheads. *A. karataviense* has a large globe of pinkish white flowers, and generally only two, opulent grey-green leaves. H 20cm (8in) S 30cm (10in) Z4 [ill.p.109]. Prefers an open situation. *A. triquetrum* THREE CORNERED ONION carries a loose umbel of greeny-white flowers. The flowering stem is distinctively triangular in section. Likes a damp, shady position, where it can self-seed invasively. H 40cm (15in) S 15cm (6in) Z4

Anaphalis triplinervis PEARL EVERLASTING Perennial with a mound of grey foliage covered with white 'everlasting' flowers in late summer. Prefers sun but will grow in partial shade. H 45cm (18in) S 60cm (24in) Z4 [ill.p.181]

Anthemis
Good varieties of this sun-loving perennial include *A. punctata* subsp. *cupaniana* which quickly

forms a low mound of finely cut silvery foliage, with white daisy-flowers, H 30cm (12in) S 60cm (24in) Z7 [ill.pp.95,98]; and *A. tinctoria* 'Alba' which has ferny, dark green foliage and white daisies over a long summer season, H and S 90cm (3ft) Z4

Anthericum liliago ST BERNARD'S LILY
Perennial. Grassy grey-green leaves and spikes of white trumpet flowers in early summer. Needs a sunny site and soil that dries out in summer. H 60cm (24in) S 30cm (12in) Z5

Antirrhinum SNAPDRAGON
An old faithful for the summer border, this annual has long-lasting flowers like closed lips that bees push through to reach the nectar. Seedsmen stock numerous varieties of different heights and flower forms including 'White Wonder' which has a splash of yellow at the flower throat. H 45cm (18in) S 25cm (10in) [ill.p.95]

Argyranthemum foeniculaceum (of gardens) MARGUERITE Perennial with finely cut blue-green leaves and many white daisies which flower over a long period. It is pretty in a pot, and can be trained as a standard. Requires sun. H and S 90cm (3ft) Z9 [ill.p.151]

Aruncus dioicus GOAT'S BEARD
A hearty perennial, tolerant of most conditions except deep shade. Makes a handsome clump of rich ferny leaves, with creamy

plumes in early summer. H 1.8m (6ft) S 1.2m (4ft) Z3 [ill.p.167]

Astilbe 'Brautschleier' (syn *A.* 'Bridal Veil') Perennial that forms clumps of bright green, ferny foliage and throws up elegant sprays of pure white flowers. Requires partial shade and rich soil. Best left undisturbed. H and S 75cm (30in) Z4 [ill.p.178]

Bellis perennis DOUBLE DAISY
The perennial cultivated daisy flowers over a long season. Tolerates sun and partial shade. H and S 20cm (8in) Z4

Camassia leichtlinii subsp. *leichtlinii* (syn. *C. l.* 'Alba') Bulb with flowers like ivory stars on slender stems; will naturalize deep, moist soil. Tolerates sun and partial shade. H 90cm (3ft) S 30cm (12in) Z4

Campanula
Perennial that tolerates both sun and shade. *C. lactiflora alba* has large, branching flowerheads which need staking in windy areas. H 1.5m (5ft) S 60cm (2ft) Z5 [ill.p.182]. *C. persicifolia alba* flowers for a long time, and is a good companion for old roses. H 90cm (3ft) S 30cm (1ft) Z4 [ill.p.174]

Carpenteria californica TREE ANEMONE Evergreen shrub whose heavy dark green foliage is justified by the richness of its flowers, which have pure white petals around long stamens. Best against a sunny wall. H 1.8m (6ft) S 1.5m (5ft) Z8

Centranthus ruber albus WHITE VALERIAN Perennial with fleshy leaves and large heads of white flowers all summer, can self-seed invasively and is often natural-ized on limestone walls. Requires sun and will tolerate poor, alkaline soil. H 75cm (30in) S 60cm (24in) Z5 [ill.p.174]

Cerastium tomentosum SNOW IN SUMMER Perennial producing mats of grey foliage smothered in white in late spring. Clip back after flowering. Requires sun, and is well situated on a hot, dry bank. H 8cm (3in) S 45cm (18in) Z4 [ill.p.109]

Choisya ternata MEXICAN ORANGE BLOSSOM Evergreen shrub with shiny three-lobed leaves, aromatic when cut or crushed, with scented white flowers in late spring. Requires sun or partial shade. H and S 3m (10ft) Z8

Cimicifuga BUGBANE
Perennial requiring partial shade and moist soil. *C. racemosa* BLACK SNAKEROOT has branching stems of bottlebrush flowers over divided, fresh green leaves. H 1.5m (5ft) S 60cm (2ft) Z4 [ill.p.81]. *C. simplex* is smaller, and flowers later, in the autumn. H 1.2m (4ft) S 60cm (2ft) Z4

Cistus x hybridus (syn. *C. corbariensis*) WHITE ROCK ROSE Shrub with wavy-edged leaves and reddish buds which open to white. Very floriferous. Requires sun. H and S 1.2m (4ft) Z8

Tulipa 'Spring Green'

Allium triquetrum

Argyranthemum foeniculaceum

Carpenteria californica

Cimicifuga racemosa

Clematis
Good climbing varieties include 'Alba Luxurians' with flowers that white with green markings, with a dark eye, H and S 3.7m (12ft) Z4; 'Huldine' has greeny-white stamens, and the white flowers are mauve on the reverse, H and S 4m (13ft) Z4; 'Marie Boisselot' (syn.'Mme le Coultre') has broad leaves and flowers like flat plates, flushed pink on opening but becoming pure white, H and S 3m (10ft) Z4; and *C. var. montana sericea* (syn. *C. m.* 'Spooneri') has only four petals, and a large tuft of greenish yellow stamens, H and S 9m (30ft) Z6. Good herbaceous varieties include *C. recta* with pinnate foliage and panicles of small white flowers in summer [ill.pp.98,167], and *C. r.* 'Purpurea' which has purple young foliage. H 1.8m (6ft) S 50cm (20in) Z3.

Cornus kousa var. chinensis KOUSA DOGWOOD An elegant spreading tree or large shrub. It is the bracts of the flowers which are conspicuously white. The foliage is a rich colour in the autumn. Tolerates sun and partial shade. Dislikes a shallow chalk soil. H 9m (30ft) S 6m (20ft) Z5

Crambe cordifolia
Perennial that makes a mound of rather coarse green foliage, from which arise bare branching stems, exploding in a cloud of white stars in midsummer.

Requires sun. H 2m (6ft6in) S 1.2m (4ft) Z6 [ill.p.174]

Dahlia
Tuberous perennial that flowers late in the season and carries on until the first frost; then tubers need lifting and storing in frost-free conditions. Elegant white varieties include the Cactus-flowered 'My Love' H and S 75cm (30in) Z9 [ill.p.163]

Delphinium
Perennials that are invaluable to provide an eye-catching vertical thrust to a border. Young growth may need protection from slugs. Best in full sun. [ill.p.176] Good white varieties include the Galahad Group [ill.p.174] and 'Butterball'. H 1.5m (5ft) S 40cm (15in) Z2

Deutzia gracilis
A dense, small shrub, flowering best in full sun but requiring protection from spring frosts. H and S 90cm (3ft) Z5

Dicentra BLEEDING HEART
Perennial requiring partial shade and moist, rich soil. *D. eximia* 'Snowdrift' has grey-green, divided leaves, topped by stems of narrow white flowers. H and S 30cm (12in) Z4. *D. spectabilis* 'Alba' has creamy-white lockets that dangle above finely cut foliage of a fresh green. H 75cm (30in) S 50cm (20in) Z3

Dictamnus albus BURNING BUSH
Perennial with spires of white flowers, which become star-shaped seed pods, and lemon-

scented foliage. Requires sun. H 90cm (3ft) S 60cm (2ft) Z3

Digitalis purpurea f. **albiflora**
FOXGLOVE Biennial producing spires of flowers, spotted on the inside. Requires partial shade. H 1.5m (5ft) S 45cm (18in) Z3 [ill.pp.94,98]

Epilobium angustifolium album
WHITE WILLOWHERB Perennial with slender spires that open their flowers gradually; the seedpods forming below before the last buds are mature above. Roots can be invasive in light soils. Requires sun. H 1.5m (5ft) S 50cm (20in) Z3 [ill.p.19]

Galium odoratum (syn. *Asperula odorata*) SWEET WOODRUFF A spreading perennial with ruffs of small spiky leaves topped by clusters of white stars from late spring. Grows well in partial shade, but tolerates sun. H 15cm (6in) S 30cm (12in) Z4

Galtonia candicans SUMMER HYACINTH Bulb producing tall stems of drooping, white bells in late summer. Requires sun. H 1.2m (4ft) S 23cm (9in) Z6

Gaura lindheimeri
Perennial whose pinky white flowers seem to flutter through the border; best staked or supported by a stouter plant such as a sedum. Requires sun. H 1.2m (4ft) S 90cm (3ft) Z6

Geranium CRANESBILL
Reliable perennials for the border. *G. clarkei* 'Kashmir White' has prettily cut foliage

and veined white flowers. Can spread rapidly by roots and seed. Best in sun. H and S 60cm (2ft) Z4. *G. renardii* makes a solid dome of quilted sage green leaves. Best in sun. H and S 30cm (12in) Z6. *G. sylvaticum* f. **albiflorum** WOOD CRANESBILL makes clumps of fingered leaves and branching stems of small flowers in late spring. Requires partial shade. H 90cm (3ft) S 60cm (2ft) Z4

Gladiolus callianthus 'Murieliae' (syn. *Acidanthera m.*) Perennial corm producing spikes of graceful, sweetly scented flowers with dark blotches. Requires sun and fertile soil. H 90cm (3ft) S 15cm (6in) Z9. Good varieties of the large-flowered *Gladiolus* hybrids include *G.* 'Ice Cap' H 1.7m (5ft6in) S 30cm (12in) Z9

Gypsophila paniculata BABY'S BREATH Rhizomatous perennial making a mound of tiny white stars. Plant so it can froth forward and cover bare ground in late summer. Requires sun and deep soil. Tolerates poor soil. H and S 90cm (3ft) Z4 [ill.p.25]

Hesperis matronalis var. **albiflora**
WHITE SWEET ROCKET Perennial with very fragrant, stock-like flowers on tall branching stems. Seeds itself freely. Does best in sun. H 75cm (30in) S 60cm (2ft) Z4

Hydrangea
Most of these useful shrubs require partial shade and moist

soil. *H. arborescens* 'Grandiflora' has greenish-white globe-shaped heads of flowers which become creamier as they mature. H and S 1.8m (6ft) Z4. *H. paniculata* 'Kyushu' has slender terminal panicles of sterile florets and quite glossy leaves. H 2.5m (8ft) S 1.8m (6ft) Z4 [ill.p.95]. *H. anomala* subsp. *petiolaris* CLIMBING HYDRANGEA will climb up a sunless wall, as it prefers cool soil. Flattened, greenish-white flowers appear early summer. H and S to 15m (50ft) Z5. *H. quercifolia* OAK LEAVED HYDRANGEA has large, lobed leaves that turn a good colour in the autumn if grown in the sun, although it will grow in full shade. H 1.5m (5ft) S 1.8m (6ft) Z5

Lamium maculatum album
SPOTTED DEADNETTLE Creeping and carpeting perennial with silver-patterned leaves and white deadnettle flowers. Tolerates full sun and partial shade and prefers moist soil. H 20cm (8in) S 90cm (3ft) Z3 [ill.p.175]

Lathyrus PEA
L. latifolius 'Albus' PERENNIAL SWEET PEA is a perennial climber with robust, almost lush, flowers over a long period, but lacking scent. H and S 1.8m (6ft) Z5 [ill.p.149]. *L. odoratus* SWEET PEA is an annual climber with a unique scent. H and S 1.8m (6ft) Both require full sun and rich, moist soil.

Clematis 'Marie Boisselot'

Dicentra spectabilis 'Alba'

Gaura lindheimeri

Gladiolus callianthus 'Murieliae'

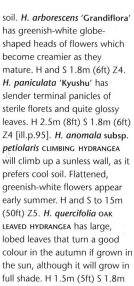
Hydrangea quercifolia

Lavandula angustifolia 'Alba' LAVENDER Shrub with fine, evergreen grey foliage and strongly aromatic flower spikes. Best in sun and well-drained soil. H and S 75cm (30in) Z6 [ill.p.95]

Lavatera trimestris 'Mont Blanc' Bushy annual smothered in large white trumpets. Requires sun. H 75cm (30in) S 45cm (18in)

Leucanthemum x superbum 'Esther Read' (syn *Chrysanthemum x s.* 'E. R.') SHASTA DAISY Perennial that produces glistening white double daisy flowers. Requires sun. H and S 45cm (18in) Z4 [ill.p.174]

Libertia grandiflora NEW ZEALAND SATIN FLOWER Rhizomatous perennial with strong clumps of long narrow leaves that send up stiff sprays of white flowers in midsummer. H 75cm (30in) S 60cm (2ft) Z8

Lilium LILY
Summer-flowering bulbs that do best in sun. *L. candidum* MADONNA LILY has foliage that appears in autumn and lasts all winter, followed by fragrant white flowers with yellow stamens in early summer. Prefers lime-rich soil. Z4. 'Casa Blanca' has large, clear white blooms Z5. *L. martagon* var. *album* MARTAGON LILY has nodding flowers with reflexed petals, variously spotted Z4. *L. regale* Album Group REGAL LILY has a bewitching scent, particularly in the evening Z4 [ill.p.183].

'Sterling Star' has clusters of creamy white flowers spotted with brown Z2. All H 90cm (3ft)

Lobularia 'Snow Carpet' (syn. *Alyssum* 'S.C.') Annual that makes low mats of long-lasting tiny white flowers. Quick and easy to grow, so it is a good plant for children, and it makes a frilly edging to a path or border. Requires sun. H 10cm (4in) S 30cm (12in) Z7

Lychnis coronaria Alba Group WHITE ROSE CAMPION Biennial or short-lived perennial with much-branched stems carrying a succession of single white flowers above tufts of downy grey foliage. Requires sun. H 50cm (20in) S 30cm (12in) Z4 [ill.pp.98,175]

Lysimachia LOOSESTRIFE
Perennials that tolerate sun and partial shade in moist soil. *L. clethroides* GOOSENECK LOOSESTRIFE has arching spikes of tiny grey-white flowers in late summer. H 90cm (3ft) S 60cm (2ft) Z4. *L. ephemerum* has slender spires of close-set white flowers and cool grey foliage. H 90cm (3ft) S 30cm (1ft) Z7

Malva moschata alba MUSK MALLOW Short-lived perennial easily raised from seed. Fresh green, divided foliage and abundant cup-shaped white flowers. Requires sun. H 75cm (30in) S 60cm (2ft) Z4 [ill.p.176]

Myrrhis odorata SWEET CICELY
Perennial with flat flowerheads

and foliage that is finely-cut and aromatic. Tolerates both sun and shade. H and S 60cm (2ft) Z4

Nicotiana FLOWERING TOBACCO
Perennials usually grown as annuals. *N. affinis* has pure white star-shaped blooms that are particularly fragrant in the evening. H 75cm (30in) S 30cm (12in). *N. x sanderae,* a bushy annual, comes in a range of colours including white. H 60cm (2ft) S 30cm (1ft) [ill.pp.121,163]. *N. sylvestris* is a towering plant with drooping, tubular flowers that is good for the back of a border. Often self-seeds. H 1.5m (5ft) S 75cm (30in) [ill.pp.107,163] All do best in sun.

Olearia x *macrodonta* NEW ZEALAND HOLLY Evergreen shrub with sage-green, spiny leaves. It is smothered in broad heads of scented white daisies in midsummer. Requires full sun. H and S 3m (10ft) Z9 [ill.p.179]

Osteospermum caulescens
Evergreen perennial with large, many-rayed white daisies with a blue eye. Requires sun. H and S 45cm (18in) Z9 [ill.p.132]

Paeonia PEONY
P. lactiflora 'Duchesse de Nemours' is a perennial, free-flowering double white peony with a good scent. H and S 75cm (30in) Z3. *P. suffruticosa* subsp. *rockii* ROCK'S TREE PEONY, first introduced by Joseph Rock, has enormous white blooms

with maroon blotches at the base of the petals, and a big bunch of yellow stamens. Very special but also very rare, as it is difficult to propagate. Prefers sun but will tolerate light shade. H and S 2.1m (7ft) Z5

Papaver orientale 'Black and White' ORIENTAL POPPY Perennial whose flowers have petals like white crepe paper with black blotches. Foliage dies back by midsummer. Does best in sun. H 90cm (3ft) S 30cm (1ft) Z4

Petunia
Annuals requiring a sunny position sheltered from wind. A good variety is 'White Cloud' H 20cm (8in) S 30cm (12in) [ill.p.150]

Philadephus 'Belle Etoile' MOCK ORANGE Shrub whose creamy white flowers have a mauve centre, and the scent carries well around the garden. Cut out old, twiggy wood immediately after flowering. Requires sun and fertile soil. H and S 2.4m (8ft) Z5 [ill.pp.98,151]

Phlox paniculata
Elegant border perennial with large heads of fragrant white flowers. Tolerates both sun and partial shade. H 90cm (3ft) S 45cm (18in) Z4. *P. p.* 'Mount Fuji' is taller with large, snow-white flowers. H 1.5m (5ft) S 60cm (2ft)

Potentilla fruticosa 'Abbotswood' Shrub with small grey-green leaves and frilly pure white

flowers over a long season. Can be hard pruned if it gets leggy. Requires sun. H 75cm (30in) S 90cm (3ft) Z3

Romneya coulteri CALIFORNIAN TREE POPPY Perennial with glaucous, divided foliage on long stems, topped with huge white poppies. Requires a warm, sunny position and deep soil. Difficult to establish, this plant resents being moved. H and S 1.8m (6ft) Z8

Rosa ROSE
Most do best in an open, sunny position. Good climbing varieties include 'Bobbie James' a vigorous rambler with large trusses of creamy white flowers, H 9m (30ft) S 6m (20ft) Z5; 'Mme Alfred Carrière' which is vigorous, tolerates partial shade, and has full, blush white blooms that repeat well, H 4m (13ft) S 3m (10ft) Z6; 'The Garland' with clusters of many small, fragrant flowers, H and S 4.6m (15ft) Z5; and 'Wedding Day' with heads of single, creamy flowers and good hips; it is tolerant of shade and poor soil, H 9m (30ft) S 4.5m (15ft) Z5. Good shrub varieties include 'Iceberg' (syn.'Schneewittchen') which has little scent but flowers constantly, H 1.5m (5ft) S 90cm (3ft) Z5 [ill.p.176]; 'Margaret Merril' with white scented flowers delicately tinged pink, H 90cm (3ft) S 60cm (2ft) Z5; and *R. soulieana* with neat grey

Lilium candidum

Lysimachia ephemerum

Olearia macrodonta

Papaver orientale 'Black and White'

Rosa 'The Garland'

foliage and masses of single flowers which are followed by small orange hips, H 3m (10ft) S 1.8m (6ft) Z7

Rubus 'Benenden'
This relative of the blackberry makes a broad shrub with large lobed leaves and showy white flowers in great quantity in early summer. Best in sun. H and S 3m (10ft) Z6

Solanum jasminoides 'Album' POTATO VINE A vigorous wall shrub with neat, dark foliage that shows off the loose heads of white jasmine-like flowers. Blooms from earliest summer until the frosts. Requires full sun. H and S to 6m (20ft) Z9

Syringa vulgaris 'Mme Lemoine' LILAC Shrub with plump racemes of heavily fragrant, double white flowers in early summer. Needs sun and deep, preferably alkaline soil. H and S 4m (13ft) Z4

Verbascum chaixii 'Album' MULLEIN Perennial producing long spikes of white flowers with pink eyes, over dark foliage. Often self seeds. Tolerates shade, but prefers an open sunny site. H 90cm (3ft) S 60cm (2ft) Z5 [ill.p.176]

Verbena tenuisecta f. alba MOSS VERBENA Perennial with finely cut leaves and dense white flowerheads. Requires sun. H 40cm (15in) S 75cm (30in) Z9 [ill.p.174]

Viburnum
V. opulus 'Roseum' SNOWBALL TREE has balls of creamy flowers in early summer and rich foliage colour in the autumn. H and S 5m (16ft) Z4 [ill.p.94]. *V. plicatum* **'Mariesii'** has a very elegant, distinctively horizontal pattern of growth, emphasized by the flat heads of flowers opening all along the branches H and S 4m (13ft) Z6 [ill.p.94]. Both tolerate full sun and partial shade.

Viola cornuta Alba Group WHITE HORNED VIOLET Perennial that makes good groundcover, with perky flowers in quantity in early summer. Cut over after flowering and a second crop will appear in late summer. Tolerates sun or partial shade. H 40cm (15in) S 60cm (2ft) Z4 [ill.pp.18, 114,176]

Wisteria floribunda 'Alba'
Vigorous twining climber, with good pinnate foliage and long racemes of white pea flowers in early summer followed by velvety pods. Requires sun. H and S to 30m (100ft) Z5

Yucca gloriosa SPANISH DAGGER Evergreen shrub with bold spiky, succulent leaves and tall panicles of creamy white flowers. Makes a bold pot plant or architectural feature, and needs full sun. H 1.8m (6ft) S 1.5m (5ft) Z7

Zantedeschia aethiopica ARUM LILY Perennial with preference for having its toes in the mud of a pond. Glossy green leaves are the perfect backdrop to the great white spathes. H 1m (3ft3in) S 45cm (18in) Z8

AUTUMN

Anemone x hybrida 'Honorine Jobert' JAPANESE ANEMONE Perennial making hearty clumps of lobed leaves which throw up branching stems of rounded white flowers. Tolerates full sun and partial shade in humus-rich soil. H 1.5m (5ft) S 60cm (2ft) Z5

Aster divaricatus
Evergreen perennial with wiry dark stems that spray forth masses of starry white flowers with yellow centres. Tolerates sun and partial shade in moist soil. H and S 60cm (2ft) Z4

Leucanthemella serotina (syn. *Chrysanthemum uliginosum*) Perennial with erect stems that carry many white daisy-flowers which turn to follow the sun. Requires a sunny site. H 2.1m (7ft) S 60cm (2ft) Z4

BERRIES

Actaea alba (syn. *A. pachypoda*) WHITE BANEBERRY Shrub whose Fluffy flowers turn into curious, poisonous, white berries on stout red stalks. Requires shade and moist, peaty soil. H 90cm (3ft) S 50cm (20in) Z4

Sorbus cashmiriana ROWAN Drooping clusters of large white berries remain on the tree long after the pinnate leaves have coloured and fallen. Tolerates sun and partial shade. H and S 9m (30ft) Z5

Symphoricarpos albus SNOWBERRY Shrub whose suckering, wiry stems form a thicket liberally scattered with pulpy white berries in autumn. Tolerates sun and partial shade H 1.2m (4ft) S 90cm (3ft) Z4

WINTER

Erica carnea 'Springwood White' WINTER HEATH Evergreen sub-shrub covered with clusters of tiny white tubular flowers for up to six months through winter and spring. Tolerates lime soil and some shade. Makes good groundcover. H 30cm (12in) S 45cm (18in) Z5

Galanthus SNOWDROP
Bulb requiring a cool position in partial shade and moist soil. Can be quick to increase. *G. elwesii* has broad glaucous leaves, with inner petals marked green. H and S 20cm (8in) Z4 [ill.p.97]. *G. nivalis* **'Flore Pleno'** DOUBLE COMMON SNOWDROP has many white petals with a sprinkling of green. H 15cm (6in) S 8cm (3in) Z3 [ill.p.113]

Helleborus niger CHRISTMAS ROSE Evergreen perennial with nodding flowers, often flushed pink on the outside, held well above the dark green leathery leaves. Requires partial shade and moisture retentive soil. H and S 30cm (12in) Z4

Lonicera x purpusii 'Winter Beauty' This deciduous shrub, densely covered in small dark leaves in the summer, has gloriously fragrant creamy flowers in winter. Tolerates sun and partial shade. H and S 1.5m (5ft) Z5

Viburnum tinus LAURUSTINUS Shrub with dark evergreen leaves on reddish stems. Pink buds open to white flowerheads that last all through the winter. *V. t.* **'Eve Price'** has more plentiful flowers and buds of a richer pink [ill.p.170]. Tolerates partial shade, but flowers more freely in sun. H and S 3m (10ft) Z8

STEMS

Betula utilis var. jacquemontii HIMALAYAN BIRCH A graceful deciduous tree lightened by the effect of its peeling bark which is of the purest white, and extends to the branches too. Requires a sunny position in moist soil. H 18m (60ft) S 9m (30ft) Z6

Rubus biflorus BRAMBLE
Shrubs for winter interest. *R. biflorus* with stout, prickly stems with angular branches covered with a white bloom, fully revealed after leaf fall. H and S 1.8m (6ft) Z6 [ill.p.171]. *R. cockburnianus* has long arching stems also with a grey-white bloom that shows up well in winter. H 2.4m (8ft) S 3.7m (12ft) Z6. Both require full sun.

Rubus 'Benenden'

Wisteria floribunda 'Alba'

Sorbus cashmiriana

Helleborus niger

Lonicera x purpusii 'Winter Beauty'

HARMONIES

Colour harmonies are the result of putting together closely related colours, such as those that are next to each other on the colour wheel (see page 15). Therefore, if you want to base a harmony on blue, you could add the adjacent mauves and violets. Similarly, you might start with red, and add orange and yellow. Other harmonies might be based on pink, which is one of the most widespread flower colours. It does not appear on the colour wheel, since it is not one of the pure spectral colours. It is a mixture of red with white and traces of other hues such as blue or yellow. A particular pink looks good with colours that relate to its own dominant constituents.

White and grey contribute to colour harmonies in a more passive way. They are both inert colours, and so do not actively affect the hue of their neighbours. They both 'go' with all other colours, making the overall effect of any planting lighter and brighter.

Colour temperature also plays a part in harmonious relationships. When blues or blue-violets dominate, the planting is a 'cold' one and is generally subdued and calming. When reds and oranges take the lead, the opposite is true: the harmony will be 'hot' and vibrant and far from relaxing. These are the two extremes. Between them lies an enormous range of 'cool' and 'warm' schemes. Pinks, for instance, hover on the border that divides warm and cool colours. Pinks that contain blue harmonize with cool schemes of blues and violets, while yellow-pinks work better with warmer colours.

When all the colours in a planting are the same lightness or darkness, the result is a harmony of tone. Evergreen foliage tends to be dark-toned, so for example, by putting together dark green holly with the deepest blue delphiniums and dark crimson roses, you will make a sombre dark-toned harmony. At the other end of the scale, silver-grey with pastel pinks and blues will make a shimmering and cheerful light-toned harmony. Silver foliage, which dominates the picture shown here, is not only lighter than most green foliage but also cooler, because it lacks the warming yellow that green contains. So, although silver is a neutral hue, it tends to cool down a scheme by replacing the slightly warmer green foliage colour.

RIGHT The blue catmint in the foreground and echoing blue delphiniums in the border beyond the lawn establish this scheme as a cold harmony, which is underlined by the relatively cool silver foliage that dominates the border. The white flowers, which are of neutral colour temperature, make the planting lighter overall, but in this cool context, they also resemble a dusting of snow. (Full planting details of this scheme are given on page 174.)

Harmonies with Blue

Harmonies dominated by cool blues or colours with a blue bias are subtle and unostentatious. These cool harmonies create a restful, even slightly contemplative mood. You can use blues with blue-violets and icy whites, perhaps including the occasional plant with blue-pink flowers or cool primrose yellow ones. Green foliage is neutral: its context determines whether it is going to be warm or cool. But to contribute to cool harmonies, you can select silver-green foliage plants and those with blue-green leaves, such as some hostas, dicentras, and irises.

The cool blues, violets, and silvers seem to recede into the distance, suggesting space that is not really there. Use this to make a border appear deeper than it actually is, by putting your cool colours at the back and warm ones, which appear to come forward, toward the front. To make the whole garden look bigger, mass the cool harmonies at the far end.

In shade, light has a blue cast which enhances cool colours, while sunlight tends to warm them up, making blues look violet and violets look pink. So for the best results, plant your cool harmonies in the shade. For the same reason, in the bluish light of dusk, you can discern cool colours longer than warm ones, so it is also a good idea to place cool plantings in a part of the garden that you see at that time of day.

But the colour relationships in a garden are constantly changing. A planting that is a cool harmony one week may easily become a warm harmony the next, when the cool blue plants decline and their role is taken over, say, by warmer-coloured pink ones. By getting to know the flowering times of your plants, you can control the associations as they wax and wane through the season.

Remember too that the colours of the hard landscape of your garden – walls, paths, even the paintwork on doors and garden structures – will affect the balance of harmonizing plantings. A single coat of paint may be enough to bring a gate or garden door into harmony with adjacent plantings.

Another idea, especially suited to smaller gardens, is to group a collection of cool-coloured plants in pots to achieve a concentration of colour that is harder to obtain in a border.

RIGHT The colours of the white willowherb (*Epilobium angustifolium album*) and its accompanying blue catmint (*Nepeta* 'Six Hills Giant') still stand out even though it is well after sunset. This willowherb goes on to produce fluffy white seeds, but because they are infertile, it will not invade your garden in the same way as the more common pink form. Nevertheless it will spread by runners under the soil. The catmint will flower again later in the season if the flowering stems are cut back to ground level as soon as they begin to fade.

ABOVE A lick of blue paint has transformed a garden door from what might have been an eyesore into an intrinsic element of a cool planting that includes blue-violet pansies, the green foliage of *Daphne laureola* in the centre and *Cleome hassleriana* to the left of the door, with a very pale pink *Anemone* x *hybrida* and tall, white tobacco (*Nicotiana sylvestris*).

ABOVE Tender and exotic plants would struggle to survive in the competitive situation of a border. Here they have been planted in a group of containers to make a cool harmony that is in sympathy with the border behind. (Full planting details of this scheme are given on page 175.)

Blues, Mauves and Violets

You can safely put blues with mauves, purples and violets to make a resonant jumble of cool summer colour. Summer-flowering bulbs such as alliums are useful ingredients in plantings like this. They come in a range of suitable colours, from deepest purple through lilac and pink, to blue and white, and in heights from a few centimetres to more than a metre. Plant them among perennials that will provide them with the support they need, and you will not need to stake them. Their seedheads, which dry naturally, remain as a structural feature in the border, even when the colour has drained out of them. The perennial wallflower 'Bowles' Mauve' is a good companion to choose because it has blue-green leaves as well as a prolific output of mauve flowers from spring to autumn. Even ornamental cabbages can be incorporated into a planting of these colours. Their purple ribs echo the purple of adjacent flowers. Bronze fennel makes a harmonizing background. Its feathery foliage sets into relief the brighter spots of colour of the flowers and emphasizes their sharper outlines.

RIGHT ABOVE Seen in early summer, the globes of *Allium sphaerocephalon* are supported by *Eryngium* x *tripartitum* which has flowers of the same shape, but blue rather than red-purple. Pink opium poppies (*Papaver somniferum*), *Phlox paniculata* 'Eventide' and *P. p.* 'Franz Schubert', and *Nepeta racemosa* complete this rich planting.

RIGHT Shaped like purple shuttlecocks, the flowers of *Lavandula stoechas* subsp. *pedunculata* pick up the colour of the flowerheads of the *Allium aflatunense* 'Purple Sensation'. There are also suggestions of purple in the bronze fennel (*Foeniculum vulgare* 'Purpureum') beyond.

LEFT In a border that has been specially created for a flower show, two alliums of different heights – tall white *Allium nigrum* and *A. karataviense* with grey flowers and broad blue-green leaves – are combined with *Erysimum* 'Bowles' Mauve' and *Hesperis matronalis*, which has flowers of a similar colour. There are also some sun-loving plants – *Lavendula stoechas* subsp. *pedunculata*, purple sage and rosemary. These last plants do not really thrive in such cramped quarters, but need well-drained soil, open to full sunlight.

BELOW Pots can be regarded as small raised beds. Take advantage of their height by planting trailing plants like verbenas around their edges. Here, deep purple-pink *Verbena* 'Hidcote Purple' and the smaller-flowered *Verbena tenuisecta* accompany *Osteospermum* 'Pink Whirls', with flowers shaped like a watersplash, and the kale 'Red Peacock'. At the base of the container, the silver foliage of *Cerastium tomentosum* gives a cool context to the scheme. In containers you can break all the rules about the required distance between plants as long as you keep up the routine of watering and feeding.

LEFT When planning an ambitious border like this one, it pays to take account of the shapes and sizes of your colour masses, so the result is structured but full of variety and interest. This border is masterfully controlled, from its loosely trained backdrop of climbing pink roses to the clusters of lamium and catmints that tumble onto the gravel at the front. Interspersed among the mounds of colour are vertical accents of pink foxgloves which find their reflection, both in colour and form, in the pink penstemons in the foreground. The huge flowerheads of *Allium christophii* – each one a mass of individual flowers – are visually balanced by clumps of pinks. The repeated grey foliage of the lychnis is a cooling influence and helps to hold the planting together. (Full planting details of this scheme are given on page 175.)

Harmonies with Pink

The pinks are such a diverse family of colours that you cannot apply a general rule of colour association to all of them. Broadly, the pinks can be divided into two groups, the cool pinks and the warm ones. The larger proportion of pinks in the garden tend to be cool pinks that are derived from crimsons and have a touch of blue in them. These pinks look good with other colours with a blue bias, such as violet, blue itself, and with neutral white. The warm pinks, on the other hand, are those that are derived from mixtures of vermilion and orange-red with white; these seem to have a trace of yellow in them, and they make harmonies with other colours with a yellow bias such as yellow-greens and apricots.

The pinkness of flowers is often underlaid with other hues that modulate the overall colour, especially when they are seen at a distance. Some pink peonies, roses such as 'Ballerina', and tulips such as 'Angélique' have white centres that lighten the overall effect as well as providing a link with neighbouring white flowers. Other pink flowers, like rock roses, have yellow centres that tend to push the overall colour toward the warmer pinks.

The cool pinks that dominate the plantings shown on these two pages associate comfortably with their blue and violet companions, while the white flowers make links with the implied white content of the pinks and also lighten the composition.

ABOVE With blue and white forget-me-nots at their feet, Peony-flowered 'Angélique' and Lily-flowered 'White Triumphator' tulips, and pink 'Guinevere' primulas are backed by *Rhamnus alaternus* 'Argenteovariegata'. Later, pink and magenta geraniums will occupy the middle ground, and *Crambe cordifolia* will replace the vertical white element.

ABOVE Pink *Dicentra* 'Stuart Boothman', *Lamium maculatum,* blue *Pulmonaria* and forget-me-nots make a harmonious jumble of spring foliage and flower colour in the shade. The only white accents are the variegations of the honesty (*Lunaria annua* 'Alba Variegata')*,* and the grass at the back. Both of these will make stronger contributions when they are taller.

111

Pinks and Whites

Pink and white associations always work well. The palest pinks of some roses and peonies are light enough to combine in harmonies with white, which enhances their brilliance so that from a distance they appear as a unity. However, you need to beware of planting pale pink and white on a large scale: the effect can be over-sweet.

For a sharper, crisper effect, use dark pink with white; the contrast of tone prevents the colours from merging together. Although white flowers are inert in colour terms, they act as tonal highlights, lightening and brightening the overall effect.

Pink and white is a colour combination that you can use all the year round, starting in early spring with snowdrops and deep pink cyclamen, and moving on with clouds of cherry blossom and ribbons of tulips. The peak season for this colour pairing is in early summer, when festoons of roses, spires of foxgloves, and banks of peonies, all in pinks and whites, come into glorious bloom.

ABOVE A ribbon of tulips – a mix of 'Peerless Pink', white 'Pax', and purple 'Negrita' – is threaded with bicoloured flowers of *Dicentra spectabilis*. Although this planting is in a public park, it is far from municipal in its approach.

ABOVE Perennial white *Viola cornuta* underplants a pink rose, *Rosa* 'Yesterday'. The colour of the yellow-throated flowers of the tender perennial *Rehmannia elata* is reflected in the smaller yellow-pink flowers of the *Diascia* 'Ruby Field' growing beside them.

BELOW The nodding deep pink flowers of *Cyclamen coum* are good companions for double snowdrops (*Galanthus nivalis* 'Flore Pleno') because of their synchronized flowering time in early spring and their roughly equal height. In suitable undisturbed ground, such as under deciduous trees, both plants will naturalize and mingle into a carpet of pink and white. You can speed up the process by splitting the clumps of snowdrops while the leaves are still green, and sprinkling the cyclamen seeds. The *Crocus tommasinianus*, seen here in bud, naturalize well without help.

ABOVE White foxgloves add a vertical accent to the horizontal sprawl of heavy-headed peonies, *Paeonia lactiflora* 'Ballerina'.

ABOVE At the height of summer, old fashioned pink roses (*Rosa* 'Mary Rose' with paler pink *Rosa* 'Gruss an Aachen'), are surmounted by foxgloves, and underplanted with sweet williams in colours from cerise extending to white with a pink 'eye'. Together they make a harmonious combination, with the three plants contributing a range of pinks. The foxgloves here are cultivated hybrids that have flowers arranged all round the stems.

113

Pinks, Blues and Violets

Midsummer offers the gardener the widest possible choice of flowering plants. It is also the season when scented plants come into their own, since most need warmth to release their fragrance. A cool planting of harmonizing muted pinks, blues, and violets is the perfect antidote to the heat of summer. And when the colours are repeated along a lengthy garden feature, a calming colour rhythm is established.

LEFT TOP Annual cosmos in deep pink through pale pink to white, with self-seeding violet-blue campanula and long-flowering *Viola cornuta* make a harmonious drift of summer colour.

LEFT CENTRE Dark pink foxglove flowers with spotted paler pink throats make perfect companions for the climbing *Rosa* 'Blairii Number Two' in which the colour becomes paler towards the outer edges of the flowers. Clambering through the rose – that also provides it with a cool root-run – is violet-blue *Clematis* 'Lasurstern' which harmonizes with the foxgloves and roses.

LEFT BOTTOM This subtle harmony is partly fortuitous because the colours of the mixed biennial sweet williams could not be predicted when they were planted out, and it was pure luck that the poppy (*Papaver somniferum*) seeded itself here where it combines so well with the pinky-blue perennial *Penstemon heterophyllus* and the silver foliage of *Artemisia* 'Powis Castle'.

RIGHT Clumps of blue catmint (*Nepeta* 'Six Hills Giant') have been planted at regular intervals along a path beneath a wooden pergola. They are interspersed with lower-growing mounds of violet-blue and white *Viola cornuta*. The tall delphiniums, planted outside the pergola so that they benefit from more sun, pick up a similar blue colour. Different roses and clematis in a variety of pinks clothe the pergola and contribute to the rhythm of the colour. (Full planting details of this scheme are given on page 176.)

Strong Pinks and Blues

Clear, strong pink is an exuberant colour, bold and uncompromising, and almost as strong as magenta. It is at its best in the company of blue which brings out its essential blueness.

If this rich harmony is to your taste, you can enjoy it in your garden from spring through to autumn. Begin the season with naturalized corms and bulbs such as dark pink cyclamen, partnered with the cool blue of *Scilla siberica*. A little later, you can enjoy vivid pink anemones and rhododendrons, introduced on the edge of woodland to coincide with bluebells. As the summer unfolds in your borders, you can partner deep pink roses and geraniums with blue perennials – dark blue delphiniums, anchusa and campanulas. For growing over walls and trellises, try a combination of large-flowered deep pink and violet-blue clematis. At the waterside, you could try clumps of purple loosestrife (*Lythrum salicaria*) in the company of blue *Pontederia cordata*. For autumn colour in the same vein, partner a vivid mauve Michaelmas daisy, such as *Aster novae-angliae* 'Andenken an Alma Pötschke', with late-flowering dark blue monkshood (*Aconitum carmichaelii*).

FACING PAGE: Colour relationships are strongest when companion hues are close in tone. The deep pinks are almost as dark as the blues. Vivid pinks like these are often regarded as 'hot', but they contain a strong ingredient of blue, which places them among the cool pinks.

TOP LEFT In late spring, bluebells (*Hyacinthoides non-scripta*) mingle with the lower branches of a dark pink rhododendron.

TOP CENTRE The perennial wallflower (*Erysimum* 'Bowles' Mauve') will still be flowering long after its blue late spring companions, the forget-me-nots, fade in early summer. To continue the harmony, plant blue annuals such as California bluebell (*Phacelia campanularia*).

TOP RIGHT Coming to their peak in late summer, the graceful flowers of *Dierama pulcherrimum* wave in the slightest breeze, setting up a shimmering association with the blue *Agapanthus campanulatus* nearby.

BOTTOM LEFT The bugloss (*Anchusa* 'Loddon Royalist') has flowers of the most intense blue and they make good companions for the apothecary's rose (*Rosa gallica* var. *officinalis*). The rich pink colour of the rose has plenty of blue in it, but the yellow stamens, reflecting on the petals, make the colour appear warmer than the other pinks on this page.

BOTTOM CENTRE The creeping *Campanula portenschlagiana* will weave through hummocks of *Geranium sanguineum* so that their colours blend together like a piece of rich embroidery.

BOTTOM RIGHT The thistle *Cirsium rivulare* has flowers that match the pink flowers of a bicoloured pink and blue lupin.

ABOVE It is worth the trouble of finding named dark pink varieties of the spring-flowering *Anemone coronaria* for a woodland setting where you can plants drifts of the tubers among naturalized bluebells and wild white wood anemones. Many spring bulbs and perennials originate in woodland, drawing their energy from the sunlight that reaches them before the leaves appear on the trees. In summer, when they are dormant, the trees' canopy protects them from being dried out by the sun.

Magenta, Purples and Maroons

These are some of the darkest colours available to the gardener. They all derive from the crimson reds – colours with at least a touch of blue in them. The blue component may be the merest nuance, as in the flowers of knautia, or it may be the dominant element, as in those of purple salvias. The near-black foliage of plants such as purple basil contain red pigments too, but the redness is tempered by the waxy shine on the leaves that reflects back the blue of the sky. The result is a deep purple colour with ink-black shadows. It is not a good idea to use deep-coloured flowers with dark foliage on a large scale; the result might be too sombre. But in a small area, such as in a container, these rich colours can make a powerful and profound effect.

LEFT Drifts of *Salvia nemorosa* 'Ostfriesland' – violet in the shade and magenta where the sunlight reaches it – are densely planted with other perennials including dusky red *Knautia macedonica,* two penstemons ('Stapleford Gem' and 'Hidcote Pink'), and catmint (*Nepeta* x *faassenii*).

RIGHT ABOVE A terracotta pot of dark burgundy petunias and purple-leaved basil (*Ocimum basilicum purpurascens*) creates a link with the paler magenta flowers of *Geranium* x *riversleaianum* 'Russell Prichard' and *G. sanguineum* beyond.

RIGHT In a section of a graduated colour border, the lupin (*Lupinus* 'Thundercloud') has been selected to make a colour match with the maroon rose (*Rosa* 'William Lobb'). A ribbon of darkest red sweet williams (*Dianthus barbatus* Nigrescens Group) ties the two together and links them with the purple *Salvia nemorosa* 'Lubecca'.

Silver-Greys and Pastels

Combinations of silver and variegated foliage with pastel flowers are harmonious in two distinct ways. First, the grouping of mainly pale colours makes a harmony of tone. Second, the colours are muted in hue, so that they give a harmony of saturation. This harmony on two levels makes the combination especially easy on the eye.

It requires a good eye to put such subtle harmonies together. As far as possible, use light-toned variegated plants or, best of all, silver-leaved plants with pastel flowers. Pink and silver are natural partners. There is a metallic sheen on some pink flowers which underlies their affinity – acknowledged in the name *Verbena* 'Silver Anne'.

You need a structural component to give backbone to such subdued compositions. Strong vertical elements, such as repeated spires of mullein, a tall, bold grey-leaved thistle or, for a more permanent arrangement, an obelisk supporting white sweet peas or a clematis, will help to stabilize informal plantings like these.

ABOVE The roses, *Rosa* 'Mevrouw Nathalie Nypels' and *R. glauca* (towards the back) form the shrubby support of a wide, sunny border, dominated by the spires of white *Verbascum chaixii* 'Album'. The silvery foliage of artemisia and lychnis lightens the effect and binds the composition together. (Full planting details of this scheme are given on page 176)

ABOVE An early autumn flowering bulb, *Amaryllis belladonna*, planted in a sunny border, makes a colour link with the tender perennial *Verbena* 'Silver Anne' in a container in front of it. The darker pink *Verbena* 'Sissinghurst' trails from an adjacent container together with the silver-leaved *Helichrysum petiolare*. White-flowered tobacco (*Nicotiana* x *sanderae*) and argyranthemum daisies lighten the tone. At the back, currently in an interval between flowering, the rose 'Ballerina' will contribute its distinctive bicoloured pink to the scheme.

LEFT Pale apricot foxgloves and a giant thistle provide the vertical element in a border dominated by silvers, whites and pinks. The variegated plants – which include a pittosporum and a grass – reinforce the lightening effect of the artemisias and santolina in the foreground. Roses are limited to white and pale pink. The strongest colours are the lilac-pink alliums that echo the low-growing tussock of thrift beside the brick path. (Full planting details of this scheme are given on page 176.)

Harmonies with Red

Sparks seem to fly when reds, oranges and yellows are concentrated together in the garden. These three colours are adjacent on the colour wheel, and so they harmonize well together, but unlike most other, cooler, harmonies, they are not restful. Instead, by putting together three of the brightest, most intense colours, you increase their vitality and encourage each to 'sing out' at full strength. Hot plantings can be so powerful that they eclipse more subdued ones, so it is best to keep them quite separate from the rest of the garden. For maximum impact, place a pair of hot borders within a hedged or walled enclosure. The effect will be all the more startling to your visitors when they come unexpectedly upon it.

Foliage has an important part to play in hot plantings. The dusky foliage of red-leaved varieties of berberis, cotinus, acer or corylus will 'tone down' a hot planting and make the colours less strident. Bear in mind, though, that these 'red' foliage colours are very dark. Too much dark foliage can make the garden gloomy. You can lighten the overall effect by mixing in some yellow-green foliage, such as 'golden' grasses and bamboos.

Hot colours look best soon after dawn or before sunset in the flattering warm light of low sun. By coincidence, perennials that lend themselves to hot plantings flower predominantly in late summer when the sun is relatively low in the sky all day. You can put together flame-coloured dahlias, kniphofias and crocosmias, with yellow rudbeckias and golden rod, to make a fiery late-season display that will meld into the fireworks of autumn foliage.

RIGHT An inspirational planting, in which drifts of bright yellow rudbeckias, bidens and perennial sunflowers lighten the scene and prevent the dark red flowers and foliage from dominating and making it gloomy. The balance of the planting is so clever, with the scarlet dahlias and lobelias limited to quite small accents of colour whereas the looser, brighter yellows have been allowed to spread out into more open drifts. Although most of these hot-flowered plants are sunlovers, these borders are shaded at the beginning and end of the day. You might expect this to make the plants slightly 'leggy' as they tend to stretch to reach the light. To compensate, they have been carefully supported here, but so discreetly that there is not a cane or a twig to be seen. (Full planting details of this scheme are given on page 177.)

LEFT *Crocosmia* 'Lucifer' adds its scarlet flames to the foreground of a hot planting, with the more orange *Crocosmia masoniorum* towards the back. A pale orange daylily (*Hemerocallis fulva* 'Green Kwanso') separates two true lilies – the apricot-orange *Lilium* African Queen Group and the bright yellow *L.* Citronella Group. Behind the lilies is the yellow-green foliage of *Cornus alba* 'Aurea'.

Russet Reds and Yellows

BELOW Evening sunlight burnishes the colours of a planting on the edge of a rivulet. The light catches the yellow spires of ligularia and mimulus, and the tall flowerheads of Candelabra primulas. It polishes foliage of hostas and the metallic yellow-tinged autumn fern (*Dryopteris erythrosora*) and brings up the copper highlights of the red-leaved acers and prunus at the far end. (Full planting details of this scheme are given on page178.)

In late spring, many perennials have new foliage that has a yellow-bronze cast. At the same time, the strengthening light picks out the bare cinnamon-coloured stems and bark of shrubs and trees. Later in the year, evening sunlight bathes the garden in a warm yellow glow. You can build on these natural colour effects by choosing plants within the limited range of yellows, oranges, rust-browns, and reds to make warm colour harmonies.

'Red' shrubs look especially good in early summer when red-leaved prunus, berberis, acer and cotinus have the colour and translucence of malt or dark toffee. This dark foliage makes an effective backing for light yellow Candelabra primulas or orange wallflowers. Yellow-green foliage is useful too in this context. You can introduce yellow-leaved valerian, golden feverfew or golden grasses to make a link with the yellow flowers of trollius or potentilla.

BELOW Early morning sunlight casts a unifying mellow glow over a harmonious spring scene. The russet reds and yellows include euphorbia with fox-red foliage and orange flowers, rusty orange wallflowers and tulips, yellow trollius and, in the distance, yellow azaleas. Golden feverfew fills the odd patch of bare ground. (Full planting details of this scheme are given on page 178.)

FAR LEFT A bearded iris (*I.* 'Kent Pride') makes a clever colour association with its neighbour, *Verbascum* 'Cotswold Queen'.

LEFT The rusty brown stems of *Euphorbia griffithii* 'Dixter' have infiltrated bulbs of yellow *Erythronium* 'Pagoda'. In a close planting like this, the stronger partner – here the euphorbia – will need occasional judicious dividing to prevent it from crowding out its companions.

CONTRASTS

Contrasts in the garden are stimulating. They happen when colours are paired in such a way that each intensifies the other. You can achieve contrasts in several ways, depending on how dramatic an effect you want. To create bright, strong schemes, combine fully saturated colours and those that are at the extremes of light and dark. To make more subtle, quieter contrasts, use more muted colours and keep the tonal contrasts more subdued.

The strongest colour contrasts of all are the result of putting together complementary colours – that is, those colours opposite each other on the colour wheel (see page 15): red with green, blue with orange, and yellow with violet. Variations on these three combinations can produce less obvious contrasts such as plum-red with grey-green, or pale blue with apricot, or creamy yellow with lilac. In general, it is better to keep colour contrasts simple, sticking to a single pair of contrasting colours throughout a particular area of the garden. Several colour contrasts together can be confusing.

Contrasts of light and dark (tone) can be used in much the same way. The backdrop of a dark yew hedge, for example, will make contrasting white and silver plants seem even lighter and brighter. In the garden shown here, the strongest tonal contrasts are made by the dark purple-red prunus hedge setting off the lighter pink roses and irises planted in front of it. More subtly, the light grey-green mounds of santolina and artemisia are juxtaposed with dark red berberis and pittosporum.

Colour temperature also plays a role in colour associations. It can have a major effect when two closely related colours, one warm and one relatively cool, are planted together. Hot orange and cool pink, for example, can have a jarring effect on each other. Shocking contrasts like this can be deliberately used as arresting incidents within a larger, more soothing framework. Gentler effects occur when differences in colour temperature are used to heighten the difference between two colours. In the garden shown here, the colours derived from red – the pinks and purple-reds – are made to to look warm by contrast with the relative coolness of the grey-greens.

RIGHT Contrasts of colour, tone and temperature are all present in this subtle scheme. The mounds of berberis and the prunus hedge are muted red, in contrast with the grey foliage of artemisias, santolina and stachys, which are unsaturated versions of green. The reds are dark in tone and warm in temperature, and they make the silver-greens seem lighter and cooler by comparison. (Full planting details of this scheme are given on page 179.)

Reds and Greens

Red and green make one of the strongest colour contrasts, not only because the two are complementary colours but also because they are very close in tone, and this emphasizes their colour difference. In the garden, red flowers are usually seen against a backdrop of green foliage, so part of the drama of an all-red planting comes from the red and green contrast. This is why red-flowered climbers, such as *Tropaeolum speciosum,* look so striking when grown into green-leaved shrubs or hedges.

In spring, scarlet tulips look brightest when they are seen against a background of bright green foliage, such as a box hedge. Autumn is the season when red and green contrast comes into its own. Red berries ripen against the foliage of evergreen hollies, pyracanthas and cotoneasters. Deciduous trees, like acers, turn red while their neighbours, such as conifers, stay green. You can take a cue from nature by growing evergreens alongside plants with foliage that turns red in autumn. It is a good idea, for example, to grow ivy among Virginia creeper against a house. Through the summer the ivy leaves are invisible among those of the creeper, but in autumn, when the creeper turns red, the contrast against the evergreen ivy makes the red all the more intense.

ABOVE *Tropaeolum speciosum* is useful for brightening up dark evergreen hedges and topiary shapes. It climbs well through yew because the yew has so many small stems and leaves for its tendrils to grasp.

ABOVE A multiple planting in terracotta pots of *Pelargonium* 'Paul Crampel' with the tender perennial *Verbena peruviana* and *Petunia* 'Red Joy' all of matching scarlet flower colour. The colour and material of the containers make a connection with the brick background, while the colour contrast between flowers and foliage is a good match for the red and black patterns of the brickwork.

ABOVE For the longest lasting autumn effects, it is a good idea to plant climbers that will change colour at slightly different times. Here a *Vitis coignetiae* is turning colour early. Its redness is made more pronounced by the contrast with the green of its companion Virginia creeper (*Parthenocissus quinquefolia*) which is yet to turn.

RIGHT The autumn foliage colour of maples looks most intense when they are interplanted with evergreens, such as these *Pinus parviflora*, growing between two varieties of *Acer palmatum*. It is often striking, too, how green the grass of lawns looks in autumn. This is not only because the grass grows long and lush in mild damp weather; it is also the effect of contrast with the surrounding autumn tints.

Muted Reds and Grey-Greens

Combining plants with flowers or foliage that are muted, unsaturated versions of red and green creates subtle contrasts. If you choose reds that are either very dark or so pale that they become pink, the intensity of the red is reduced and will make a less startling contrast than, for example, a bright vermilion when seen against adjacent green foliage. To make a corresponding reduction in the strength of green, you can choose plants with grey-green or 'silver' foliage.

Foliage combinations of plum red and grey-green are particularly beautiful. They incorporate the complementary contrast of red and green in an understated form, but tonal differences also come into play. The leaves of some cotinus and prunus are very dark in tone, for example, and look almost black against silver foliage.

Pink flowers are the perfect accessories for this foliage combination. Pink is half-way between plum and silver – you can imagine that a mixture of plum and silver paints would give you a metallic pink. The pink flowers of verbenas, diascias and some roses have a sheen that reflects the light almost like metal, and so these flowers look especially appropriate with silver foliage.

BELOW One of the best small trees with plum foliage is the *Cercis canadensis* 'Forest Pansy', seen here against a grey-green background of *Artemisia ludoviciana* 'Silver Queen' and a dwarf pampas grass, *Cortaderia selloana* 'Pumila'. The stronger, green contrast in the foreground comes from foliage of broom and *Helianthus salicifolius*.

ABOVE If you cut the smokebush *Cotinus coggygria* 'Royal Purple' right back in early spring, its new growth will have larger leaves, closer to the ground, so they will be better partners for silver-leaved *Artemisia ludoviciana*.

ABOVE Stems of the lightly-variegated *Berberis thunbergii* 'Rose Glow' reach up into the overhanging branches of the silver pear (*Pyrus salicifolia* 'Pendula'). The pear might need trimming to prevent it becoming dominant.

RIGHT Rex begonias with large purple- or pink-tinged leaves take centre stage in a stone container. They are accompanied by two clovers – the dark, four-leaved *Trifolium repens* 'Purpurascens Quadrifolium' and lighter-coloured *Trifolium repens* 'Harlequin' – a spiderwort (*Tradescantia* 'Zebrina'), *Stachys citrina*, and hare's tail grass *(Lagurus ovatus)* with fluffy flower heads. This rich planting is a small-scale study in unsaturated reds and grey-greens.

BELOW At the front of a midsummer border of muted reds and greens are the black cherry colours of sweet william (*Dianthus barbatus* Nigrescens Group*)*, snapdragons (*Antirrhinum* 'Black Prince'), a black-leaved beet (*Beta vulgaris* 'Bull's Blood') and *Atriplex hortenis* var. *rubra*. These colours are echoed by the purple-leaved berberis (*B. thunbergii* 'Red Chief') at the top right. Warm pinks come from the rose ('Pink Perpétué') towards the top left, pink valerian (*Centranthus ruber*) on the left, foxgloves (*Digitalis* x *mertonensis*) in the centre, and *Diascia rigescens* towards the right. Greens range from the foliage of the meadowsweet (*Filipendula rubra*) on the left to that of the variegated figwort (*Scrophularia auriculata* 'Variegata') on the right.

Oranges and Blues

Orange is one of the most vibrant colours in the gardener's palette. Seen alongside blue, which is its complementary colour, it is all the more intense. Orange and blue combinations are not for the faint-hearted. They bring a brassy exuberance to the border and the colour effect carries a long way. If you feel that a massed planting of orange and blue is too strong for you, you could try a more restrained approach by using spot plantings of orange to animate an expanse of blue. For spring you could enjoy the sight of orange wallflowers above a haze of forget-me-nots, or orange tulips pushing through a mass of purple-leaved bugle. For summer, individual bulbs of orange lilies, planted among clumps of blue perennial aconitums or delphiniums, or with annuals such as echium or clary, will bring the blue flowers to life and intensify their colour by contrast. Reversing the proportions may not be so effective. The impact of a mass of orange flowers may swamp a scattering of blue flowers among them.

ABOVE The orange turkscap flowers of *Lilium henryi* hang from a long arching stem above a massed planting of the annual blue clary (*Salvia viridis* 'Blue Beard') whose colour comes from long-lasting bracts around the tiny flowers. Unlike many lilies, this one prefers alkaline soil, and it will increase each year once it is established.

ABOVE A theatrical planting is dominated by the blue backdrop of a *Ceanothus* 'Cascade' trained against the back wall and echoed by the blue-grey brickwork of the path. The flashes of bright orange wallfowers in the wings bring the scene to life. They lead the eye to the standard *Cordyline australis*, underplanted with the perennial wallflower (*Erysimum* 'Bowles' Mauve') and the tender daisy-flowered *Osteospermum caulescens*, all planted in a container made from a baker's cast-iron dough mixing bowl. Training a ceanothus against a wall ensures it some protection over winter.

ABOVE A rim of blue and violet-blue flowers, composed mainly of violas (*V. cornuta* and *V.* 'Maggie Mott') and a clump of *Veronica austriaca* 'Crater Lake Blue', edges a collection of orange flowers round a stone trough. These include *Anthemis sancti-johannis, Inula orientalis,* the dark orange hawkweed (*Pilosella aurantiaca*) which has flowers like a dandelion, *Geum* 'Fire Opal' and *G.* 'Prince of Orange', with double-flowered *Meconopsis cambrica* var. *florepleno* in the foreground. The anthemis flowers intermittently all summer, but the other plants have a relatively short flowering season. To extend the effect, you could supplement them with annuals. For orange, try Californian poppies, marigolds, and nasturtiums; for blue try *Echium* 'Blue Bedder', *Nigella damascena* 'Miss Jekyll' and *Salvia farinacea* 'Victoria'.

TOP An orange rock rose (*Helianthemum nummularium*) provides a shrubby mound of colour for the creeping lilac-blue *Campanula poscharskyana* to thread its way through. Both plants like sunny, well-drained soil, and will thrive in the cracks between the stones in a terrace garden.

ABOVE In spring, elegant orange species tulip and orange wallflowers grow through purple-leaved *Ajuga reptans* 'Atropurpurea'.

Oranges and Blue-Green

You can moderate the contrast between complementary colours orange and blue by using muted versions of one or both. There are many plants, like irises and achilleas, whose foliage has just a hint of blue – enough to provide a gentle contrast with neighbouring orange flowers. In the planting *right*, care has been taken with the shapes and sizes of the blocks of colour. The brilliant orange wallflowers need a large expanse of blue-green iris foliage to balance them. The more diffused orange of the euphorbias looks most effective in a large drift, whereas the sharp stab of colour of the tulips works best in compact clumps.

For muted orange colours you could use bronze foliage varieties of phormiums or cordylines. Trees with orange-brown bark such as *Acer griseum* and arbutus are also enhancing companions for blue flowers.

RIGHT This colour scheme suits a garden in full sun, not only because wallflowers, irises, and achilleas thrive in this situation, but also because the hot colours, orange, red, and yellow, look brightest in sunshine. In a few weeks' time the scene will change completely: the vivid blue-green of the iris and achillea foliage will be eclipsed by their own flowers, and by orange, red, and yellow lilies, daylilies, and dahlias. (Full details of this scheme are given on page 179.)

BELOW The 'red' cabbage (*Brassica* 'Scarlett O'Hara') in this planting of vegetables among flowers is actually distinctly blue with purple veining. More blue comes from the petunias and sea lavender (*Limonium latifolium*). The upright *Solanum pyracanthum* has orange spines that echo the colour of the French marigold (*Tagetes* 'Tangerine Gem'), and together they 'lift' the blues, increasing their blueness by contrast and lightening up the composition.

Yellows and Violets

Yellow and violet plant associations create intense contrasts both of colour and of tone. Nature herself exploits these in bicoloured flowers, particularly irises and violets. Yellow and violet are complementary colours and also, since violets tend to be darker than yellows, violet flowers make yellow companions appear lighter. This means that in associations such as the primroses and violets seen below right, the primroses will seem to dominate the violets because their colour is much brighter. The yellow colour is also warmer and so catches the eye more than the recessive, cooler colour of the violets. To make the colours balance, you would need many more violets than primroses.

Schemes based on yellows and violets are particularly appealing, and can be carried through the garden for most of the year. They are especially successful in spring when yellow prevails both in flowers and in the yellowish tinge of the fresh new foliage of trees and shrubs. Spring brings yellow crocuses and miniature narcissi; these could be combined with violet dwarf irises and *Anemone blanda*. Forsythia, corylopsis or broom would add another layer of yellow or yellow-green above them. Later in the spring the choice of plants widens and includes a range of yellow tulips, Imperial fritillaries, and yellow-green euphorbias that could be teamed with violet alpine clematis. In a sunnier situation, yellow cowslips could be combined with aubrieta. In early summer there is scope to extend this scheme with bearded irises, which are available in both yellow and violet varieties. You could grow both together, or else underplant violet ones with yellow *Allium moly*, or with Welsh poppies.

ABOVE The pale yellow stripes of *Iris pallida* 'Variegata' draw the eye to the violet flowers of the *Anemone blanda* at their feet. Both plants have been allowed to spread in an area of dappled shade. This early spring partnership between horizontal and vertical accents of colour is a risk, because the iris would prefer full sunlight in summer, and the anemone full shade. Although this iris, which has pale blue flowers in the summer, may not flower out of the sun, the risk has been worth taking because it has been grown here primarily for its foliage effect.

ABOVE Primroses and violets are natural early spring partners since they frequently appear growing together in the wild. Although they are easily cultivated, they are – like spring-flowering bulbs too – best left to naturalize.

RIGHT Yellow Welsh poppies and *Corydalis lutea* have seeded themselves around violet irises, creating a contrast of complementaries. The new foliage of the ginkgo tree picks up the yellow theme, while its sparse branches allow the irises to get the sun they need. Further back, the faded blue of the forget-me-nots makes them seem more distant than they really are. The silvery buds of *Nectaroscordum siculum* are about to open into rusty green flowers, and the *Clematis montana* in the background has just come into bloom.

Yellows and Warm Violets

Warm violets – those with a tinge of red – come in all tints and shades from palest pink-lilac to strong purple-violet. They all combine well with yellows, but the gentlest associations occur when cream or pale yellow flowers are teamed with the soft violet colours of plants such as wisteria, lilac, lavender, or buddleja. These colours come into their own in the summer. Hanging yellow racemes of laburnum with lilac alliums would make a stunning start to the season, which might finish in the autumn with lilac Michaelmas daisies and pale yellow dahlias. This is a colour combination, too, that lends itself to massed plantings of annuals and tender perennials.

LEFT The sun of late evening can change the appearance of pale yellows and soft violets, making the yellows more yellow and the violets more pink. Under the laburnum tunnel, the true lilac colour of the *Allium aflatunense* is only seen in the shade. Their flowerheads echo the shapes of the box globes, which the slanting rays of the sun have lit up, giving them yellow rims that link up with the laburnum flowers above them. The setting sun also catches the delicate-looking creamy spires of *Tellima grandiflora*. Deeply shaded (but receiving dappled light earlier in the day) *Hosta sieboldiana* var. *elegans* contributes a bluish cast to the foliage colours.

RIGHT ABOVE The loose, frothy flowerheads of x *Solidaster luteus* 'Lemore' create a haze of pale yellow beneath the more sharply-defined flowers of the *Buddleja davidii* 'Glasnevin'.

RIGHT BELOW In a formal massed planting of long-lasting annuals, warm violet *Verbena rigida* contrasts with pale yellow snapdragons. The topiary bird of golden yew (*Taxus baccata* 'Aurea'), contributes a sharper yellow contrast, but its curves and right angles are reflected in the shapes of the box-edged beds.

Yellows and Blues

Yellows and blues make potent and popular colour contrasts. Although not exactly opposite each other on the colour wheel, they behave as if they were true complementaries, each enhancing the other. They act together like light and shade. Yellow is bright and prominent; blut is comparatively dim and withdrawn.

Given the wide range of blues and yellows in flowers and foliage, it is possible to use the blue-yellow contrast through the seasons and across all plant groups. In spring you can use yellow narcissi and tulips, accompanied by blue scillas, chionodoxas and forget-me-nots. As summer progresses you can bring in yellow roses, lupins and verbascums and partner them with blue delphiniums, catmint, and salvias. In autumn you can pair yellow rudbeckias and kirengeshoma with late aconitums and blue asters. Even in winter you can keep the blue-yellow theme alive with the foliage of 'blue' cedars and spruces combined with yellow-leaved evergreens.

RIGHT This yellow and blue border is one of a pair that are planned to make a sumptuous show for about six weeks in summer. The yellows range from bright lysimachias, heleniums and French marigolds to pale verbascums, evening primrose and the poached egg flower (*Limnanthes douglasii*) which has white flowers with yellow centres. Soft yellow is also present in the lime-greens of tobacco flowers and *Alchemilla mollis*. Delphiniums and catmint are the dominant blues, with blue-violet erigerons and ageratums nearer the front. This border is labour-intensive, with annuals used to fill spaces between permanent plantings of perennials. The plants are graded for height and carefully staked when necessary. (Full planting details of this scheme are given on page 180.)

RIGHT Creamy yellow *Lupinus* 'Chandelier' with *Iris orientalis, Verbascum* 'Gainsborough' and *Rosa* 'Graham Thomas' of similar hues, are set off well by dark blue delphiniums and aconitums and the paler violet-blue *Nepeta* 'Six Hills Giant'.

BELOW LEFT Pale blue *Veronica gentianoides* accompanies bright yellow doronicums in an early summer planting. Reaching about 45cm (18in), this veronica is usually grown at the front of a border. It is daring to break convention and plant it among the taller doronicums, which create a frame through which the shorter flowers can be seen.

BELOW RIGHT The elegant *Narcissus* 'Hawera' surrounded by a haze of blue forget-me-nots, accompanies double yellow tulips. This blue and yellow spring display anticipates the colour theme of a summer-flowering herbaceous border.

Lime-Greens and Blues

The yellow that you see in some foliage and in the bracts surrounding euphorbia flowers is sharp and acidic, like the colour of limes. It is a colour that is seen in abundance in spring and early summer, when the newly-emerged leaves of many shrubs and trees are tinged with yellow; later in the year foliage yellows tend to lose their sparkle and become drab. Use blue spring bulbs like hyacinths, scillas and grape hyacinths to enhance the sharp yellow of spring foliage and euphorbia flowerheads. Later, blue summer-flowering plants, such as anchusa, campanula, delphinium and nigella make good companions for the yellow leaves of 'golden' maples, robinia and gleditsia. The yellow-leaved forms of yew, philadelphus or physocarpus would also make good backdrops of yellow foliage.

An audacious and very effective variation on the blue with lime-yellow scheme involves introducing blue as paintwork on garden structures and furniture, and using lime-green foliage in the plantings around them. A dark blue painted metalwork arbour, rose arch, or wooden trellis screen, can look fabulous draped with yellow ivy or golden hop. Dark blue ornate metal gates with euphorbias and golden grasses around the gateposts make an inviting overture to a garden. Blue can also be a relatively unobtrusive and restful colour to paint your garden furniture.

LEFT Boldly painted bright blue, a Lutyens bench looks superb in the company of the lime yellow flowerheads of *Euphorbia characias* subsp. *wulfenii*. The blue of the bench also harmonizes with the forget-me-nots alongside. The blue and yellow theme will be extended into summer when the rosette of felty grey leaves of *Verbascum bombyciferum* puts out spikes of yellow flowers.

ABOVE A clump of dark blue *Delphinium* Black Knight Group is effective against a backdrop of the Japanese maple, *Acer shirasawanum* 'Aureum'. This sharp yellow foliage holds its colour well, but the maple is very slow-growing. For quicker-growing yellow trees, consider *Robinia pseudoacacia* 'Frisia' or *Gleditsia triacanthos* 'Sunburst.' Grown in a border with perennials, these two will need to be kept within bounds by careful pruning.

ABOVE Self-seeded *Nigella damascena* 'Miss Jekyll' grows through the vines of the golden hop (*Humulus lupulus* 'Aureus') accompanied by New Zealand flax (*Phormium cookianum* 'Cream Delight') and the variegated *Euonymus fortunei* 'Silver Queen'. This hop has foliage of a beautiful colour early in the season, but needs to be kept in check as it is something of a horticultural thug that can overwhelm its neighbours. Restricted to its own section of wall, fence or trellis, it will make a yellow-green curtain during the course of one summer.

Scarlet, Pink and Orange Shocks

You often see startling combinations of colour in paintings, textile design and fashion, but only rarely in gardens and then often as accidents. Blue-pink with vermilion, magenta with orange – these are colours that react together so shockingly that their effect is often described as a 'clash'. This pejorative word can obscure the fact that colour shocks do sometimes have a place in the garden. They are the equivalent of the clash of cymbals in a symphony – a vital element of the music, but one that makes the audience wake from slumber or jump with astonishment.

Colour shocks occur between colours that are quite close together both in hue and tone, such as pink and red, or pink and orange. They share a common ingredient – red, and thus might be expected to harmonize. The reaction between them has to do with the cooling blue content of the pink, and the warming yellow content of the red or orange. So, when you look at the two colours together, the conflicting messages of harmony and contrast can be disturbing to the eye. This is exacerbated when there is little or no foliage to dilute or neutralize the flower colour.

The pleasure (or pain) that colour shocks can give depends very much upon the context and the light conditions in which they are seen. Shocking schemes might be appropriate in a public park that is the setting for games and entertainment, but would be out of place in a private garden intended for repose. Shocking contrasts look wonderful in the intense light of the tropics, but can seem too strong in the pallid light of temperate regions.

Some of the most effective colour shocks can be created among single-colour plantings. Try pink or magenta in a red border to make you jump, or shocking scarlet in a pink border to shake off any any feelings of calm and sweetness that the pinks may induce. Generally, shocking contrasts are best used as isolated incidents to enliven a planting and to prevent it from becoming predictable. They should be like a clap of hands in a silent room; sudden, short and surrounded by silence.

LEFT A cascade of exuberant colour has been created by planting the climbing rose 'Dorothy Perkins' with *Tropaeolum speciosum*.

FACING PAGE: Each picture contains its own colour shock: seen together the four have a cumulatively arresting effect.
TOP LEFT The dark pink spires of purple loosestrife (*Lythrum salicaria*) are seen against a drift of mottled yellow and orange *Helenium autumnale*. The loosestrife grows in boggy soil while the helenium favours the well-drained conditions of a slightly higher patch of ground.
TOP RIGHT The strength of the colour shocks that deciduous azaleas can produce together, or in combination with other flowering plants – here wild bluebells – is even greater due to their almost complete lack of neutral green foliage at flowering time in late spring.
BOTTOM LEFT The annual verbenas – the scarlet 'Nero' and the pink 'Cleopatra' – provide long-lasting colour in summer bedding schemes. For similar effects with perennial verbenas, choose red 'Lawrence Johnston' with pink 'Sissinghurst'.
BOTTOM RIGHT For a spring scheme of bold colour shocks, you can plant double orange tulips with mixed pink and scarlet *Bellis perennis*.

Autumn Colour Shocks

When leaves turn and berries ripen in late summer and autumn, nature takes a stronger hand in controlling garden colour and may overturn some of your carefully planned colour schemes. Bright scarlet berries, vivid orange and yellow leaves and the strong pink of autumn-flowering colchicums and cyclamen can dominate parts of the garden that were previously devoted to totally different colours. This can result in some surprising juxtapositions and happy accidents.

These colour partnerships can be mildly shocking, but are somehow acceptable, even to those who normally prefer more muted effects. Maybe it is because we take delight in seeing the same natural colour changes in our gardens that we enjoy in the parks and woods outside. Maybe, too, it is because the sun is low in the sky in the autumn, and bathes everything in a uniform warm yellow light, touching each colour and having a softening influence on even the strongest contrasts.

ABOVE Scarlet and magenta petunias in a terracotta container extend nature's autumnal contrasts. The magenta petunia shown here is one of the new Surfinia Hybrids, grown for their intensity of colour, prolific flowering and their trailing habit.

ABOVE RIGHT The scarlet berries of *Arum italicum* subsp. *italicum* 'Marmoratum' make a rich combination with the deep pink autumn-flowering *Colchicum speciosum*.

RIGHT Mellow pink *Sedum* 'Herbstfreude' creates a vibrant colour combination for the autumn with violet-flowered *Verbena rigida*.

ABOVE Autumn-flowering *Cyclamen hederifolium* combines with the fallen leaves of *Parrotia persica* to make an unexpected bold colour marriage. For a similar effect plant the cyclamen under maples or fothergillas which also have red and yellow autumn foliage.

RIGHT Shrubs in a mixed border, like this *Acer palmatum* var. *dissectum*, evergreen *Ligustrum ovalifolium* 'Aureum', *Euphorbia griffithii,* and dark-leaved *Cotinus coggygria* 'Royal Purple', give a backbone of foliage interest. This contributes dazzling colour changes through late summer and autumn, setting up vivid new colour partnerships with the dark pinks of Michaelmas daisies and the last lingering flowers of a purple heliotrope (*Heliotropium* 'Marine'), and the purple sage (*Salvia officinalis* Purpurascens Group). The gentle autumnal light softens what might otherwise be harsh colour contrasts.

Blacks and Whites

Putting light and dark plants together in the garden creates contrasts of tone. The greatest possible tonal contrast would be between the two extremes, black and white, but you rarely see these pure colours in nature. 'Black' flowers or foliage have a hint of red or purple in them that makes them lighter in tone than pure black. White flowers often have coloured centres, and a hint of green: the effect of this is to make them seem darker in tone than pure white.

Tonal contrasts that are nearly black and white are pleasing to the eye because the limitation of colour makes their relationship relatively ordered and formal. Black and white combinations in the garden are striking and smart, just as they are in formal dress.

As with pairs of complementary colours on the colour wheel, black and white enhance each other, the black bringing out the 'whiteness' of the white, and vice versa. You could plant 'black' tulips with artemisias or cardoons, for instance, to emphasize the lightness of their silvery foliage. On the other hand you would make a purple-leaved cotinus, hazel or berberis look all the darker by growing a white climber through it, such as a clematis or a sweet pea.

You can easily incorporate the architecture of your garden and its furniture into a black and white scheme. Use a white wall as a backdrop for black hollyhocks, or train a white clematis through a black-painted wrought-iron fence or gate.

BELOW The white flowers of *Cornus florida* make an intense tonal contrast with the black tree trunks that recede into the woodland beyond. The risers of the steps are black-stained railway sleepers which echo the tree trunks and make a horizontal feature that balances the vertical one. *Berberis thunbergii* 'Atropurpurea Nana' makes a bold dark-toned shape in the foreground.

RIGHT A perennial sweet pea (*Lathyrus latifolius* 'Albus') clambers through *Berberis* x *ottawensis* f. *purpurea* making the deep purple foliage appear even darker.

BELOW Purple *Salvia officinalis* Purpurascens Group makes an excellent two-toned underplanting for clumps of 'Queen of Night' tulips and the light-toned young foliage of *Cynara cardunculus*. A vegetable garden might normally be thought of as home to the cardoon and sage, but they can make an attractive foliage contribution to the flower garden.

LEFT Variegated grass (*Holcus mollis* 'Albovariegatus') with purple clover (*Trifolium repens* 'Purpurascens Quadrifolium'), *Sedum sieboldii* 'Mediovariegatum', and the oval seedheads of *Tulipa tarda*, make a striking black and white combination in early summer.

Violets, Blues and White

White flowers give the lightest and brightest colour in the garden, violets some of the darkest. Planted together, the white flowers will make the coloured ones seem even darker than they really are. This is because the white stimulates the eye to see a contrasting dark tone beside it that reinforces any dark colour that really is there. So when you look at any colour relationship involving white, the first thing that strikes you, subliminally, is the strong tonal contrast. Any subtle relationships within a scheme can simply be overpowered.

Besides exaggerating tonal differences, white has an invigorating effect on dark colours. The best way to see this effect is to imagine the plantings on these pages without the white flowers. Take them away, and the violets and blues would sink into gloom, the dark flowers merging with the dark foliage. The overall effect would be much more sombre. Restore the whites, and the colour schemes are instantly lighter and more cheerful, with highlights that draw the eye. You could create a lighter scheme without whites by using lighter colours overall, such as pale lilac clematis and light blue petunias, but the result would be totally different. Such a scheme would be harmonious and restful on the eye, but would lack the energy that the contrast with white creates. Besides, you would be passing up the chance to use the rich and velvety hues of pure blues and violets.

LEFT The late summer-flowering *Clematis viticella* covers a wall beside a white door. This tonal contrast is taken up in a stronger form by violet and white petunias. There is a secondary and unplanned link between the *Corydalis lutea* which has seeded itself in the dry stone wall at the front and the yellow-variegated ivy (*Hedera helix* 'Oro di Bogliasco') on the back wall.

LEFT In spring, the dark violet-blue groundcover made by *Ajuga reptans* is lightened with white lily-of-the-valley (*Convallaria majalis*). Both moisture-loving plants are invasive, but are equally matched, so one will not swamp the other.

RIGHT Blue *Clematis* 'Prince Charles' flowers at the same time as mock orange (*Philadelphus* 'Belle Etoile'). Growing clematis through shrubs is a good way to introduce colour after the shrubs have finished flowering.

RIGHT This richly-planted midsummer scheme of white, violets, and blues consists of hardy perennials – *Geranium* 'Johnson's Blue', paler violet-blue *Viola cornuta* and sea lavender (*Limonium latifolium*), with the tender white marguerite (*Argyranthemum foeniculum*); annuals – bright violet-blue clary (*Salvia viridis*) and deep blue *Delphinium grandiflorum;* together with the grey-leaved shrub, *Santolina chamaecyparissus.* It takes great gardening skill to make such a planting look natural and effortless.

MIXED COLOURS

Gardens filled with myriad colours are the result either of highly sophisticated planning or no planning at all. To take the first approach, you can orchestrate colours to achieve a complex symphony of colour. For instance, you could lay out a border across the full spectrum of colours to make a rainbow effect. Another ambitious approach would be to combine two separate harmonizing plantings that together create a contrast: a harmony of yellows, creams and lime-greens, for example, could be intermixed with an opposing harmony of blues, blue-violets and even blue-pinks. Associations like these look colourful but remain controlled. The colour palette is broad but it still excludes certain colours, in this case reds and oranges. Alternatively, a judicious sprinkling of the 'wrong' colours in an otherwise harmonious planting – a few bright red or yellow flowers, for example, among soft violets and pinks – will add zest and a welcome element of surprise. But even this needs control.

At the other extreme is the *laissez-faire* approach of the cottage gardener. Here, all colour is welcome, the more the merrier. The effect can be exhilarating, but it is worth analysing the reasons why. First, whereas the exuberance is thrilling on a small scale, it could become tiresome and even disturbing over a large area. Second, by virtue of its rural location, the traditional cottage garden merges with its natural surroundings, its colourful plantings contiguous with the random colours of the natural vegetation around them. In an urban or suburban context cottage garden colour is less convincing. When a garden is surrounded by a formal grid of buildings, a structured use of colour is more appropriate, with repetitions of simple blocks of colour, for instance, to echo the background.

RIGHT At first glance, this cottage garden looks like an explosion of random colour, in which all the colour conventions have been ignored. But although a wide range of colours has been used, the liberal use of white, the cooling green surroundings and, most especially, the repetition of colours and shapes transforms what might have been a haphazard arrangement into a rhythmical pattern. This quality makes the eye accept the broken conventions, such as the partnering of a salmon-pink poppy with a blue-pink geranium. (Full planting details of this scheme are given on page 180.)

Blues and Pinks with Yellow

LEFT Clumps of delphiniums and geraniums make a harmonious thread of blues, lilacs and pinks, which weaves together these long double borders. There is a contrasting weft of yellows, provided by the tall cephalarias and thalictrums, with repeated patches of bright yellow *Anthemis tinctoria* along the front. Some gardeners might have chosen the paler yellow *Anthemis tinctoria* 'E.C. Buxton', which would make a softer impact with the bright pink geraniums, but then some of the exuberance would be lost. (Full planting details of this scheme are given on page 181.)

Mixing a harmonious planting with a contrasting one is an ambitious undertaking, but can be very successful, especially in a large garden. The overall energy of such a combination can override the occasional unhappy juxtaposition of colour.

For a long border, start with the colour blue, achieved by repeated plantings of, for example, delphiniums or agapanthus. Next, think of blue as part of a harmony with pinks and violets, and make repeated plantings of these colours, using perhaps alliums or lupins. Finally, treat the blue as part of a blue and yellow contrast and put together a series of yellow flowers or foliage – achillea or potentilla are possibilities – to partner it. In the double border *below*, the yellow-green hedges provide the yellow component. The harmony and contrast combination is comfortable as long as the yellows butt up against blues, violets and even lilac. But a strong yellow combined with a strong pink makes an energetic colour 'shock'.

ABOVE Faced with the problem of planting double borders between existing yellow-green hedges of holly and yew, the designer composed a harmonizing scheme of cool pinks and blues and blue-green foliage. The predominant blue bias of the borders sets up a contrast with the yellowness of the hedges, and this gives an energizing tension to the design. (Full planting details of this scheme are given on page 181.)

ABOVE Understated splashes of yellow from lime-green tobacco flowers and euphorbias introduce touches of contrast to an otherwise harmonious planting of blue-green, silver, pink and magenta. Only the clump of deep red sweet williams breaks the gentle transitions between the colours. Note how the patina of the copper container makes a link with the predominantly blue-green foliage around it. (Full planting details of this scheme are given on page 182.)

Deep Pinks, Blues and Violets with Yellows

A harmonious theme of pinks, mauves, violets, and grey-blues – of roses, delphiniums, ornamental onions, sweet peas – is the common thread linking the three plantings here. Woven through these predominantly dark, cool harmonies is a secondary contrasting theme of pale yellow, lime-green, and creamy white. By acting as a subtle contrast, the yellows enhance the blues and violets of the main colour scheme. They also lighten the plantings, making them less sombre than they would be without them.

Beware of introducing too much yellow to a cool colour scheme, however. Large drifts of strong yellow would set up a sense of conflict, and the cooler colours could easily be overpowered. To counteract this effect, use pale, unsaturated tints of yellow as in some of the varieties of verbascum or marguerites, or choose flowers in which the colour is dispersed in small dots, such as dill. Or use variegated foliage in which the yellow is a mere suggestion.

RIGHT ABOVE Sweet peas, restricted to mixtures of mauves and violets, scramble across the corner of a border planted with yellow *Achillea filipendulina* 'Gold Plate', dill (*Anethum graveolens*), creamy yellow *Anthemis tinctoria* 'E.C.Buxton', Shasta daisies (*Leucanthemum* x *superbum*), a yellow daylily (*Hemerocallis* 'Stella de Oro') and angelica (*Angelica archangelica*).

RIGHT Compared with the dense dollops of deep-pink of the rose 'Charles de Mills' and the violet-blue of the delphiniums, the pale yellows of the *Nepeta govaniana* on the right, *Verbascum* 'Gainsborough' on the left, and iris foliage (*Iris pallida* 'Variegata') are diffuse and understated. Blue *Eryngium alpinum* and pink *Penstemon* 'Evelyn' help to disperse the dense colours.

157

Blues and Violets with Red and Yellow

BELOW In this apparently informal garden, plants have been carefully chosen to make diaphanous pastel clouds. Dots of bright red salvia, smoky red knautia and clear yellow Welsh poppies and *Allium moly* add spice to the colour without breaking up the overall harmony. (Full planting details of this scheme are given on page 183.)

Imagine the two gardens shown here stripped of their red and yellow flowers. They would still be beautiful plantings – perfect harmonies of blues, violets, lilacs, and whites. But they would have lost an important element – that slight agitation supplied by the red and yellow that pre-

vents the eye settling on the harmonious colours and becoming too relaxed.

However, when you add contrasts to harmonies, you need to be careful. Here, the contrasting colours are used quite differently from the harmonizing ones. The harmonious plants are grown in relatively

dense drifts and patches of colour, each melding into the next, or into an equally solid patch of green. The red and yellow flowers, on the other hand, are used as separate dots and splashes of colour. They are present as a suggestion of contrast, not as lead players in the overall scheme. In the border *opposite*, the yellow Welsh poppies, red salvias, and deeper red knautia add just

a few touches of sharp contrast to the ethereal haze of blue and violet.

To achieve this, you have to have a good eye and a knowledge of which plants produce scattered, less densely-packed flowers. Then plant them as highlights in a border, rather than in solid blocks or drifts so that they make their contribution without becoming overwhelming.

BELOW The pastel pinks, violets and blues flow through this cottage garden border like a meandering stream. Crimson peonies, and yellow Welsh poppies bob about on the surface and energize the otherwise placid effect. In such an informal scheme, you can allow the aquilegias and geraniums to cross and self-seed, pulling out any colours that do not fit in. (Full planting details of this scheme are given on page 183.)

Greens and Yellows with Pink

In the plantings shown here, the greens make a framework for flowers in a single hue of pink. But these borders rely for their effect chiefly upon tonal contrasts, the highlights provided by yellows. In the informal border *below*, there is a satisfying rhythm of contrasting light and dark set up by the deep purple foliage of the *Atriplex hortensis* var. *rubra*, the pale cream variegated leaves of the physostegia and the cream flowers of the santolina. There are also more subtle tonal contrasts between the dark green and the grey-green foliage. In the more formal garden *opposite*, the tonal contrasts come chiefly from the garden's foliage backbone. If you shape box into globes and spirals, and choose dome-shaped plants like sedum, their effect is to create patterns of highlight and shadow, even when the sun is not shining. These tonal contrasts are the equivalent of the dark and light foliage contrasts in the other planting.

RIGHT The tonal contrasts created by light falling on the box shapes add an extra dimension to the colour contrast between two plantings of pink and yellow-orange. (Full planting details of this scheme are given on page 184.)

BELOW Clumps of purple-leaved *Atriplex hortensis* var. *rubra* grow between mallows and a lupin with matching pink flowers. Variegated phlox, physostegia and santolina flowers give a contrasting note of pale yellow. (Full planting details of this scheme are given on page 184.)

Pinks and Yellows with White

Pink and yellow can make an uncomfortable partnership because they set up a tension between warmth and coolness. They are two of the most common flower colours, so it is often difficult to avoid using them together. But there are ways you can minimize the discord between the two, and even turn it to your advantage.

If you are using flowers of a saturated yellow, use them in small quantities relative to the amount of pink; otherwise the yellow, being a stronger colour, will overpower the pink. Another way to reduce the tension between the two colours is to limit the use of yellow to pale, unsaturated tints. A third technique is to create a buffer of white, silver, or green to keep the colours apart. Silver foliage is good in this respect as it makes a good partner for both yellow and pink. You can also exploit the natural buffer in particular flowers, such as yellow-centred daisies fringed with white.

BELOW A sunny summer border is dominated by pink roses – the deep cerise English rose 'Chianti', vivid pink 'De Rescht' at its foot, and pink and white striped *Rosa gallica* 'Versicolor', grown here as standards. The pink flowers outnumber those of the strong yellow *Phlomis fruticosa*, preventing its highly saturated colour from becoming overpowering. The white rose 'Yvonne Rabier' and white foxgloves act to keep the two colours apart, and even the white stripes of the *Rosa gallica* 'Versicolor' contribute to the effect.

RIGHT The potential impact of the egg yolk yellow centres of the flowers of the daisy *Anthemis tinctoria* 'Alba' is neutralized by the surrounding white rays, so that the flowers combine peaceably with even the strongest of pinks. Here a perennial pea (*Lathyrus grandiflorus*) scrambles through a clump of the daisies, and their colours combine with impunity.

BELOW Between espaliered apples and a box hedge, a cottage garden planting offers a mellow cornucopia of colour in late summer. In the foreground are the muted yellow flowers and amber buds of *Crocosmia* 'Golden Fleece' in front of pink, red, and white annual cosmos. Further back, *Penstemon* 'Chester Scarlet' grows with orange nasturtium, white tobacco (*Nicotiana x sanderae),* white campanula and white *Dahlia* 'My Love'. Beyond, pink *Rudbeckia* 'Brilliant Star' mixes with pink and white tobacco, and the taller white *Nicotiana sylvestris*. The all-embracing presence of green and the white flowers prevent the riot of colour from becoming overwhelming.

Lime-Green with Blues, Violets and Deep Red

Violet and yellow are complementary colours, and so they form the basis of one of the main contrasting schemes available to the gardener. You can elaborate on this pair of colours – or on other complementary pairs – by thinking of each colour as the centre of a harmonizing planting. You could use the violet as a starting point for harmonizing pockets of blues, violets and crimsons. Next you base a yellow scheme around the lime-greens of foliage plants. Put the two plantings together, and where they meet they will make a strong contrast.

This is a colour scheme that can work throughout the spring and summer. Start the season with contrasting yellow and purple tulips, and with blue forget-me-nots, all planted in the spaces between perennials, among shrubs with lime-green foliage, so that when the bulbs are going over the perennials are ready to take their place. Fill any gaps with annuals, such as blue cornflowers and magenta cosmos, so that these will be ready to take over when the earlier perennials, such as anchusas, and geraniums start to go over. One attraction of this successional scheme is the subtle change in dominant colour over the season.

ABOVE AND RIGHT Two views of the same border: in the early summer, *above*, the blue and violet theme is taken up by alliums, anchusas, iris and geraniums. Weaving through them is a thread of lime-green, provided by foliage of golden hop, robinia and philadelphus. (Full planting details of this scheme are given on page 184.) Later in summer, *right, Clematis* 'Perle d'Azur' makes a lavender-blue backdrop, with the contrasting robinia and philadelphus meeting in front of it. A swathe of blue annual cornflowers mingles with the deep smoky red flowers of perennial *Knautia macedonica* at the front.

Red and Yellow with Cream and Purple

Bright red flowers always stand out in the garden. Red roses and poppies attract attention like warning flags. One way to make them less dominant is to partner them with strong yellows and oranges so that they become equal partners in 'hot' plantings. But a more subtle approach, as seen in the plantings shown here, is to use the red as a basis for colour harmonies with unsaturated versions of the hot colours. Yellow appears throughout these plantings, but in a muted form – diluted with white in the cream-coloured flowers, or with green in the lime-greens. Red itself reverberates through the muted reds and purples of the foliage.

The brilliant reds of the roses and poppies harmonize with the muted yellows and reds of the accompanying flowers and foliage. But there is an extra dimension in this relationship. The pale yellows are very light in tone, and the reds and purples of foliage are very dark. Together they make a powerful contrast of tone, which is almost the equivalent of black and white. This strong tonal contrast, submerged within the colour harmony, helps to draw the eye away from the intensity of the red flowers, and creates a balanced composition.

The most sophisticated use of colour in the garden, whether achieved by instinct or artifice, depends on establishing a balance between saturated and unsaturated colours, and between light and dark tones. The principles that underlie the plantings shown here could be extended to other colour schemes. You could replace the red roses or poppies with brilliant blue delphiniums, and surround them with muted versions of harmonizing colours such as deepest mauves and purples, with light pinks and pale blues for tonal contrast.

RIGHT Deep red poppies (*Papaver orientale* 'Beauty of Livermere') peer through a thicket of honesty (*Lunaria annua*), whose ripening seedheads have a touch of purple in them, echoed in the *Salvia officinalis* Purpurascens Group towards the bottom. These three plants make a muted harmony of blue-red and purple, which contrasts with the other plants, all of which are variants on a theme of yellow. The muted yellow leaves of *Lonicera nitida* 'Baggesen's Gold' at the back, *Limnanthes douglasii,* wispy Bowles' golden grass (*Milium effusum* 'Aureum') and wallflowers, all bring lightness to the scheme as well as a contrast with the purple.

OPPOSITE The deep scarlet rose 'Frensham' repeated at intervals, sets a high note in a border at midsummer. Without it, this planting would be dominated by the tonal contrast between white *Clematis recta*, pale cream *Sisyrinchium striatum*, lime-green *Alchemilla mollis,* and fluffy white *Aruncus dioicus* 'Kneiffii', and the dark purple-red foliage of *Lysimachia ciliata* 'Firecracker' and the almost black sweet williams *Dianthus barbatus* Nigrescens Group. You might expect the rose to make this border a 'hot' one, but it is cooled down by the creamy yellow flowers and the silver foliage of *Artemisia* 'Powis Castle'. White and deep orange lilies (*Lilium regale* and *L. henryi,* seen here in bud), the trumpet-shaped flowers of *Phygelius aequalis* 'Yellow Trumpet' and *P.* x *rectus* 'African Queen', and the lime-green foliage of *Symphoricarpos orbiculatus* 'Foliis Variegatis' will carry the colour theme through into early autumn.

ABOVE In early summer, the pale yellow flowers of a tree lupin (*Lupinus arboreus*) radiate light and make a link with the hint of yellow in the iris, whose cool lilac-pink colour also harmonizes with the *Geranium* 'Johnson's Blue'. The grey-green foliage of both lupin and iris contributes to the overall subtlety of the scheme. To maintain this planting you would need to keep the lupin in check by judicious pruning to prevent it shading the iris and geranium, both of which need sun.

Yellows and Creams with Muted Reds

When you put together muted, unsaturated colours, the resulting harmonies or contrasts are likely to be low-key too. It can be very effective to use muted colours almost exclusively, both in flowers and foliage, with occasional strong hues for emphasis. This way, you are likely to have success even when mixing contrasts with harmonies.

The plantings shown on these pages all employ red that is so unsaturated that it is difficult to recognize that it is red at all. 'Queen of Night' tulips certainly have a hint of red in them, but they are so deep that they are usually described as purple, or even black. Similarly, the irises, seen *left*, are such a subtle mixture of hues, from dark pink, through lilac, to pale yellow, that their relationship to red is tenuous. By contrast, the yellows shown here are all recognizably yellow although most of them are unsaturated too, apart from the bright, saturated yellow 'West Point' tulips. The yellow of the tree lupin, *left*, and wallflowers, *right*, is lightened with white, which makes them primrose melding into cream. On the other hand, the yellow of the robinia foliage, *right*, is slightly darkened with an overlay of green. This gives the colour a slightly acid quality, and spices up its relationship with its muted red foliage companion.

When you use unsaturated yellow or red foliage, remember that the yellow is always light in tone and will always have a lightening effect in the garden, while the red – even if it has patterns of pink variegation, like 'Rose Glow' berberis – is almost always dark in tone, and will make the garden darker. If you use a lot of trees and shrubs with red foliage, you might find that you need to 'lift' the tone with some light yellow-green or grey foliage.

ABOVE There is a subtle balance between the muted foliage colours of the yellow-green *Robinia pseudoacacia* 'Frisia', the pink-variegated berberis (*B. thunbergii* 'Rose Glow') and the greyish-green Jerusalem sage (*Phlomis fruticosa*), seen here in early autumn. In summer the flowers of the phlomis will add brilliant yellow highlights to the composition.

RIGHT These late spring-flowering tulips, the yellow lily-flowered 'West Point' and the near-black 'Queen of Night' create light and shade in a border, even on a dull day. In fact these tulips, together with primrose-yellow wallflowers, have been planted in a heavily shaded spot. The shade has made them grow taller and lean towards the light. You can treat bulbs and annuals in this way as they can be dug up after flowering and the bulbs replanted somewhere more favourable for next year. But generally, successful colour in the garden, especially with perennials and shrubs, depends upon plants receiving the correct amount of light for them to thrive.

Note how the fence behind this border has been stained deep green, so that it creates a dark and muted backdrop. Imagine how intrusive it would be if it had remained the chestnut-brown of the raw wood.

Winter Schemes

Many gardeners are content to leave winter colour for nature to resolve, and you will have no choice if your climate serves up constant snow and ice. In milder regions, though, you can plan for winter colour. As well as useful evergreens, you can exploit the little incidents of colour that winter brings – vividly coloured tree bark, for example, the sparse but sweetly-scented flowers of a winter-flowering shrub, sheets of winter aconites or clumps of early crocus. You can also create striking effects by massed plantings of evergreen grass with repeated sprays of red- stemmed dogwoods or white-stemmed brambles. If you do not have the space or the inclination to make a special winter planting, then garden for colour in a more passive way. Resist the urge to tidy up in the autumn and when frost and snow settle on the shapes of brown and gray and dark green (which are prrobably all that remain of your colourful summer borders), they will be transformed into subtle confections of silvers, cold whites and blue-greens.

LEFT ABOVE The broad, floppy leaves of *Bergenia cordifolia* turn crimson in cold weather, making a colour connection with the pink heather (*Erica x darleyensis* 'Furzey'). The bare stems of the dogwood (*Cornus alba* 'Sibirica') give vivid flashes of red against the predominantly yellow-variegated foliage of the large-leaved ivy (*Hedera colchica* 'Sulphur Heart'). This in turn makes an effective groundcover as it clambers among plants, filling the spaces between them.

LEFT The evergreen *Viburnum tinus* 'Eve Price' begins flowering in late autumn and produces flowers through any mild interludes in winter. Here the viburnum is underplanted with *Bergenia cordifolia*, whose pink flowers pick up the colour of the viburnum buds in spring.

ABOVE The bare white stems of *Rubus biflorus* make a shapely network that catches the low winter light. The whiteness comes from a thin layer of 'bloom' on the stems. Behind it is *Viburnum* x *bodnantense* 'Dawn' which produces pink flowers on bare stems through the late winter and early spring. Grasses are a great asset in the winter garden. Here, the evergreen grass, *Stipa arundinacea*, turns a russet colour in winter, giving off a warming glow in sunlight.

RIGHT The pepperpot seedheads of *Phlomis russeliana* collect a layer of hoarfrost that transmutes them into out-of-season flowers unknown to science. The same dusting of frost adds pallor to the dark pink flowerheads of *Sedum* 'Herbstfreude'. Even the browns and yellows of decaying stems and leaves contribute to their colour. If you wait until spring before tidying your borders, the dead perennial material acts like a blanket to protect the living roots below ground.

Keylines of Major Plantings

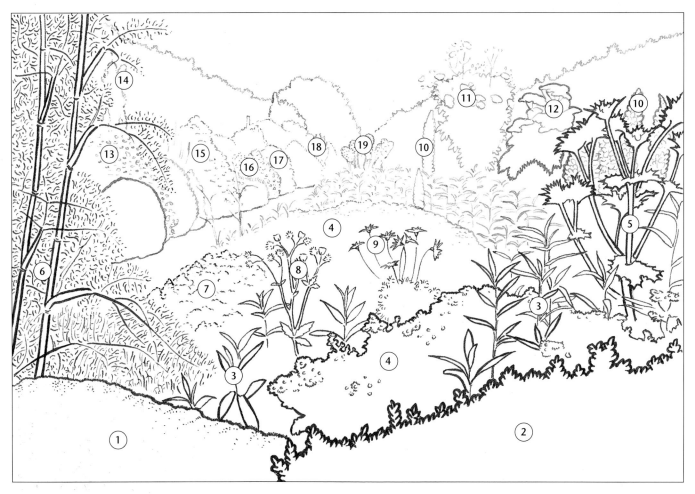

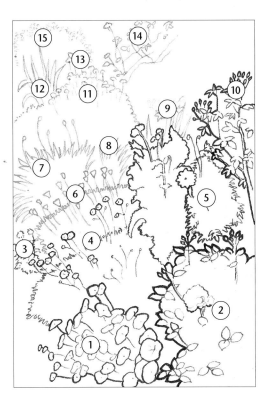

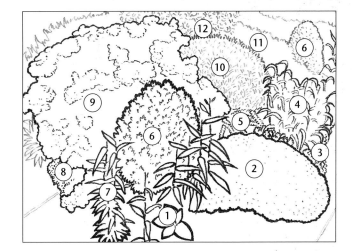

LEFT PAGE 46

1 *Beta* (Ruby Chard)
2 *Nicotiana* x *sanderae*
3 *Pelargonium* 'Lord Bute'
4 *Aeonium* 'Zwartkop'
5 *Beta*
6 *Verbena* 'Lawrence Johnston'
7 *Begonia* x *tuberhybrida*
8 *Iresine herbstii*
9 *Penstemon* 'Schoenholzeri'
10 *Monarda* 'Mrs Perry'
11 *Sedum telephium* subsp. *maximum* 'Atropurpureum'
12 *Dahlia* 'Bishop of Llandaff'
13 *Dahlia* 'Blaisdon Red'
14 *Ricinus communis* 'Carmencita'
15 *Dahlia* 'Anchor Light'
16 *Cotinus coggygria* 'Notcutt's Variety'
17 *Berberis* x *interposita* 'Wallich's Purple'
18 *Corylus maxima* 'Purpurea'
19 *Vitis coignetiae*

LEFT PAGE 47

1 *Tropaeolum majus* with *Geum* 'Mrs J. Bradshaw'
2 *Rosa* 'Lilli Marlene'
3 *Dianthus barbatus* Nigrescens Group
4 *Geum* 'Mrs J. Bradshaw'
5 *Dahlia* 'Bishop of Llandaff'
6 *Arctotis* x *hybrida* 'Flame'
7 *Agapanthus* foliage
8 *Crocosmia* 'Lucifer' (foliage)
9 *Lilium* 'Enchantment'
10 *Rosa* 'William Lobb' (in bud)
11 *Lychnis chalcedonica*
12 *Phormium tenax*
13 *Papaver somniferum*
14 *Rosa* 'Parkdirektor Riggers'
15 *Ligustrum lucidum* 'Tricolor'

ABOVE PAGE 79

1 *Digitalis purpurea*
2 *Thymus* x *citriodorus* 'Aureus'
3 *Trifolium repens* 'Purpurascens'
4 *Milium effusum* 'Aureum'
5 *Polemonium pauciflorum*
6 *Buxus sempervirens* 'Elegantissima'
7 *Campanula persicifolia alba*
8 *Artemisia schmidtiana*
9 *Euphorbia polychroma*
10 *Lavandula angustifolia*
11 *Artemisia pontica*
12 *Geranium sanguineum*

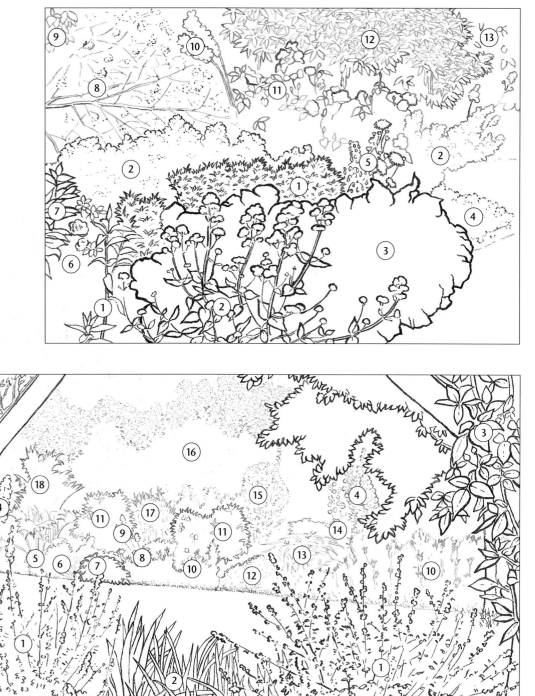

LEFT PAGE 96

1 *Phlox paniculata* 'White Admiral'
2 *Centranthus ruber albus*
3 *Bergenia cordifolia*
4 *Verbena tenuisecta* f. *alba*
5 *Borago officinalis* 'Alba' with *Leucanthemum* 'Esther Read'
6 *Rosa* 'Madame Plantier'
7 *Symphytum* x *uplandicum*
8 *Crambe cordifolia*
9 *Rosa* 'Madame Alfred Carrière' (foliage)
10 *Delphinium* Galahad Group
11 *Rosa* 'Souvenir de St Anne's'
12 *Piptanthus nepalensis*
13 *Aralia cachemirica*

LEFT PAGES 104-105

1 *Nepeta* 'Six Hills Giant'
2 *Iris pallida*
3 *Rosa* 'Veilchenblau'
4 *Delphinium* Pacific Hybrids
5 *Stachys byzantina*
6 *Dianthus*
7 *Salvia officinalis* Purpurascens Group
8 *Campanula persicifolia alba*
9 *Polemonium caeruleum* var. *lacteum*
10 *Eryngium bourgatii* with *Campanula persicifolia*
11 *Phlox paniculata* 'White Admiral' (foliage)
12 *Parahebe catarractae*
13 *Tradescantia* x *andersoniana* 'Osprey'
14 *Anemone* x *hybrida* 'Honorine Jobert' (in bud)
15 *Thalictrum flavum* subsp. *glaucum*
16 *Elaeagnus* 'Quicksilver'
17 *Lysimachia ephemerum* (foliage)
18 *Cynara cardunculus*

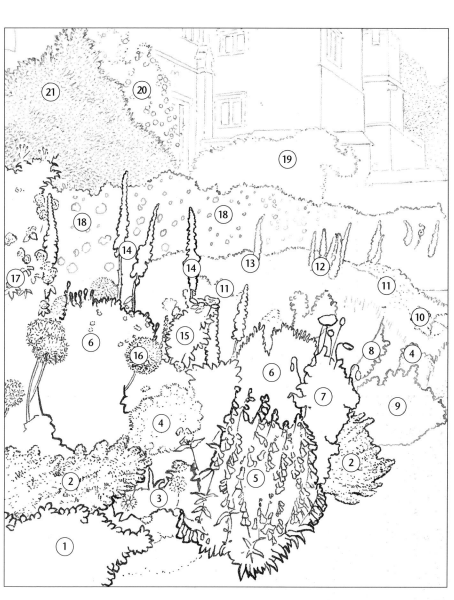

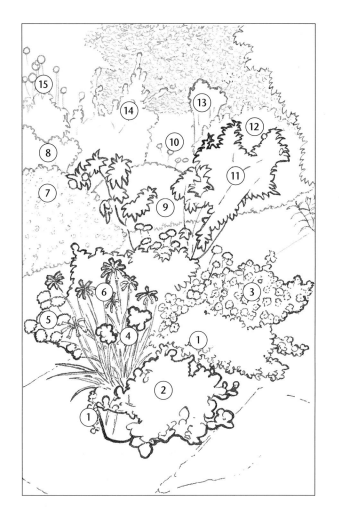

ABOVE **PAGE 107**

1　*Helichrysum petiolare*
2　*Mertensia simplicissima*
3　*Malva sylvestris* 'Primley Blue'
4　*Heliotropium* 'Chatsworth'
5　*Verbena*
6　*Agapanthus* 'Midnight Blue'
7　*Nigella damascena* 'Miss Jekyll'
8　*Geranium pratense* 'Plenum Caeruleum'
9　*Geranium* 'Johnson's Blue' (foliage)
10　*Papaver somniferum*
11　*Solanum rantonnetii*
12　*Salvia pratensis* Haematodes Group
13　*Lathyrus odoratus* 'Noel Sutton'
14　*Delphinium* Pacific Hybrids
15　*Echinops bannaticus* 'Taplow Blue'

ABOVE **PAGE 110**

1　*Lamium maculatum* cv.
2　*Nepeta* x *faassenii*
3　*Centaurea montana carnea*
4　*Dianthus* 'Rainbow Loveliness'
5　*Penstemon* 'Pennington Gem'
6　*Lychnis coronaria* Alba Group
7　*Papaver somniferum*
8　*Penstemon* 'Stapleford Gem'
9　*Lamium maculatum* cv.
10　*Penstemon* 'Garnet'
11　*Tanacetum parthenium* 'Plenum'
12　*Digitalis purpurea* f. *albiflora*
13　*Digitalis purpurea*
14　*Digitalis purpurea* 'Sutton's Apricot'
15　*Rosa* 'Magenta'
16　*Allium christophii*
17　*Rosa* 'Pink Prosperity'
18　*Rosa* 'Felicia'
19　*Rosa banksiae* 'Lutea' with *Fallopia baldschuanica*
20　*Rosa* 'François Juranville'
21　*Ceanothus impressus* (foliage)

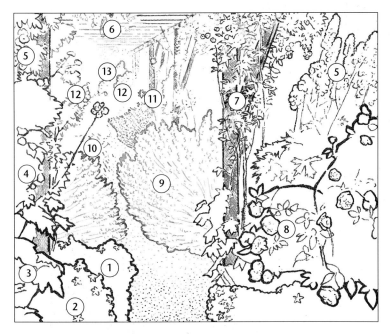

LEFT PAGES 114-115

1 *Viola cornuta*
2 *Viola cornuta* Alba Group
3 *Anemone* x *hybrida* (foliage)
4 *Rosa* 'Commandant Beaurepaire'
5 *Delphinium* Pacific Hybrids
6 *Rosa* 'Violette'
7 *Rosa* 'Veilchenblau'
8 *Rosa* 'Comte de Chambord'
9 *Nepeta* 'Six Hills Giant'
10 *Anthemis punctata* subsp. *cupaniana*
11 *Clematis* 'Bees' Jubilee'
12 *Rosa* 'Ballerina'
13 *Rosa* 'Penelope'

ABOVE PAGE 120

1 *Rosa* 'The Fairy'
2 *Penstemon* 'Apple Blossom' (in bud)
3 *Artemisia ludoviciana*
4 *Origanum laevigatum* 'Hopleys'
5 *Artemisia abrotanum*
6 *Rosa* 'Mevrouw Nathalie Nypels'
7 *Papaver somniferum*
8 *Malva moschata alba*
9 *Verbascum chaixii* 'Album'
10 *Rosa glauca*
11 *Lychnis coronaria* Oculata Group
12 *Lavatera* 'Barnsley'
13 *Spiraea* x *billiardii*

ABOVE PAGE 121

1 *Rosa* 'White Meidiland'
2 *Santolina pinnata* subsp. *neapolitana*
3 *Artemisia arborescens*
4 *Allium nigrum*
5 *Rosa* 'Boule de Neige'
6 *Hosta* 'Francee'
7 *Buxus*
8 *Onopordum nervosum*
9 *Armeria maritima*
10 *Acanthus mollis*
11 *Miscanthus sinensis* 'Variegatus'
12 *Digitalis purpurea* Foxy Hybrids
13 *Alchemilla mollis*
14 *Helichrysum italicum*
15 *Artemisia* 'Powis Castle'
16 *Allium aflatunense* 'Purple Sensation'
17 *Delphinium* x *belladonna* 'Casa Blanca' (in bud)
18 *Rosa* 'Iceberg'
19 *Thalictrum aquilegiifolium*
20 *Milium effusum* 'Aureum'
21 *Hesperis matronalis* var. *albiflora*
22 *Weigela* 'Praecox Variegata'
23 *Sambucus nigra*
24 *Rosa* 'New Dawn'
25 *Prunus lusitanica* 'Variegata'
26 *Pittosporum tenuifolium* 'Silver Queen'

ABOVE **PAGE 123**

1 *Lilium lancifolium* (foliage)
2 *Rudbeckia fulgida* var. *sullivantii* 'Goldsturm'
3 *Hypericum* x *inodorum* 'Summergold'
4 *Plantago major* 'Rubrifolia'
5 *Tropaeolum majus* 'Hermine Grashoff'
6 *Cuphea ignea*
7 *Hemerocallis* 'Golden Chimes'
8 *Carex comans*
9 *Crocosmia* 'Star of the East'
10 *Arctotis* x *hybrida* 'Flame'

11 *Lobelia* 'Queen Victoria'
12 *Dahlia* 'Bednall Beauty'
13 *Tropaeolum majus* 'Crimson Velvet'
14 *Heuchera micrantha* var. *diversifolia* 'Palace Purple'
15 *Bidens ferulifolia*
16 *Hosta fortunei* var. *aureomarginata*
17 *Crocosmia masoniorum*
18 *Pleioblastus auricomus*
19 *Monarda* 'Cambridge Scarlet'
20 *Salvia elegans* 'Scarlet Pineapple'

21 *Ligularia dentata* 'Desdemona'
22 *Inula hookeri*
23 *Rheum palmatum*
24 *Lobelia* 'Dark Crusader'
25 *Atriplex hortensis* var. *rubra*
26 *Helenium* 'Wyndley'
27 *Ricinus communis* 'Gibsonii'
28 *Lobelia* x *speciosa*
29 *Dahlia* 'Arabian Night'
30 *Crocosmia* 'Vulcan' with
   C. x *crocosmiiflora* 'Lady Hamilton'

31 *Fagus sylvatica* 'Dawyck Purple'
32 *Ligularia* 'The Rocket'
33 *Helianthus* 'Monarch'
34 *Sinacalia tangutica*
35 *Berberis thunbergii* f. *atropurpurea*
36 *Helianthus decapetalus* 'Triomphe de Gand'
37 *Dahlia* 'Bishop of Llandaff'
38 *Colutea* x *media*
39 *Acer platanoides* 'Crimson King'

177

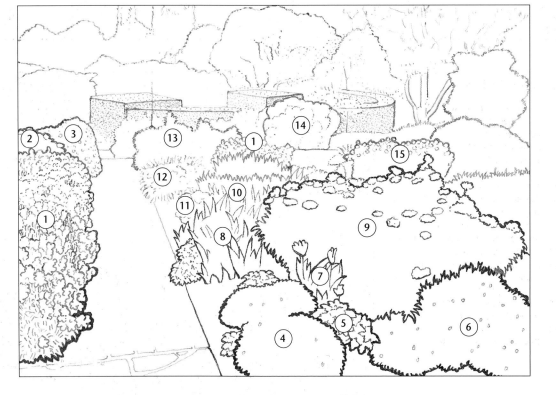

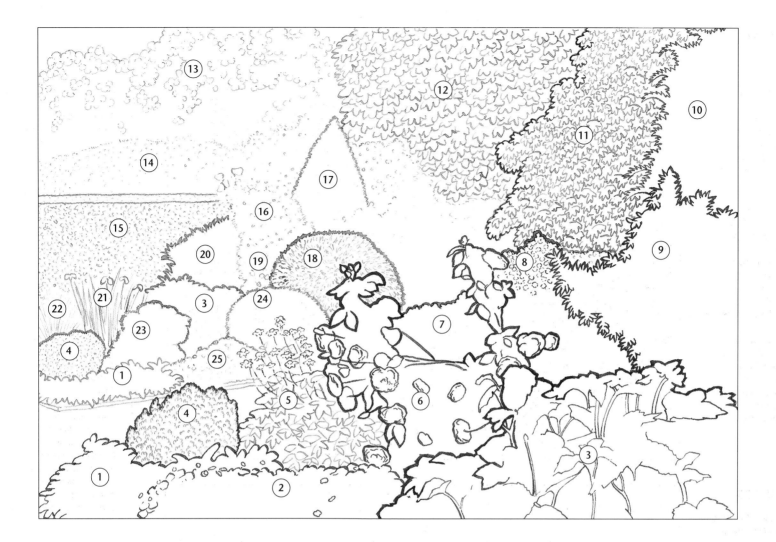

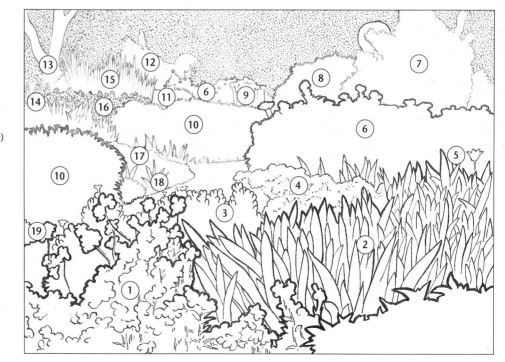

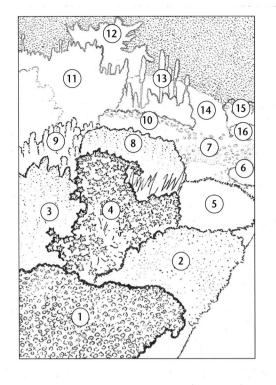

RIGHT **PAGE 140**

1   *Tagetes* 'Lemon Gem'
2   *Limnanthes douglasii*
3   *Nepeta* x *faassenii*
4   *Nicotiana* x *sanderae* 'Lime Green'
5   *Solidago* 'Queenie'
    (syn. 'Golden Thumb')
6   *Alchemilla mollis*
7   *Erigeron* 'Sincerity'
8   *Ageratum* 'Blue Horizon'
9   *Lysimachia punctata*
10 *Helenium* cv.
11 *Verbascum* Harkness Hybrid
12 *Cornus mas* 'Variegata'
13 *Delphinium* 'Blue Nile'
14 *Achillea filipendulina* 'Gold Plate'
15 *Oenothera biennis*
16 *Solidago* 'Goldenmosa'

BELOW **PAGES 152-153**

1   *Rosa* x *alba*
2   *Nigella damascena* 'Miss Jekyll' (in bud)
3   *Campanula latiloba*
4   *Geranium* x *oxonianum* 'Wargrave Pink'
5   *Papaver orientale* 'Mrs Perry'
6   *Digitalis purpurea*
7   *Dianthus barbatus*
8   *Nepeta* 'Six Hills Giant'
9   *Helianthemum* 'Fire Dragon'
10 *Campanula punctata*
11 *Helianthemum* 'Rhodanthe Carneum'
12 *Anthemis punctata* subsp. *cupaniana*
13 *Tanacetum parthenium* 'Aureum'
14 *Gladiolus communis* subsp. *byzantinus*
15 *Geranium* 'Johnson's Blue'
16 *Gladiolus* 'The Bride'

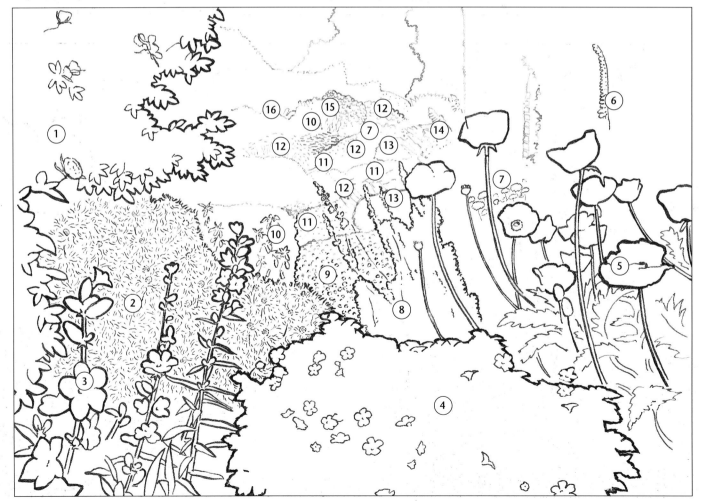

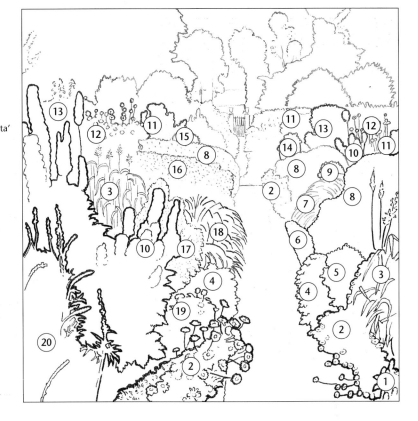

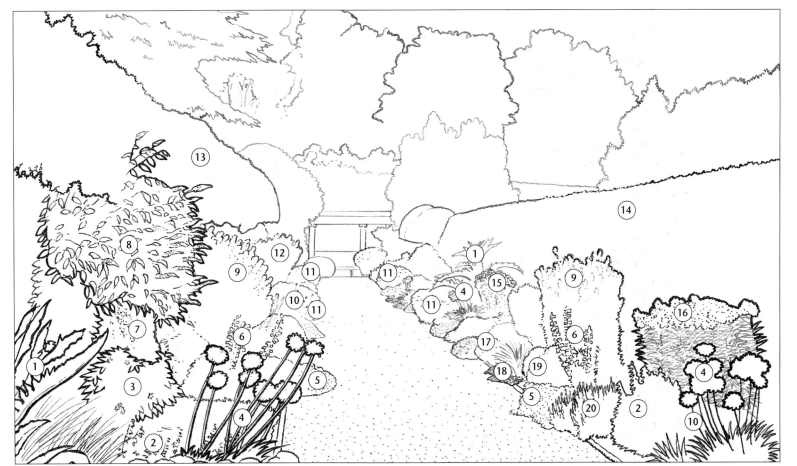

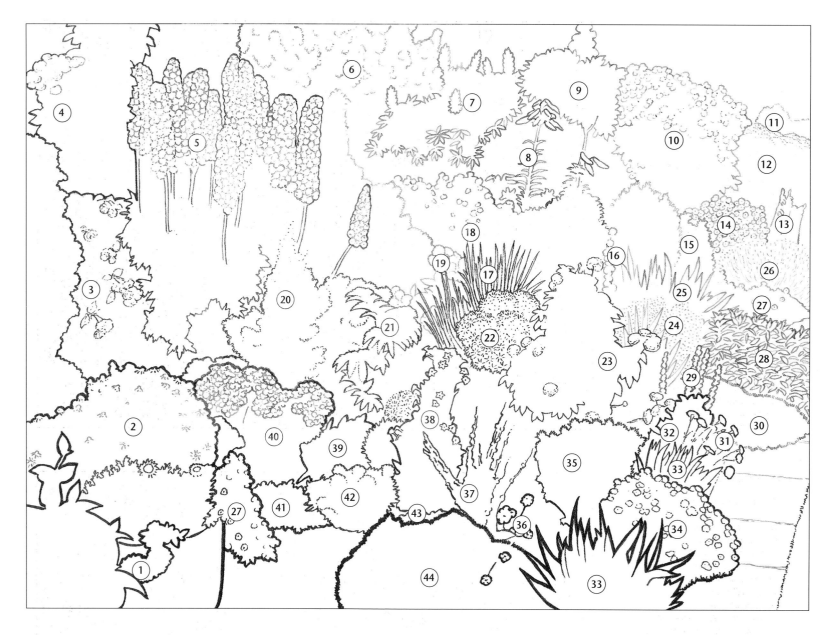

ABOVE **PAGE 156**

1 *Heliotropium* 'Princess Marina'
2 *Argyranthemum* 'Vancouver' and *A. foeniculaceum*
3 *Rosa* 'Madame Lauriol de Barny'
4 *Rosa* 'Constance Spry'
5 *Delphinium* 'Blue Jade'
6 *Campanula lactiflora*
7 *Lupinus* 'Noble Maiden'
8 *Lilium regale*
9 *Rosa* 'May Queen'
10 *Geranium psilostemon*
11 *Alchemilla mollis*
12 *Sedum* 'Herbstfreude'
13 *Penstemon crandallii* subsp. *glabrescens*
14 *Viola* 'Mercury'

15 *Fuchsia magellanica* var. *molinae* Sharpitor'
16 *Campanula latiloba* 'Hidcote Amethyst'
17 *Iris sibirica* 'Ego' (foliage)
18 *Mimulus lewisii*
19 *Rosa* 'Penelope'
20 *Thalictrum delavayi*
21 *Melianthus major*
22 *Allium christophii*
23 *Rosa* 'La Ville de Bruxelles'
24 *Calamintha nepeta* subsp. *nepeta*
25 *Iris* 'Jane Phillips' (foliage)
26 *Crepis incana*
27 *Petunia integrifolia* var. *integrifolia*
28 *Salvia officinalis* Purpurascens Group
29 *Ballota acetabulosa*

30 *Phlox subulata* 'Emerald Cushion Blue' (foliage)
31 *Dianthus* 'Valda Wyatt'
32 *Dahlia* 'Mount Noddy' (foliage)
33 *Iris* (foliage)
34 *Geranium sanguineum* 'Jubilee Pink'
35 *Eryngium bourgatii*
36 *Verbena* 'Sissinghurst'
37 *Salvia argentea*
38 *Nicotiana* x *sanderae* 'Lime Green'
39 *Lobelia fulgens* x *speciosa* (foliage)
40 *Dianthus barbatus* 'Auricula-eyed'
41 *Campanula portenschlagiana*
42 *Euphorbia nicaeensis*
43 *Viola* 'Universal Cream'
44 *Artemisia schmidtiana*

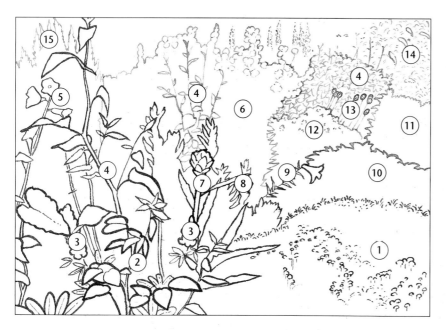

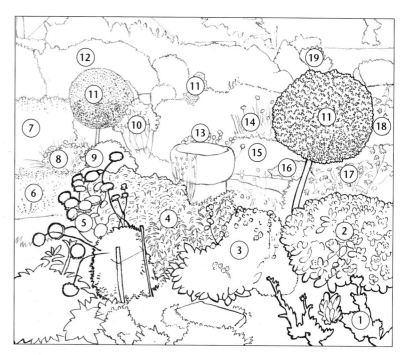

ABOVE PAGE 160

1   *Santolina pinnata* subsp. *neapolitana*
    'Edward Bowles'
2   *Rosa* 'Wife of Bath' (foliage)
3   *Lupinus* 'The Chatelaine'
4   *Atriplex hortensis* var. *rubra*
5   *Lavatera* 'Rosea'
6   *Sidalcea* 'Rose Queen'
7   *Cynara cardunculus* Scolymus
    Group 'Purple Globe'
8   *Physostegia virginiana* 'Variegata'
9   *Lilium* Pink Perfection Group
10 *Chaerophyllum hirsutum* 'Roseum'
    (foliage)
11 *Phlox paniculata* 'Norah Leigh'
12 *Geranium phaeum* (seedling)
13 *Allium sphaerocephalon*
14 *Buddleja davidii* 'Nanho Purple'
15 *Artemisia lactiflora*

ABOVE PAGE 161

1   *Silene compacta*
2   *Sedum telephium*
3   *Lychnis yunnanensis*
4   *Lysimachia clethroides* (foliage)
5   *Pyrethrum*
6   *Myosotis*
7   *Nepeta nuda* 'Rosea'
8   *Allium schoenoprasum*
9   *Sidalcea* 'Loveliness' (foliage)
10 *Aquilegia vulgaris* var. *stellata* (double)
11 *Buxus sempervirens* 'Notata'
12 *Physocarpus opulifolius* 'Luteus'
13 *Armeria alliacea* Formosa Hybrids
14 *Pavaver* spp.
15 *Helianthemum* 'Amy Baring'
16 *Sedum kamtschaticum* 'Variegatum'
17 *Aquilegia vulgaris* var. *stellata* (single)
18 *Aquilegia formosa*
19 *Corylus avellana* 'Aurea'

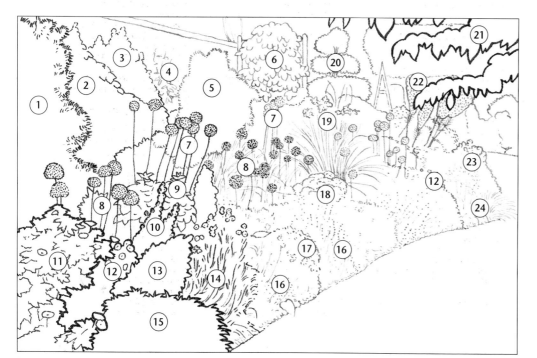

LEFT PAGE 164

1   *Taxus baccata*
2   *Clematis* 'Etoile Violette' (foliage)
3   *Hedera helix* 'Buttercup' and *H.h.* 'Oro di Bogliasco'
4   *Cornus alba* 'Aurea'
5   *Robinia pseudoacacia* 'Frisia'
6   *Humulus lupulus* 'Aureus'
7   *Allium rosenbachianum*
8   *Allium aflatunense* 'Purple Sensation'
9   *Philadephus coronarius* 'Aureus'
10 *Anchusa azurea* 'Loddon Royalist'
11 *Geranium psilostemon*
12 *Geranium* 'Johnson's Blue'
13 *Lunaria annua* 'Alba Variegata'
14 *Erysimum cheiri*
15 *Penstemon heterophyllus* 'Heavenly Blue' (foliage)
16 *Myosotis*
17 *Viola cornuta*
18 *Euphorbia polychroma*
19 *Iris sibirica*
20 *Ilex* x *altaclerensis* 'Lawsoniana'
21 *Cornus controversa*
22 *Euphorbia characias* subsp. *wulfenii*
23 *Geranium* x *magnificum*
24 *Milium effusum* 'Aureum' and *Carex morrowii* 'Variegata'

BIBLIOGRAPHY

Garden Colour

Hobhouse, Penelope *Colour in Your Garden* Collins, London, 1985

Jekyll, Gertrude *Colour Schemes for the Flower Garden* Windward/Frances Lincoln, London, 1992

Jekyll, Gertrude *Wood and Garden. Notes and thoughts, practical and critical, of a working amateur* Longmans, London, 1899, 1981

Keen, Mary *Colour Your Garden. A Portfolio of Inventive Planting Schemes* Conran Octopus, London, 1991

Lacey, Stephen *The Startling Jungle. Colour and Scent in the Romantic Garden* Viking, London and New York, 1986

Verey, Rosemary *Good Planting* Frances Lincoln, London, 1990

Colour for Artists

de Sausmarez, Maurice *Basic Design: The Dynamics of Visual Form* The Herbert Press, London, 1992

Gage, John *Colour and Culture. Practice and Meaning from Antiquity to Abstraction* Thames & Hudson, London, 1993

Homer, William Innes *Seurat and the Science of Painting* The MIT Press, Massachusetts, 1964

Itten, Johannes *The Art of Color* 1961. Reprinted, Van Nostrand Reinhold, New York, 1973

Nicholson, Winifred *Unknown Colour. Paintings, Letters, Writings* Faber & Faber, London, 1987

Wilcox, Michael *Colour Theory. For Artists working in Oil colours or Acrylics* Colour Mixing Ltd., London 1981

Information on Plants

Hillier's Manual of Trees & Shrubs David & Charles Publishing, Devon, 1984

Hobhouse, Penelope *Flower Gardens* Frances Lincoln, London, 1991

Lawson, Andrew *Performance Plants* Frances Lincoln, London, 1992

Phillips, Roger & Martyn Rix *The Pan Garden Plants Series*: *Bulbs* 1981, reprinted 1989; *Perennials*, 2 vols. 1991; *Roses* 1988. Pan, London

RHS Gardeners' Encyclopedia of Plants and Flowers Dorling Kindersley, London, 1989

RHS Plant Finder 1995/6 Edition Moorland Publishing Co. Ltd., Derbyshire, 1995

Thomas, Graham Stuart *Perennial Garden Plants or The Modern Florilegium* Dent, London, 1976, reprinted, 1993.

Miscellaneous

Birren, Faber *Color Psychology and Color Therapy* University Books, New York, 1961

Gregory, R.L. *Eye and Brain. The Psychology of Seeing* Weidenfeld & Nicolson, London, 1990

Jackson, Carole *Color Me Beautiful* Ballantine Books, New York, 1981

L. regale Album Group REGAL LILY 31 [W]102 *167 182 183*
L. speciosum var. *rubrum* [P]59 *59*
L. 'Sterling Star' [W]102
L. x testaceum NANKEEN LILY 40 [O]43 *43*
L. tigrinum 177
lily 24 95 132 134 160 173 179 SEE ALSO *Lilium*
arum, SEE *Zantedeschia aethiopica*
canna, SEE *Canna indica*
daylily, SEE *Hemerocallis*
kaffir, SEE *Schizostylis coccinea*
Peruvian, SEE *Alstroemeria aurea*
plantain, SEE *Hosta*
St Bernard's, SEE *Anthericum liliago*
St Bruno's, SEE *Paradisea liliastrum*
lily-of-the-valley 151 SEE ALSO *Convallaria majalis*
lilyturf SEE *Liriope muscari*
Limonium latifolium SEA LAVENDER [V]69 *134 151*
Limnanthes douglasii POACHED EGG PLANT [Y]35 *140 167 179 180*
Linaria purpurea TOADFLAX [V]68 *183*
Linum perenne PERENNIAL FLAX [B]76
Liquidambar styraciflua [R]50
liquorice plant SEE *Helichrysum petiolare*
Liriope muscari BLUE LILYTURF [V]68 *68*
Lithodora 23
L. diffusa 74
L. d. 'Cambridge Blue' [B]74
L. d. 'Heavenly Blue' [B]74
Lobelia 122
L. cardinalis CARDINAL FLOWER 45 [R]49
L. c. 'Dark Crusader' 177
L. 'Cherry Ripe' 45
L. erinus TRAILING LOBELIA [B]76
L. e. 'Blue Cascade' [B]76
L. e. 'Cambridge Blue' [B]76
L. fulgens 182
L. 'Queen Victoria' [R]49 *80 177*
L. x speciosa 17 *177*
Lobularia 'Snow Carpet' [W]102
Lonas annua 40
Lonicera HONEYSUCKLE:
L. japonica 'Halliana' JAPANESE HONEYSUCKLE [Y]37
L. nitida 'Baggesen's Gold' 32 78 *78* [G]86 *167 172*
L. periclymenum 'Belgica' HONEYSUCKLE & WOODBINE 56 [P]61
L. pileata PRIVET HONEYSUCKLE [G]84
L. x purpusii 'Winter Beauty' [W]103 *103*
L. x tellmanniana [O]42 *42*
loosestrife SEE *Lysimachia, Lythrum*
Lotus hirsutus [S]93
love-in-a-mist 80 *133* SEE ALSO *Nigella*
Lunaria annua HONESTY [V]68 *167*
L. a. 'Alba Variegata' VARIEGATED WHITE HONESTY [G]88 *111 183 184*
lungwort SEE *Pulmonaria*
lupin (*Lupinus*) 6 23 *23* 25 28 116 *119* 140 155 160 168 172 182 184
Lupinus LUPIN:
L. arboreus TREE LUPIN 6 25 [Y]37 *168*
L. 'Chandelier' [Y]37 *141 172*
L. 'Noble Maiden' 182
L. 'The Chatelaine' [P]60 *184*
L. 'Thundercloud' 119
Lychnis 22

L. chalcedonica MALTESE CROSS 47 [R]49 *173*
L. coronaria ROSE CAMPION [P]58 *58* 90 [S]93 *98 120*
L. c. Alba Group [W]102 *110 175*
L. c. Oculata Group *176 178 184*
L. viscaria 'Splendens Plena' DOUBLE GERMAN CATCHFLY 181
L. yunnanensis 184
Lysichiton americanus SKUNK CABBAGE [Y]34
Lysimachia LOOSESTRIFE 140
L. ciliata 'Firecracker' 167
L. clethroides GOOSENECK LOOSESTRIFE [W]102 *184*
L. ephemerum [W]102 *102 174*
L. nummularia 'Aurea' 32
L. punctata YELLOW LOOSESTRIFE 32 [Y]35 *180*
Lythrum salicaria PURPLE LOOSESTRIFE 116 144 184

Macleaya microcarpa 'Kelway's Coral Plume' PLUME POPPY 80 *81* [G]87
Magnolia x loebneri 'Leonard Messel' [P]60 *60*
M. x soulangeana [P]60
M. stellata STAR MAGNOLIA 96 [W]99 *99*
Mahonia aquifolium [Y]34
M. japonica [G]84 *84*
M. x media 'Charity' [Y]36
maidenhair tree SEE *Ginkgo biloba*
mallow 95 160 SEE ALSO *Lavatera, Malva, Sidalcea*
Maltese cross SEE *Lychnis chalcedonica*
Malus CRAB APPLE:
M. floribunda JAPANESE CRAB APPLE [P]60
M. hupehensis [W]99
M. 'John Downie' [O]43
M. x moerlandsii 'Profusion' [P]58
Malva moschata 'Alba' MUSK MALLOW [W]102 *176*
M. sylvestris var. *mauritiana* TALL MALLOW [P]58
M. s. 'Primley Blue' 175
manna grass, variegated SEE *Glyceria maxima* var. *variegata*
manzanita, green SEE *Arctostaphylos patula*
maple 142 SEE ALSO *Acer*
marguerite 151 157 SEE ALSO *Anthemis, Argyranthemum*
marigold 20 *133* 140
French 140 SEE ALSO *Tagetes*
pot, SEE *Calendula*
marjoram SEE *Origanum*
marsh marigold SEE *Caltha palustris*
Matteuccia struthiopteris OSTRICH FEATHER FERN 9 [G]85
meadow clary SEE *Salvia pratensis* Haematodes Group
meadow rue 62 SEE *Thalictrum*
meadowsweet *Filipendula* 131
Meconopsis POPPY 72 [B]76
M. betonicifolia HIMALAYAN BLUE POPPY [B]76
M. cambrica WELSH POPPY [Y]35 *136 136 183*
M. c. var. *flore-pleno* 133
M. grandis [B]76
Melianthus major HONEYBUSH [G]87 *87 182*

Mentha suaveolens 'Variegata' APPLEMINT [G]89 *89*
Mertensia simplicissima [G]87 *175*
Mexican orange blossom SEE *Choisya*
Mexican sunflower SEE *Tithonia rotundifolia*
mezereon SEE *Daphne mezereum*
Michaelmas daisy 116 139 *147* SEE ALSO *Aster*
Milium effusum 'Aureum' BOWLES' GOLDEN GRASS 78 *79* [G]86 *86 167 173 176 184*
Mimulus 124
M. aurantiacus MONKEY MUSK [O]43
M. guttatus 32 *172*
M. lewisii 182
M. luteus 178
Miscanthus sinensis 'Gracillimus' [G]85 *85*
M. s. 'Variegatus' [G]88 *176*
Miss Willmott's ghost SEE *Eryngium giganteum*
mock orange [G]86 *98 151* SEE ALSO *Philadelphus*
mock privet SEE *Phillyrea*
Moluccella laevis BELLS OF IRELAND 79 [G]87
Monarda BERGAMOT [R]50
M. 'Beauty of Cobham' 57 [P]61
M. 'Cambridge Scarlet' [R]50 *50 177*
M. didyma [R]50
M. 'Mrs Perry' [R]50 *173*
monkey musk SEE *Mimulus*
monkshood SEE *Aconitum*
morning glory SEE *Ipomea*
Mount Etna broom SEE *Genista aetnensis*
mullein 120 SEE ALSO *Verbascum*
Muscari GRAPE HYACINTH [B]74 *97*
M. armeniacum 70 [B]74
M. latifolium [B]74
Myosotis FORGET-ME-NOT [B]74 *183 184*
Myrrhis odorata SWEET CICELY [G]85 [W]102

naked ladies SEE *Colchicum speciosum*
nankeen lily SEE *Lilium x testaceum*
Narcissus DAFFODIL 10 31 [Y]34 *72 73 140*
N. 'Actaea' [W]99
N. 'February Gold' [Y]34 *34*
N. 'Hawera' [Y]36 *141*
N. 'Jack Snipe' [Y]36 *36*
N. 'Peeping Tom' [Y]34
N. 'Tête-à-Tête' [Y]34
N. 'Thalia' [W]99
N. 'White Lion' 95 [W]99
N. 'Yellow Cheerfulness' JONQUIL [Y]34
nasturtium 38 44 *47 133 162 163 173 177* SEE ALSO *Tropaeolum majus*
Nectaroscordum siculum 136
Nemesia lilacina 181
Nemophila menziesii BABY BLUE EYES [B]76 *76*
Nepeta CATMINT [B]76 *184*
N. x faassenii [B]76 *119 175 180*
N. govaniana [Y]37 *157*
N. nervosa [B]76
N. nuda rosea 184
N. racemosa 108
N. sibirica [B]76
N. s. 'Souvenir d'André Chaudron' [B]76 *172 183*

N. 'Six Hills Giant' 7 [B]76 *106 114 141 174 176 180*
Nerine bowdenii [P]60
New Zealand cabbage palm SEE *Cordyline*
New Zealand flax (*Phormium cookianum*) 143
New Zealand satin flower SEE *Libertia grandiflora*
Nicotiana TOBACCO PLANT, FLOWERING TOBACCO:
N. affinis [W]102 *121*
N. langsdorffii 79 [G]88 *88*
N. x sanderae 9 [P]60 [W]102 *163 173*
N. x s. 'Domino Lime' 80
N. x s. 'Domino Salmon Pink' 57
N. x s. 'Lime Green' 44 79 [G]88 *180 182*
N. sylvestris [W]102 *107 163*
Nigella damascena LOVE-IN-A-MIST [B]76 *80*
N. d. 'Miss Jekyll' [B]76 *133 143 175 180*

Ocimum basilicum var. *purpurascens* PURPLE BASIL [R]51 *119*
Oenothera EVENING PRIMROSE:
O. biennis [Y]37
O. macrocarpa [Y]35
Olearia x macrodonta NEW ZEALAND HOLLY [W]102 *102 178*
oleaster SEE *Elaeagnus*
Omphalodes cappadocica NAVELWORT [B]74
O. c. 'Cherry Ingram' 71
onion, ornamental 108 139 *157* SEE ALSO *Allium*
Onopordum acanthium SCOTCH THISTLE [S]93
O. nervosum 176
Ophiopogon planiscapus 'Nigrescens' [R]51
oregano SEE *Origanum*
Origanum laevigatum 'Hopleys' OREGANO *176*
O. vulgare 'Aureum' GOLDEN MARJORAM [G]86
Ornithogalum nutans DROOPING STAR OF BETHLEHEM [S]93
O. umbellatum STAR OF BETHLEHEM [W]99
Orontium aquaticum GOLDEN CLUB 32 [Y]35
ostrich feather fern SEE *Matteuccia struthiopteris*
Othonna cheirifolia 179
Our Lady's thistle SEE *Silybum marianum*
oval leaved mint bush SEE *Prostanthera ovalifolia*
oxeye SEE *Buphthalmum salicifolium*

Pachysandra 83
Paeonia PEONY:
P. delavayi var. *ludlowii* 179

P. lactiflora [P]60
P. l. 'Ballerina' [P]60 *113*
P. l. 'Bowl of Beauty' [P]60 *60*
P. l. 'Duchesse de Nemours' [W]102
P. x lemoinei 'Madame Louis Henri' 17
P. mlokosewitschii 178
P. officinalis 'Rubra Plena' [R]50 *183*
P. suffruticosa subsp. *rockii* ROCK'S TREE PEONY [W]102
pampas grass SEE *Cortaderia selloana*
pansy 24 54 62 63 *107* SEE ALSO *Viola*
Papaver POPPY 184
P. commutatum 'Lady Bird' [R]49 *49*
P. orientale ORIENTAL POPPY 8 39 [R]49 [P]61
P. o. 'Beauty of Livermere' [R]49 *167*
P. o. 'Black and White' [W]102 *102*
P. o. 'Cedric Morris' [P]61
P. o. 'May Queen' 17
P. o. 'Mrs Perry' [P]61 *180*
P. o. 'Patty's Plum' 48
P. somniferum OPIUM POPPY [V]68 *108 114 173 175 176*
paper flower SEE *Bougainvillea glabra*
Paradisea liliastrum ST BRUNO'S LILY 41
Parahebe catarractae 174
P. perfoliata DIGGER'S SPEEDWELL [B]76
Parrotia persica 147
Parthenocissus quinquefolia VIRGINIA CREEPER [R]50
pea (sweet, everlasting) SEE *Lathyrus*
pear, willow leaf 82 SEE ALSO *Pyrus*
pearlbush SEE *Exochorda x macrantha*
pearl everlasting SEE *Anaphalis triplinervis*
Pelargonium GERANIUM [R]49 *128*
P. 'Lord Bute' 173
P. 'Paul Crampel' 44 [R]49 *128*
Penstemon 22 [R]49 [R]50 *69 110*
P. 'Apple Blossom' 176
P. barbatus [R]49
P. 'Blackbird' [V]68
P. 'Burgundy' 147
P. 'Chester Scarlet' 163
P. crandalli var. *glabrescens* 182
P. 'Evelyn' 53 [P]60 *157 181*
P. 'Flame' [R]49
P. fruticosus 'Purple Haze' [V]68
P. 'Garnet' [R]50 *175*
P. heterophyllus [B]76 *114 183*
P. h. 'Blue Gem' [B]76
P. h. 'Heavenly Blue' [B]76 *184*
P. 'Hidcote Pink' 119
P. 'Midnight' [V]68
P. 'Pennington Gem' 175
P. 'Raven' [V]68
P. 'Rubicundus' [R]49
P. 'Schoenholzeri' [R]49 *173*
P. 'Sour Grapes'[V]69
P. 'Stapleford Gem' [V]69 *111 175 181*
P. virens [V]69
peony SEE ALSO *Paeonia* 111 112 159 174 178 179
Perilla frutescens rubra [R]51
periwinkle SEE *Vinca*
Perovskia 'Blue Spire' RUSSIAN SAGE [B]76
Persicaria campanulata 81

HARDINESS ZONE CHART

Hardiness depends on factors such as the depth of a plant's roots, the rate at which temperature falls, duration of cold weather and wind force. The ratings are allocated to plants according to their tolerance of winter cold in the British Isles and Western Europe. In climates with hotter and\or drier summers, as in Australia or New Zealand, some plants will survive colder temperatures.

° CELSIUS	ZONE	° FAHRENHEIT
below -45	1	below -50
-45 to -40	2	-50 to -40
-40 to -34	3	-40 to -30
-34 to -29	4	-30 to -20
-29 to -23	5	-20 to -10
-23 to -18	6	-10 to 0
-18 to -12	7	0 to 10
-12 to -7	8	10 to 20
-7 to -1	9	20 to 30
-1 to 4	10	30 to 40

PUBLISHERS' ACKNOWLEDGMENTS

Planting keyline artwork Joanna Logan
Horticultural consultant Tony Lord
Index Penny David
Editorial director Erica Hunningher
Art director Caroline Hillier
Production director Nicky Bowden

The publishers are also grateful to Alison Freegard, Hilary Hockman, Antonia Johnson and Penelope Miller for editorial help.

AUTHOR'S ACKNOWLEDGMENTS

Frances Lincoln's team has included the most inspiring and thorough of editors who has coached me over the jumps and hurdles with the lightest of touches, and a designer with a very sensitive feel for the material. Judy Dod and Gillian Naish have done an immaculate job of word-processing my scruffy typescript, produced on a broken-down manual typewriter (vintage 1961), crunching it into a miniscule computer disk.

The plant lists are the equivalent of a complete book in themselves and I have had great help with the research from Carolyn McNab, Judy Dod, Jane Douglas, Sue Smith and Hetty Sookias, and I am especially grateful for the expertise of Antonia Johnson. Pennie Cullen came up with some bright ideas over lunch at Claridges. Tony Lord has very kindly checked the nomenclature of plants. To them all, my warmest thanks.

PHOTOGRAPHER'S ACKNOWLEDGMENTS

I am most grateful to garden owners and gardeners who have permitted me to take pictures. Many of them have also taken great pains to help with the identification of plants. My special thanks to the following, whose plantings appear in the more general views (*a* = above, *b* = below, *c* = centre, *l* = left, *r* = right): Lesley and John Jenkins, Wollerton Old Hall, Shropshire 1; The National Trust, Sissinghurst Castle, Kent 6,57*l*,125*b*,134-5; Fiona and John Owen, The Old Chapel, Gloucestershire 7,106,141*t*; Mr and Mrs H. Wakefield, Bramdean House, Hampshire 8; Laura Fisher, White Meadows Farm, Katonah, New York 9*t*; Winterthur Gardens, Delaware 9*b*; Gothic House, Oxfordshire 10-11,5*l*,62,73*l*,109*r*,111*l* and *r*,119*r*,121*r*,164-165,169*r*; Wendy and Michael Perry, Bosvigo House, Cornwall 18,122-3,126-7; The National Trust, Powis Castle, Powys 19*t*,52*br*,117*tr*; Clare College, Cambridge 19*b*,140; Sir Roy Strong and Dr Julia Trevelyan Oman, The Laskett, Hereford and Worcester 20; The National Trust, Tintinhull House, Somerset 21,166; Lord and Lady Saye and Sele, Broughton Castle, Oxfordshire 22*l*,110,151*b*; Randal Anderson, private garden, Oxfordshire 22*r*,118; Pam and Peter Lewis, Sticky Wicket, Dorset 2,23,108*t*,117*br*,120,131*b*,160; Nori and Sandra Pope, Hadspen Gardens, Somerset 28-9, 39*br*,45*l*,47,48*bl*,57*tr*,81*tl*,96,107*l* and *r*,119*b*,149*b*; The late Nancy Lancaster, The Coach House, Oxfordshire 30*l*; Susan Strange, Holywell Manor, Oxford 31*l*,79*r*; RHS Gardens, Wisley, Surrey 32*l*,116; Mr and Mrs Thomas Gibson, Westwell Manor, Oxfordshire 33; Keith and Ros Wiley, The Garden House, Devon 38,128*l*; Het Loo, Apeldoorn, Holland 39*t*; Frank and Marjorie Lawley, Herterton House, Northumberland 39*bl*,133*l*,161; Stavordale Priory, Somerset 41*t*; Dr James Smart, Marwood Hill, Devon 41*b*; Planting by Sue Dickinson, private garden, Buckinghamshire 44; The National Trust, Hidcote Gardens, Gloucestershire 45*r*,83,95*l*; The Hon Mrs P. Healing, The Priory, Kemerton, Hereford and Worcester 46; Longwood Gardens, Pennsylvania 53*b*; Caroline Eckersley, Woodside Farm, Oxfordshire 65; Stobshiel House, East Lothian 72; Ralph Merton, Old Rectory, Burghfield, Berkshire 24*l*,64*r*,73*r*; Rosemary Verey, Barnsley House, Gloucestershire 78*l*,114*t*,138-9,149*tl*,168, 171*r*; Mr and Mrs R. Paice, Bourton House, Gloucestershire 35*bl*,31*r*,82,122*l*, 131*t*; Anthony Noel, 17 Fulham Park Gardens, London 90*l*; Wendy and Len Lauderdale, Ashtree Cottage, Wiltshire 90*r*,104-5,114-5; John Brookes, Denmans, Sussex 94*r*,142; Planting by Bill Frederick, Delaware 53*t*,97,148; Andy and Polly Garnett, Cannwood Farm, Somerset 98; Lynden Miller, Bryant Park, New York 112*l*; John and Caryl Hubbard, Chilcombe, Dorset 112*r*,158; Ian Kirby, The Menagerie, Northamptonshire 113*r*; Arabella Lennox-Boyd, planting at RHS Flower Show, Chelsea 121*l*; Anthony and Lynn Archer-Wills, West Chiltington, Sussex 124; Rupert Golby, Adderbury, Oxfordshire 52*l*,128*r*; Westonbirt Arboretum, Gloucestershire 129*r*; RHS Gardens, Rosemoor, Devon 130*r*; Mr and Mrs Peter Aldington, Turn End, Buckinghamshire 132*r*,136*l*; Waterperry Gardens, Oxfordshire 133*br*; Mrs Gwen Beaumont, Stoke-sub-Hamdon, Somerset 137; Levens Hall, Cumbria 139*b*; Mr and Mrs John Chambers, Kiftsgate Court, Gloucestershire 143*l*; Mrs Gerda Barlow, Stancombe Park, Gloucestershire 143*r*; Carol and Malcolm Skinner, Eastgrove Cottage, Hereford and Worcester 147*r*; Private garden, Chedworth, Gloucestershire 150; Mrs M.J. Coombe, Yew Tree Cottage, Hampshire 152-3; Mrs Margaret Farquar Ogilvie, House of Pitmuies, Tayside 114*b*,154; The National Trust, Ascott, Buckinghamshire 155; Planting by Pam Schwert and Sibylle Kreutzberger, private garden, Gloucestershire 156,157*b*; Ethne and Donald Clarke, Yaxham, Norfolk 157*t*; Nell Maydew, Daglingworth, Gloucestershire 159; Sir Hardy Amies, Langford, Oxfordshire 162; Myles Hildyard, Flintham Hall, Nottinghamshire 163*b*;Mr and Mrs John Sales, Cirencester, Gloucestershire 167; University Botanic Garden, Cambridge 170*t*,171*tl*; Mr and Mrs J. Wallinger, The Manor House, Upton Grey, Hampshire 170*b*.

My thanks too to gardeners and garden owners whose plantings appear only as details. They include: Putsborough Manor, Devon; Rousham House, Oxfordshire; Thuja Garden, Maine; Charlie and Amanda Hornby, Hodges Barn, Gloucestershire; Caroline Burgess, Stonecrop, Cold Spring, New York; University Botanic Garden, Oxford; Robert Cooper, Ablington, Gloucestershire; Veronica and Giles Cross, Stoke Lacy, Hereford; John and Eve Meares, Norton-sub-Hamdon, Somerset; Gwladys Tonge, Winslow, Buckinghamshire; Annie Huntingdon, Sudborough, Northamptonshire; Lucy Gent, London; Sir Peter and Lady Parker, Manor Farm, Oxfordshire; Peggy Jeffery, Mount Pleasant, Devon; Dan Pearson, London.